$27.50 cloth

D1553574

Men, Religion, and Melancholia

DONALD CAPPS

Men, Religion, and Melancholia

JAMES, OTTO, JUNG, AND ERIKSON

Yale University Press
New Haven and London

Copyright © 1997 by Yale University.
All rights reserved.
This book may not be reproduced, in whole or in part, including illustrations, in
any form (beyond that copying permitted by Sections 107 and 108 of the U.S.
Copyright Law and except by reviewers for the public press), without written
permission from the publishers.

The extract from "The Last Hiding Places of Snow," *Mortal Acts, Mortal Words*,
copyright © 1980 by Galway Kinnell, is reprinted by permission of Houghton
Mifflin Co. All rights reserved.

Printed in the United States of America.

Library of Congress Cataloging-in-Publication Data
Capps, Donald.
    Men, religion, and melancholia : James, Otto, Jung, and Erikson /
  Donald Capps.
      p. cm.
  Includes bibliographical references and index.
  ISBN 0-300-06971-5 (cloth: alk. paper)
    1. Psychology, Religious. 2. Psychologists of religion —
  Psychology. 3. Psychologists of religion — Religious life.
  4. Melancholy. 5. Mothers and sons. 6. Boys — Religious life.
  7. Boys — Psychology. 8. Men — Religious life. 9. Men — Psychology.
  I. Title.
  BL53.C266 1997
  200'.1'9 — dc20   96-36548
                                             CIP

A catalogue record for this book is available from the British Library.

The paper in this book meets the guidelines for permanence and durability of the
Committee on Production Guidelines for Book Longevity of the Council on
Library Resources.

10 9 8 7 6 5 4 3 2 1

To John
From a Grateful Father

My mother did not want me to be born;
afterwards, all her life, she needed me to return.
When this more-than-love flowed toward me, it brought
    darkness;
she wanted me as burial earth wants — to heap itself gently
    upon
    but also to annihilate —
and I knew, whenever I felt longings to go back,
that is what wanting to die is. That is why

dread lives in me,
dread which comes when what gives life beckons toward
    death,
dread which throws through me
waves
of utter strangeness, which wash the entire world empty.

— *Galway Kinnell, from "The Last Hiding Places of Snow,"*
Mortal Acts, Mortal Words. *Boston: Houghton Mifflin, 1980.*

Contents

Preface

This is a book in the psychology of religion. It concerns itself with four of the most influential texts in the psychology of religion over the course of the twentieth century, texts by William James, Rudolf Otto, C. G. Jung, and Erik H. Erikson. The assumption that guides my interpretations of these works is that they reflect the personal religious struggles of their authors, that they are certainly *about* religion but in addition are — more indirectly — about their own authors and their lifelong struggle with the pathology for which each used the term *melancholy*.

Because these texts are indirectly about themselves, I assume that for these four authors the psychology of religion is not primarily an objective science, if by objective science we mean that every effort is made to exclude, or at least reduce, the "contaminating" effects of the personal subjectivity of the researcher with respect to whatever happens to be the object of research. Rather, for these authors, their personal subjectivity is a necessary and vital feature of their investigations, as for them it is their most reliable and trustworthy resource.

Thus, this book cuts across the grain of what is currently understood to be the psychology of religion, and it moves in a direction quite different from the prevailing trend in the psychology of religion to view it as a behavioral and social science. My intention is not to denigrate the work of those who are taking this very scientific approach to the psychology of religion (many are my good friends), but I do attempt to make the case for a different construal of it, one that is not only based on texts (as opposed to questionnaires) but also views the texts in question as, to some degree, autobiographical.

I frequently encounter students who are attracted to the psychology of religion as an area of study but because they are more oriented toward the humanities (or arts and letters) than toward the sciences, are not drawn to the more conventional approaches to the psychology of religion. If they have been introduced to the psychology of religion via the objective-science model, they are often unaware that a very different approach to it is in fact available. Or, alternatively, they have been cursorily introduced to the approach that I take here, only to have *it* denigrated as insufficiently scientific — as failing to meet accepted objective standards of scientific investigation, as being "too philosophical" or even "theological."

The unfortunate effect of these attitudes toward the kinds of texts represented here is that many who might find in the psychology of religion precisely the approach to the study of religion that best fits their own personal proclivities and competencies are instead turned off by these initial encounters with it, even before they have had opportunity to read some of the important "classics" in the field.

Fortunately, there *are* psychologists of religion with a more humanistic bent who, while oriented toward the scientific, have a deep appreciation for these classic texts, assigning them in their courses and writing about them. Thus, in the course of writing this book, I did not view myself as a lonely prophet crying in the wilderness. The book is one of a growing number of books that address the psychology of religion from a textual orientation. What I *do* consider unique about what I have done here is my argument that there is a persistent theme running through the classic texts in the psychology of religion: the theme of melancholy. It seems as though the one thing that the major authors in the psychology of religion share in common is a disposition to be melancholic, and it is this personal disposition that prompts them to write about religion in the ways they do. One wonders, in fact, whether the disposition to address religion *from a psychological orientation* is itself a direct consequence of this personal tendency toward melancholia.

I want to thank the editorial staff at Yale University Press for doing the many things, large and small, that are involved in bringing a book to completion, but I especially want to thank Otto Bohlmann for his thoughtful support throughout the editorial process. I am grateful to the anonymous reviewer who offered many informed and insightful suggestions for strengthening the manuscript, all of which I have tried to implement. I have profited from many personal conversations in recent years with students and colleagues on the topic of this book, but those that especially stand out in my mind are ones I had with John Capps, who sensed by the rather serious tone of our conversations that the topic of melancholy has for me a personal subtext, which mercifully remained, for the most part, unspoken but understood. For all that he has been and meant to me through the years, I dedicate this book in gratitude to him. In the course of writing it, I was frequently aware of carrying on a conversation in my mind with James E. Dittes, who introduced me to the psychology of religion and thus enabled me to find my niche in life, and who has subsequently extended to me the kindnesses to which I allude in the second half of the book's conclusion. Reserved for last is my special appreciation to my wife, Karen, who is the one to whom I make reference in chapter 5 when I proclaim: "And how fortunate the son who finds in this immense world of objects one whom he can love and, in loving, can regain his capacity to believe."

Religious Melancholy and the Lost Object

In the epilogue of *Young Man Luther,* Erik H. Erikson concludes that he has been dealing throughout the book with "a Western religious movement which grew out of and subsequently perpetuated an extreme emphasis on the interplay of initiative and guilt, and an exclusive emphasis on the divine Father-Son." But then he adds, "Even in this scheme, the mother remains a counterplayer however shadowy. Father religions have mother churches" (1958, 263).

This is not a book about "mother churches," but it *is* a book about that shadowy figure—the mother herself—who remains in the background not only of the Western religious movement Erikson explores in *Young Man Luther* but also in the major texts in the psychology of religion that bear the imprint of the Western religious tradition's emphasis on the father-son relationship. Perhaps the sole exception to this relegation of the mother to shadowy status are the many psychological studies of Augustine's *Confessions* (1992). Because Augustine recognized his mother, Monica, and not his father, Patricius, as the strong counterplayer in his religious struggles, psychologists of religion have had no choice in his case but to focus on the mother-son relationship (see Capps and Dittes 1990).

Yet the very fact that Augustine does not seem to fit the father-son schema that is so central to the Western religious movement has given these studies of

Augustine, and Augustine himself, a rather anomalous status in the psychology of religion. In recent years, efforts have been made to bring Augustine and his *Confessions* into greater conformity with the father-son schema by placing more emphasis on the shadowy figure of Patricius, implying that perhaps too much attention has been given to Monica (Rigby 1990). Attempts have also been made to bring to more central attention the "symbolic fathers" in Augustine's life, such as Bishop Ambrose, Saint Anthony, and Victorinus, the several male figures whom Augustine credits with having helped him find his way to Mother Church. And there have been efforts to bring attention to Christological themes in his account of his conversion, downplaying the fact that it was his vision of a female figure — Continence — that prompted him to yield himself to God, and that it was his mother to whom he immediately went with the news of his conversion (Hawkins 1990).

For many years I have been teaching a course in the psychology of religion that rests on what I consider to be the major texts in modern psychology of religion. Four books have been central to the course: *The Varieties of Religious Experience* by William James (1982), *The Idea of the Holy* by Rudolf Otto (1958), *Answer to Job* by C. G. Jung (1958), and *Young Man Luther* by Erik H. Erikson (1958). I have used other texts to supplement these, including Sigmund Freud's *Civilization and Its Discontents* (1962) and *The Future of an Illusion* (1964), Paul W. Pruyser's *Between Belief and Unbelief* (1974) and *The Play of the Imagination* (1983), Ana-Marie Rizzuto's *Birth of the Living God* (1979), and W. W. Meissner's *Psychoanalysis and Religious Experience* (1984). But I invariably use the texts by James, Otto, Jung, and Erikson because, viewed together, they provide students with a sense of what counts as important work in the psychology of religion, what its major preoccupations have been, and how the psychology of religion has been shaped by modern Western religion, reflecting *its* preoccupations. I indicate to students, especially those who experience themselves as marginal to this religious tradition, that while they are certainly not being asked to endorse this tradition, one needs nonetheless to know what it was that got the psychology of religion under way, and why it seemed important to its founders and their successors to pursue certain issues and overlook or neglect others.

I have suggested to students that they read these four books as, in a sense, autobiographical, because the four authors appear to be writing about issues that concern them deeply, or existentially. Unlike most texts — and certainly textbooks — in the psychology of religion, these four seem to have been written with considerable self-investment, suggesting that their authors were not simply writing "about" religion but struggling to articulate their own stake in religion, its personal meaning and significance for them. While, unlike Augustine's *Confessions,* these books are not overtly autobiographical, I have suggested nonetheless that we look for what Erikson (1981) calls "the sense of 'I' " in them, to discern the ways in which the author locates himself in the text. What makes this proposal natural is that I always start the class with James's *Varieties* and point out that James included autobiographical material in his chapter "The Sick Soul" (1982, 159–61) but concealed his identity, so that his original readers may not have known that the account was his own. This has served to illustrate my point that the authors are "in" their texts, but often surreptitiously or in disguise.

These, then, are not autobiographies in the technical sense of the term, but they are personal and not, as students might have assumed, the work of scientifically oriented authors in search of objective truths. Although there are many books and articles that represent a scientific approach to the psychology of religion, this is not the psychology of religion that I choose to teach. If I prefer to teach the classics, however, it is not because I have any particular interest in preserving the so-called Western canon but because I believe that the psychology of religion is a discipline in which the "investigators," if we may call them that, are "integral" to their investigations (see Dittes 1977).

Over the years, I have been slowly evolving an argument that I present alongside the four authors' own arguments regarding religion, one that derives from the view that these texts reflect the personal interests and struggles of their authors. This argument has two interrelated points. The first is that each author is struggling with the relationship between religion and psychopathology, but, more specifically, the psychopathology they know as *melancholy* (and you and I probably know as *chronic depression*). For reasons that will become clear in the course of this book, I prefer the more traditional term *melancholy* than the more contemporary term *depression.* When one discovers "the sense of 'I' " in these texts, one finds, in my judgment, that this is a melancholic I, an I acquainted not only with sadness but also with deep negative emotions of rage, fury, and even hate. Again, the anonymous self-report in James's *Varieties* is most helpful, because it is an account of a young man who is suffering "the worst kind of melancholy" (James 1982, 159).

My second related point is that the melancholy may be traced, ultimately, to the author's relationship with his own mother. The sadness, despair, and rage characteristic of melancholy have an object, and in these four cases this object is the author's mother. This point is more difficult to establish, as none of the authors writes about his relationship to his mother. But this, I suggest to students, is precisely where their own capacities as psychologists of religion come in. It becomes their task to try to understand how religion serves as a stand-in for the mother, or for the son's relationship to his mother, and how, within his mature views on religion, there is a "pre-historic core" that has to do with this relationship. Thus, a book in the psychology of religion needs to be read psychologically, and one way to do this is to read it as a text in which the author is searching in religion for the lost object who is his natural mother as he experienced her in infancy and the earliest years of childhood. An assumption that lies behind this argument is that one would not have become "religious" had one not experienced the emotional loss of one's mother as a child.

I shall argue, however, that for these four authors the psychological (though not physical) loss of their mothers when they were small boys had complications that, while not unique, are not necessarily the experience of all children. There were traumas associated with the loss that were perhaps more severe, or more deeply felt, than is usually the case. A commonplace of the developmental literature is talk about the boy's "separation" from his mother in early childhood, and it is typically noted that the boy's separation may be more decisive or thoroughgoing than the girl's, as he needs to achieve gender differentiation from his mother and to identify with his father instead. Thus, separation is assumed, and it is considered "normal," therefore, that all boys will feel a sense of loss. But I believe that this natural separation process was more traumatic for these four boys than is normally the case (or at least as described in the literature as normal), and that it in turn disposed them, on the one hand, toward melancholia and, on the other, toward a certain receptivity to religion.

I suggest that there are in fact two losses in this regard. One is that the boy experiences a loss of his mother, that, even though she is still present and the two of them continue to relate to each other, he has in a sense lost the mother he had previously experienced, the mother who held him close and made no effort to help him achieve the separation. The other loss concerns himself, the boy who lived in the aura of her unmitigated love and experienced himself as her beloved son. In the process of separation, this self-image proves untenable and altogether too simplistic. He finds it necessary to separate from the original boy so as to become a different boy, a boy who will not take his mother's unmitigated love for granted. The new boy feels, and rightly so, that his mother's love needs now to be earned, that her love is no longer an unconditional love. If the separation is fraught with unusual anxiety, both the loss of his original mother and the loss of his original self will create a disposition toward melancholia.

I believe Erikson is correct when he observes that young adulthood allows for a return to one's origins, and especially a revisiting of the separation process, in search of grounds for trust and reassurance. At this time, the fact of his disposition to melancholia may become evident to the young man, whether or not he uses the actual word. He discovers within himself an unexplainable sadness, exacerbated, but not fully accounted for, by broken relationships, difficulties in finding what he wants to do with his life, and so on. He also discovers within himself a silent rage he did not know was there, and he has great difficulty understanding its source, because the frustrations he encounters in his struggle to come into his own do not seem to warrant such depth of feeling, such negative affect. However, the way in which he now relates to his mother, if she is still living, is a clue to its source, as he has feelings toward her that are disproportionate to her actual provocations. Such feelings are rooted, I suggest, in the early separation process, when he lost her unconditional love and experienced the unbridgeable gulf that separated him from the child he was before the separation. Now a similar two-pronged separation occurs once again as he moves into adulthood.

James's account of his melancholic episode when he was 28 years old and Erikson's focus on "young man" Luther, also a sufferer from melancholia, help to make the point that young adulthood is a critical period both in the discovery of one's disposition toward melancholy and in one's tendency to view it as a religious problem, as the symbolic universe of religion is what one turns to for new grounds for trust and reassurance. Erikson describes this search for a new grounding as the "rock-bottom attitude" of the young adult, who questions everything that he formerly believed or took for granted in "an attempt to find that immutable bedrock on which the struggle for a new existence can safely begin and be assured of a future" (1958, 103). If seen in therapy, the patient with such a "rock-bottom attitude" demands "that the psychotherapist become for him as immediate and as close, as exclusive and as circumspect, as generous and as self-denying, a counterplayer as only a mother of an infant can be" (p. 103). Thus, the search is for the lost object, and this search may entail attraction to the symbolic universe of religion, psychotherapy, or some combination of the two.

I note further the significance of the fact that the authors of these texts are writing as older men across a chasm of intervening years that now separates them, once again, from the struggles of young adulthood. Like Augustine, who wrote his *Confessions* in his early forties, at least twelve years after the last of the events recounted in his autobiography, the authors of our four texts are mature adults taking stock of the religious preoccupations of their youth and questioning the adequacy of their earlier resolutions and conclusions.

Yet to say that they are mature adults looking back on earlier struggles does not mean that they had adopted an objective, disinterested, "scientific" attitude in the writing of their texts. As young adults they struggled with

grievances relating to their early childhood; now they are mature adults struggling with grievances relating to the commitments they made in young adulthood, especially commitments that were religious or quasi-religious in nature.
The youngest of the four authors at the time of publication is Rudolf Otto, who
was 48 years old when *The Idea of the Holy* was published (b. 1869, published
1917), and the oldest is C. G. Jung, whose *Answer to Job* appeared when he
was 77 (b. 1875, published 1952). Erikson was 56 when *Young Man Luther*
was published (b. 1902, published 1958), and James was 60 when *The Varieties* appeared in print (b. 1842, published 1902). Although all were long since
bereaved or geographically separated from their mothers, the tie that continued to bind them was religion as personally (not conventionally) understood.

While I understand that, in one sense, no boy's separation from his mother is
"normal," as all separations are likely to entail exacerbating circumstances, I
believe that the four authors with whom we are dealing here *did* experience the
separation as particularly traumatic, owing to the unique situations in which
they found themselves. Jung speaks for all four when he says that he always felt
mistrustful when the word *love* was spoken, and that the feeling he associated
with *woman* was for a long time one of innate unreliability (Jung 1961, 8).

This, however, raises an issue that needs to be addressed with the utmost
sensitivity. We are being cautioned today against the tendency of an earlier
generation of psychologists to blame mothers for whatever may have gone
wrong in a child's formation. While her role in such formation is certainly
formidable, the tendency to blame mothers for "poor outcomes" (however
defined) is now being challenged, and appropriately so, for we know so little
about what makes a child turn out "well" or "badly." This explicit or implicit
attack on mothers is now recognized for what it was: a social and cultural
prejudice against women and against the social involvements and respon-
sibilities typically associated with women. As all of our authors succeeded in
life, the issue of where to place the blame is in a sense beside the point.

Yet the issue of blame cannot be so easily discounted, because it has importance *within* the mother-son relationship itself. Whether mothers are to blame
for how their boys turn out is a nonissue, a fallacy I do not wish to perpetuate.
But when we consider the relationship between *this* mother and *this* son, the
issue of blame is a very important one, as there *is* explicit or implicit blame in
the very ways in which these four authors write about their mothers or relate
to their mothers in later years. Moreover, the issue of who is to blame is at the
very core of the melancholic condition, for, as Freud makes clear in his famous
essay "Mourning and Melancholia" (1963), the core issue in melancholia is
that the sufferer has a "plaint" against another, that is, the lost object. Rightly
or wrongly, legitimately or not, the sufferer blames his mother for his plight or,

if he finds it too threatening to cast blame on her, he internalizes the blame in the form of *self*-reproach. Melancholiacs, then, are people who cannot bring themselves to blame directly the one against whom they have a grievance but instead internalize the object of blame and punish that aspect of the self with which the object is now identified.

In short, if we merely take a moral approach to this issue of mother blaming, noting the patent unfairness to mothers of placing the onus on them for whatever may go wrong or turn out badly as far as her children are concerned, we overlook an important dynamic of the melancholic condition: from the boy's own point of view, something *has* gone wrong and there is someone who is at fault. If there *was* considerable mother blaming in earlier developmental theory, we might want to ask whether this was itself an indication that male developmental theorists were closet melancholiacs, using their privileged status as developmental theorists to blame mothers in general for what they perceived — clearly or dimly — their own mothers to have done to them when they were small boys. This blaming of mothers may then be viewed as the child's revenge. Even D. W. Winnicott's term "the good enough mother" (1971b, 11), a term that developmental theorists of both genders have warmly embraced, may have a certain melancholic bite to it, as it may seem to say, subtextually, "My mother? Well, I guess you could say that she was 'good enough.'" While it reassures today's mothers that they are not expected to be perfect, the good enough mother may, from the adult male's point of view, betray a certain calculated negative judgment: "She was not the mother I needed" or even "She was not the mother I felt I deserved."[1]

In any event, this book is not focally about blaming mothers, but neither is the subject avoided, for in my view religion becomes for all of these authors the locus in which they seek what they lost in their relationships with their mothers. In turn, this recourse to religion has for them its own problems and dangers, as for all four authors there is a sense in which religion creates a "double bind": They turn to it with such need, and yet in very important ways it not only fails to assuage their pain but also adds difficulties of its own. As I have indicated, these are not men who are conventionally religious. They are men who continued to struggle with religion throughout their lives, just as they struggled with their emotions and attitudes toward their own mothers.

The pain that especially interests me here is melancholy, the subject of several important new texts, including Julia Kristeva's *Black Sun: Depression and Melancholia* (1989) and Julius H. Rubin's *Religious Melancholy and Protestant Experience in America* (1994). While melancholy is identified in the fourth edition of the American Psychiatric Association's *Diagnostic and Statistical Manual of Mental Disorders* (DSM) as a variant form of major depressive episode (1994, 383–84), it has proven to be a notoriously difficult psychopathology to define with any degree of precision, because it seems to vary so much from person to person. Rubin argues that "religious melancholy is a culturally and historically specific form of depressive disorder, a special variety of melancholy" common in America from the colonial period through the nineteenth century but rather uncommon today precisely because it was a culturally and historically specific form of depressive disorder (p. 3). Although I would not disagree with his claim that religious melancholy took a particular form in the centuries that interest him, it would be a mistake in my view to assume that melancholy itself is a thing of the past or that melancholy's association with religion must always take the form it did in earlier centuries.

Indeed, Rubin himself raises the question of melancholy's persistence in our own times in the final chapter of his book, entitled "The Passing Away of Religious Melancholy?," and makes two observations that have direct bearing on our explorations here. The first is his reference to a study by George Mark Fisher (1990), minister of the Ross Christian Church in Ross, Ohio. Fisher discovered that the "feeling of forsakenness was very prevalent among members of his church" (Rubin 1994, 237). He and Roy Fairchild (1987) concur "that a religious life founded upon the immediacy of the indwelling spirit (spirituality or God's presence in one's heart) also produced problems of 'dispirited souls,' and those who feel bereft of God in their hearts" (Rubin 1994, 238). Rubin concludes, "In the light of these findings, the future of religious melancholy unfortunately looks bright" (p. 238). The second observation, several paragraphs later, concerns his contention that some believers *chose* to live inside the "prison of ideas" that constituted religious melancholy, while others found themselves trapped in it, "not by their own choice, but by the persistent memory of childhood cruelty" (p. 238). This observation not only implies a direct connection between childhood experiences and religious melancholy but also suggests that religious melancholy will continue to persist so long as childhood cruelty and other childhood traumas persist.

These two seemingly unrelated observations indicate that something deeply psychological lies behind religious melancholy — here reflected in the sense of having been forsaken by God — for, otherwise, why would believers take this "feeling of forsakenness" so very personally? I suggest that the psychological precursor to the adult's religious experience of forsakenness is the experience of separation from one's mother, because this is the moment when the child first experiences what it means to be a "dispirited soul," to "feel bereft" in one's "heart." I suggest further that childhood cruelty, especially when its agent is the boy's mother, exacerbates the sense of forsakenness and gives religious melancholy its deeper dimensions of rage, fury, and even hate.

What makes melancholy somewhat unique among the "depressive disorders" is that it manifests — or, more commonly, hides — a deep sense of bitterness, the feeling that one has been mistreated or treated unjustly, as, for example, in the case of Job, a man who bitterly complains not only that he has been forsaken by God but also that God had no right to do this to him, as he was God's most loyal supporter and defender. I submit, therefore, that a mother's cruelty is an important variable in the formation of a melancholic personality. To experience separation from one's mother is one thing; sadness and longing will surely result. But to experience the withdrawal of her love in an especially cruel or unfeeling manner is another. Severe melancholia is the predictable outcome.

The primary text for my argument here is Freud's brief but compelling "Mourning and Melancholia" (1963). A secondary text of his that figures importantly in my interpretation is his essay "The 'Uncanny' " (1958). While I consider these two texts to be as autobiographical as the four texts that I shall be discussing in detail, I have chosen to exclude Freud himself from this exploration because the texts I regularly use in my course in the psychology of religion to reflect his views on religion — *The Future of an Illusion* and *Civilization and Its Discontents* — do not in my judgment add significantly to the argument that I am developing here.

While this decision not to focus on Freud's texts on religion, together with my use of his essays in support of my argument, may give the impression that he offers an objective standpoint from which to view the more subjective reflections of the other four authors, I hope that this is not in fact what my chapters on James, Otto, Jung, and Erikson actually communicate. In my view, there is no single standpoint we may adopt or achieve that enables us to view religious experience objectively; rather, the best we can hope for are insights gained from comparing various authors with each other. As Erikson points out in *The Life Cycle Completed,* the theory of relativity "at first had unbearably relativistic implications, seemingly undermining the foundations of any firm human 'standpoint'; and yet, it opens a new vista in which relative standpoints are 'reconciled' to each other in fundamental invariance" (1982, 96–97). I am claiming that the psychology of religion as reflected in the four authors under discussion here has one "fundamental invariance": all four "relative standpoints" reflect their authors' disposition toward the psychopathology of melancholy. And because this disposition has roots in their childhood experiences of their mothers, theirs is necessarily a *religious* form of melancholy.

If Erikson talks about the "reconciliation" of relative standpoints to each other, the literary term *intertextuality* expresses much the same thing. The four authors draw on their own personal experiences as they set forth their ideas about religious experience, but they also draw on their experiences as readers of texts written by others, and in some instances the texts written by others are among the works included here. For example, both Otto and Erikson make explicit reference to James's *Varieties*, and James's own views on religious melancholy have direct influence on Erikson's interpretation of the religious melancholy of Martin Luther. In my chapters on the four texts, I make a conscious effort to be intertextual myself, to make connections between two or more texts. This seems to me a productive way to show that there is a "fundamental invariance" in these four texts, something that holds them together besides the fact that they belong to the discipline known as the psychology of religion. This also means that I make a conscious effort *not* to discuss these texts as illustrative of their authors' general psychological theory (for example, showing how Jung's *Answer to Job* illustrates key aspects of his theory of archetypes or how Erikson's *Young Man Luther* both uses and supports his life-cycle theory). I do not wish to pit the four texts against one another; my concern is to demonstrate that all four authors wrote from the common perspective of religious melancholia.

In describing these authors as religious melancholiacs, I also hope to disabuse readers of the common misconception that melancholiacs are ineffectual people, lacking in motivation and ambition. The four authors were extremely productive individuals, and this poses precisely the opposite question — whether their melancholia fueled their productivity and, if so, in what ways. Moreover, the view of *DSM* that melancholy is a subtype of depression should not be misinterpreted to mean that melancholiacs are "chronically depressed." The vigorous lives of these four men challenge this assumption. Conversely, I would not want readers to take me as saying that chronic depression can be traced in all cases to early childhood experiences, though I *am* making that claim with respect to religious melancholia.

As my discussion of these four texts will reveal, I do not believe that the four authors are all equally melancholic. I would also emphasize that melancholia may be more severe or less severe in different periods of a person's adult life. While melancholia, much like the common cold, admits of no permanent cure, only comparatively effective remedies, there were undoubtedly phases in the lives of these four authors when they felt relatively free of melancholic symptoms, and other times when they experienced them acutely. But even to discuss melancholy in terms of symptoms and severity of "mood" is potentially distortive. Melancholia has less to do with a general mood or with symptomatology and more to do with a relationship: the boy's relationship to his mother. Thus, if someone finds himself engaged as an adult in activities having little or no psychodynamic connection with this relationship, there is every reason to believe that he will not in those instances manifest melancholic symptoms or moods. If, on the other hand, he finds himself in a relationship that is psycho-dynamically similar to that which obtained between himself and his mother or involves activities that are the symbolic equivalent of this relationship, he may then become suddenly and inexplicably melancholic. Women who marry men who view and treat their wives as "substitute mothers" will know from experi-ence what I am talking about. Frequently, such men will take out on their wives the deeply felt grievances they harbor against their own mothers, while continuing perhaps to idealize these mothers. And religion, as I have already suggested, bears a symbolic affinity to the mother-son relationship of early childhood.

A rather unexpected development that occurred in the course of writing this book is that I became aware of the importance of art — especially the visual arts — for each of these authors, precisely where their disposition to melan-cholia was concerned. While the relationship between art and melancholia has been explored by various authors (Wittkower and Wittkower 1963; Kristeva 1989, ch. 5), and there is no point in my duplicating their work here, I shall give some attention in my discussion of the four texts to matters of art and vision, as it appears that for most of these authors art is a less "binding" and "constricting" compensation for the loss of their mother's unconditional love than religion proved to be. Conversely, their melancholia made them un-usually sensitive to how things are viewed, envisioned, and re-envisioned. Although it has become almost commonplace to critique the "modern era" for its tendency to privilege vision among the sense perceptions (see Jay 1993), it may be that we should not be so quick to make a negative judgment of this tendency, for in several of the cases before us vision played an important role in clarifying and ameliorating the melancholic condition.

In my chapters on the four texts, I take them up in their chronological sequence, beginning with James's *Varieties* and concluding with Erikson's *Young Man Luther.* By discussing them in chronological order, I hope to avoid the implication that there may be another basis for the order in which I con-sider them, such as the notion (often promulgated when the psychology of religion is viewed as a science) that later works in the field reflect an *advance* over earlier works. When the psychology of religion is viewed from the per-spective of melancholy, the idea of it as an advancing science makes little sense. In each case, however, I *do* try to identify the ways in which the author achieves some genuine insights into the problem and, where it seems justi-fied, to indicate how his text clears the way for additional insights that we as readers may identify independently for ourselves. If, as I have suggested, melancholy has no cure, we should not disparage the remedies that those who have lived with religious melancholy have discovered for themselves, and we should be on the lookout for features in their texts that point to remedies of which the authors were not fully aware but to which their texts nonetheless point.

Finally, the fact that I do not always discuss the sorts of issues for which these four texts are best known to psychologists of religion has no other meaning or significance than that I have chosen to focus on the issue of melancholy instead. This is to say, I do not claim that this is a comprehensive study of the four texts. Nor should it be viewed as an introductory textbook in the psychology of religion. In fact, the existence of several excellent introductory texts has freed me from any sense of obligation to provide comprehensive discussions of the four texts or to locate them within the larger framework of contemporary psychology of religion.

"Mourning and Melancholia" and "The 'Uncanny'"

I have noted that Freud's "Mourning and Melancholia" is the primary basis, and "The 'Uncanny'" the secondary basis, for my interpretation of the texts by James, Otto, Jung, and Erikson. I shall provide a brief summary of the first essay and, from this, an elaboration of my theory of the origins of religion in the life of the male child. I shall also briefly summarize the second essay as it supports an expansion of the theory in significant ways. By focusing on Freud's "Mourning and Melancholia," I signal my judgment that it offers a more fruitful explanation than his books *The Future of an Illusion* or *Civilization and Its Discontents* for why individuals become "bound" to religion. The target of Freud's attacks on religion in the two books is in my view a secondary expression of religion (focused on the father), whereas his essay on mourning and melancholia, while not expressly about religion, provides a powerful analysis for why some individuals become and remain religious, even when they find themselves in fundamental agreement with the critiques of religion presented in the two books.

In "Mourning and Melancholia," Freud explores the similarities, and differences, between the normal grieving process ("mourning") and the pathology known to the psychiatric community of his day as "melancholia." He warns that this exploration may not bear much fruit, in part because the psychiatric definition of melancholia is so uncertain. Yet he believes that a correlation of the two is justified, because they have the same cause: Both are reactions to the loss of someone or something that was deeply loved. In the case of mourning we assume that the loss will be overcome in the normal course of time, whereas melancholia is a pathological condition that may require medical treatment. How to account for these very different outcomes?

In Freud's view, the distinguishing features of melancholia are a profoundly painful dejection, diminished interest in the outside world, loss of the capacity to love, inhibition of all activity, and a lowering of one's self-regarding feelings to such a degree that one engages in self-reproach and self-revilings, often culminating in a delusional expectation of punishment. Many of the same traits are found in grief: The same feeling of pain, the loss of interest in the outside world, the loss of a capacity to adopt any new object or objects of love, and a turning away from active effort that is not connected with thoughts of the dead person. In the mourning process, however, there is little of the self-reproach that is invariably present in melancholia, nor is there the anticipation of impending punishment. In mourning, the loss is deeply painful, yet it is experienced not as punishment but as integral to life itself.

Why this loss of self-esteem in melancholia? Why this self-abasement? Why this "delusional belittling" of self? Why this expectation of punishment and chastisement? That some of this self-criticism is justified cannot be doubted. After all, the patient is as lacking in interest and as incapable of love and of any achievement as he says he is. Moreover, in his self-criticisms, he has a keener eye for truth than those who are not melancholiacs, for others cling to views of themselves and human nature that are much too positive and sanguine.[2] The issue, however, is not whether the melancholiac's distressing self-abasement is justified in the opinion of others but whether he is in fact correctly describing not only his experience of himself but also the underlying reasons for it. If he has lost his self-respect, which seems to be the case, is there some good reason for this, as he seems to believe there is? This, and not others' objective assessment of him is the issue, and the more he protests that he has lost his self-respect for good and unassailable reasons, the more hollow these protests seem.

Given his loss of self-esteem, it might seem as though melancholia is the very antithesis of grief, for grief involves the loss of an object in the external world, whereas melancholia involves the loss of self. But, says Freud, this difference is only apparent, and further probing reveals why. Like the griever, the melancholiac has experienced the painful loss of a loved object. But while the griever mourns the loss of the loved object who has been taken from him, the melancholiac experiences the loss of the object with considerable ambivalence, as he feels that the loss he is now having to endure is the object's own fault, that the object has abandoned him. This, however, is not a feeling that he can openly acknowledge, because the feeling of abandonment is more painful than the feeling, in grief, of bereavement, where the loved one has been "taken away" against her will. So the reproachful feelings he has toward the lost object are turned against himself. The lost object is not relinquished and released, as in grief, but is internalized, becoming an aspect of the ego, so that the ego itself becomes the focus of reproach and delusions of future punishment.

Freud suggests that this is how conscience comes to be created. Reproaches against the external object are redirected against the self. Thus, "in the clinical picture of melancholia dissatisfaction with the self on moral grounds is far the most outstanding feature; the self-criticism much less frequently concerns itself with bodily infirmity, ugliness, weakness, social inferiority" (1963, 169). By viewing the self-reproachings of melancholiacs as the reproach of the lost object turned against the self, Freud suggests that another puzzling feature of melancholia also becomes more comprehensible. This is the fact that the melancholiac exhibits little if any signs of "shame before others." We would expect that anyone who genuinely felt himself to be worthless would shrink from the gaze of others. But this is not the case with melancholiacs: "On the contrary, they give a great deal of trouble, perpetually taking offense and behaving as if they had been treated with great injustice. All this is possible only because the reactions expressed in their behavior still proceed from an attitude of revolt" (1963, 169–70).

If the melancholiac is in a state of revolt, this means that he has vengeful feelings toward the lost object. In Freud's view, his revenge is the pathology itself, as his illness is the means by which he torments the one who has forsaken him. Such tormenting of the other is possible because, unlike mourning, where the other is dead, the "person who has occasioned the injury to the [melancholic] patient's feelings, and against whom his illness is aimed, is usually to be found among those in his near neighborhood" (1963, 172–73). Thus, the melancholiac's relationship to the lost object has a twofold fate: the internalization of the object, which takes the form of self-reproach, and the punishment inflicted on the actual object by means of the pathology itself.

As a therapist, Freud takes a great interest in the question of whether melancholia is curable. By way of answer, he notes that melancholia is more complicated than mourning because the lost object evokes such highly ambivalent feelings. In melancholia, there are "countless single conflicts in which love and hate wrestle together" (1963, 177). Also, unlike in mourning, where the object is finally relinquished, in melancholia the release of the object is greatly complicated because the object has become so self-identified, meaning that the melancholiac is unconscious of the causes of his pathology. On the other hand, just as the work of grief enables the ego to give up the object in time, so in melancholia each single conflict or ambivalence, by disparaging and denigrating the object, loosens the fixation to it. Thus, it *is* possible for the process in the unconscious to come to an end, either because the fury has spent itself or because the object is abandoned as no longer having value. Which of these two possibilities is the regular or more usual one in bringing the melancholia to a merciful end is impossible to determine. What *is* indisputable, however, is that, unlike grief, the melancholia ends as the sufferer experiences "the satisfaction of acknowledging itself as the better of the two, as superior to the object" (1963, 179), indicating that reproach of the other is in some sense justified.

It must be emphasized that the object in this case is the internalized other, which bears only a partial resemblance to the other in real life. The struggle is an internalized one, in which the ego (or I) wrestles ambivalently, mixing both love and hate, with the internalized other. That the struggle is internal helps to explain why the melancholiac typically experiences symptoms both of mania and of depletion. The mania is usually associated with the sense of triumph over the internalized other, while the depletion is the sense that the ego is weak and unable to hold its own against the superior power of the internalized other. When the ego feels strong, it has the ability to "slay" the object, bringing the melancholia to an end. Therapeutically speaking, the goal is to strengthen the ego so that it may defeat the internalized object, thus achieving, in an admittedly violent manner, what grief accomplishes without the need for violence.

Although Freud does not identify the lost object as the boy's mother, the very intensity of the melancholic reaction suggests that she, the boy's first love object, is the object that has been lost. This would explain, for example, why one important feature of melancholia is the formation of a conscience and the fear of punishment. The boy believes that he has done something to warrant the loss of his mother and that if he makes certain reparations and promises he might win her back. Because, for reasons of gender differentiation, the son's separation from his mother is more decisive than the daughter's, he is also more likely to form a false conscience, one more delusional as to his own personal culpability for the initial separation and the failure to restore the relationship.

If the mother is the original lost object, all subsequent experiences of loss for reasons other than death (where grieving is possible) will be reminiscent of the loss of his mother and will evoke similar feelings of shame and rage, guilt, and remorse. These subsequent losses may be other people (for example, women with whom he falls in love) or desires that are symbolically linked to his mother (for example, the desire to pursue a career in art, music, or caregiving). To assert that the lost object is the mother—that is, the mother who had nothing but love for her son—is therefore consistent with Freud's analysis of melancholia. Melancholia is a reaction to the palpable fact that this object has been taken away, replaced by a mother whose love is perceived *not* to be unconditional but dependent on his capacity and willingness to be a certain kind of boy, one whom only she is in the position to declare acceptable to her. To regain the lost object, he will do whatever is in his power to make himself acceptable in her eyes. He promises to be "good," and tries valiantly to keep this solemn promise.

While all of this is going on at the conscious or preconscious level, something else entirely is occurring unconsciously, outside his conscious awareness. The lost object—the mother who has nothing but love for her son—is internalized, and this object now becomes the focus of his ambivalent feelings of love and hate. He loves the perfect mother, the mother of his fondest and most beautiful visions, but he also hates her, because she has betrayed and forsaken him. He blames the internalized "perfect mother" for this, but in the real, objective world the blaming takes the form of self-reproach, for what he is painfully conscious of, fervently believes to be the actual case, is the "fact" that it was his actions that caused her to vanish, to be replaced by the mother who is "good enough" or "not good enough." (In this case, it does not much matter which.) The internal struggle continues, and may do so indefinitely, even long after the mother of real flesh and blood is dead and mourned, for he is contending not with the good enough or not good enough mother but with the perfect mother who had nothing but love for him. "She" is the object of his continued struggle, "she" is the one who evokes such longing and such rage, such adoring gazes and such bitter, spiteful remarks and curses.

How does religion fit into this internalized drama? As I indicated, the boy's initial desire is to win the perfect mother back. He believes that if he makes himself acceptable in her eyes she will return, and all will be well. He develops a conscience, becomes conscientious, and begins to exercise self-control over his actions and thoughts. To the real mother, everything is working well, just as the child-rearing manuals have promised: Make your love for him conditional, and he will become a good boy, even perhaps a gentle boy who is kind to his brothers and sisters and treats animals and old people with dignity and respect. But this is only the surface story. Under the surface, in the unconscious, an emotional storm is brewing. The calm, placid, well-behaved boy is inwardly furious with himself and with his shattered image of the perfect mother. He continues to cherish this image but also wants to desecrate it. Love and hate wrestle together in a seemingly endless series of skirmishes. The "religious" side of him continues to cherish the loved object, now beatified. The "pathological" or iconoclastic side of him wants to have done with the object, to destroy it, so that he might get on with his life. Thus, melancholia is more than sadness over the lost object, for it also contains a deep bitterness, a bitterness toward self and toward the perfect mother who became, at best, a good enough one.

One way that conventional religion may conceivably help him to get on with his life is by teaching him that God is a Father and that if he continues to be "a good boy," this Father God will not only *not* punish him but will reward him for his goodness. But this teaching has very little to do with, or to say to, his real distress, which is that he has lost the perfect mother. He has experienced the withdrawal of his mother's love, and he feels bereft, depleted, and angry. Thus, if it is true that "father religions have mother churches," it is also true that father religions are a convenient cover for good enough mothers as these religions deceive the sons into believing that if they appease the Father God, all will be well with them, when in fact nothing will be well with them until they come to terms with their melancholy, which has another basis entirely. The heart of the matter is the boy's image of the perfect mother. Everything else is secondary, an interesting sideshow, a useful distraction, but irrelevant to his basic distress, his underlying sense of having been forsaken by his mother.

Given the role that conscience and fear of future punishment play in melancholia, the paradigmatic experience that triggers this plunge into melancholia is the mother's decision to punish her son for misbehavior. But while this punishment scenario may be paradigmatic, other experiences may serve as catalysts for the shattering of the perfect image of his mother. Indeed, where melancholy seems especially pronounced or severe, we should look for other experiential causes besides the punishment scenario, or some combination of punishment and other factors, such as his mother's prolonged physical absence, her preferential treatment of a sibling, or a situation where she appears to her son to place her own well-being ahead of his (for example, where the father abuses both mother and son). Her own inflictions of pain on her son are therefore important, and the experience of child abuse, especially when inflicted by the mother, is often a crucial factor in the development of melancholia. But there are typically other contributing factors as well. Thus, more important to my argument than allegations of child *abuse* is that the son experiences some form of childhood *trauma,* leading him to implicate his mother in what becomes a form of self-abuse, the internalized rage whose real object is the idealized, perfect mother.

Freud's other essay that has importance for my argument here is "The 'Uncanny,'" first published in *Imago* in 1919, two years after the publication of "Mourning and Melancholia." Freud begins this essay with the observation that the psychoanalyst does not often investigate the subject of aesthetics, even when aesthetics is taken to mean not merely the theory of beauty but also the theory of feeling (1958, 122). Yet "it does occasionally happen that he has to interest himself in some particular province of that subject; and then it usually proves to be a rather remote region of it and one that has been neglected in standard works" (1958, 122). The subject of the "uncanny" is a "province" of this very sort: "It undoubtedly belongs to all that is terrible — to all that arouses dread and creeping horror; it is equally certain, too, that the word is not always used in a clearly definable sense, so that it tends to coincide with whatever excites dread. Yet we may expect that it implies some intrinsic quality which justifies the use of a special name. One is curious to know what this peculiar quality is which allows us to distinguish as 'uncanny' certain things within the boundaries of what is 'fearful' " (1958, 122).

Freud notes that little is written on this subject in treatises on aesthetics, which concern themselves with the beautiful, attractive, and sublime. In the absence of prior investigations into the subject, he proposes that two courses are open to us. Either we can find out what meaning has come to be attached to the word *uncanny* in the course of its history or we "can collect all those properties of persons, things, sensations, experiences and situations which arouse in us the feeling of uncanniness, and then infer the unknown nature of the uncanny from what they all have in common" (1958, 123). Having engaged in both investigations for the purposes of this essay, Freud claims at the very outset that "both courses tend to the same result: the 'uncanny' is that class of the terrifying which leads back to something long known to us, once very familiar" (1958, 123–24). The point of this essay is to show how this can be, how "the familiar can become uncanny and frightening" (1958, 124).

His explorations into the meaning of the word *uncanny*, which is the English translation for the German word *unheimlich*, lead to the conclusion that the word *heimlich* ("homelike") shades into its opposite, *unheimlich*, as it not only means "that which is familiar" but also "the making visible of that which ought to have remained hidden and secret." In reference to the revelation of that which should have remained secret, either the word *heimlich* or the word *unheimlich* may be used, indicating that there is an emotional tension or ambiguity in the word *heimlich*, as it has to do, on the one hand, with the familiar and congenial and, on the other, with what is concealed and kept out of sight: "Thus *heimlich* is a word the meaning of which develops towards an ambivalence, until it finally coincides with its opposite, *unheimlich*" (1958, 131). The familiar becomes unfamiliar, frightening and strange. When secrets that are heimlich (such as personal confidences, love affairs, and so forth) are disclosed, they become unheimlich (that is, conducive to fear, anxiety, panic, and terror). Precisely because heimlich "has the meaning of that which is obscure, inaccessible to knowledge," it has an aura of das Unheimliche (1958, 131).

The second course open to Freud, that of reviewing those persons, things, impressions, events, and situations that arouse in us a feeling of the uncanny in a very forceful manner, leads to the same conclusion. The feeling of the uncanny is aroused when that which is very familiar to us suddenly becomes strange and foreign. He provides many examples of this transformation of the familiar into the unfamiliar, including amputated or dismembered body parts, places one revisits after years of absence, the experience of sitting in a room that is slowly being enveloped in darkness, and his own experience of assuming that he was viewing another man in the adjoining rail car when in fact he was seeing himself in the mirror. What makes such experiences uncanny is not that they involve objects, persons, or situations that are totally unfamiliar to us (like aliens from space) but that we are suddenly confronted with the unfamiliarity of that which was originally familiar to us. A human hand is a very familiar sight, but a human hand severed from the arm makes it very unfamiliar — uncanny — especially when it continues to move.

Employing psychoanalytic theory, Freud suggests that what makes certain things seem uncanny is that objects or situations once familiar to us but since repressed have reappeared. The experience of the return of the repressed accounts for the anxiety that accompanies the uncanny. We can therefore understand "why the usage of speech has extended *das Heimliche* into its opposite *das Unheimliche*: for this uncanny is in reality nothing new or foreign, but something familiar and old-established in the mind that has been estranged only by the process of repression. This reference to the factor of repression enables us, furthermore, to understand Schelling's definition of the uncanny as something which ought to have been kept concealed but which has nevertheless come to light" (1958, 148).

Freud also suggests that animistic religion has its emotional basis in the anxiety that attends the return of the repressed, as when we imagine that the dead have come back to life in the form of spirits and ghosts. And "since practically all of us still think as savages do on this topic, it is no matter for surprise that the primitive fear of the dead is still so strong within us and always ready to come to the surface at any opportunity. Most likely our fear still contains the old belief that the deceased becomes the enemy of his survivor and wants to carry him off to share his new life with him" (1958, 149–50).

However, the example of the return of the repressed that seems most to interest Freud is "an instance taken from psycho-analytical experience." It often happens "that male patients declare that they feel there is something uncanny about the female genital organs. This *unheimlich* place, however, is the entrance to the former *heim* [home] of all human beings, to the place where everyone dwelt once upon a time and in the beginning. There is a humorous saying: 'Love is home-sickness'; and whenever a man dreams of a place or a country and says to himself, still in the dream, 'this place is familiar to me, I have been there before,' we may interpret the place as being his mother's genitals or her body. In this case, too, the *unheimlich* is what was once *heim-isch*, home-like, familiar; the prefix 'un' is the token of repression" (1958, 152–53). This statement suggests that a man's mother is associated with the very ambivalence reflected in the shading of das Heimliche into das Unheim-liche, and thus with the experience of the uncanny. Her body, especially those parts with which he was most intimately familiar, has become unfamiliar, de-familiarized, no longer congenial, and this de-familiarization, with its atten-dant anxieties, is implicated in all subsequent experiences of the uncanny.

This leads us to the conclusion that the "lost object" identified in "Mourn-ing and Melancholia" is the mother who has become unheimlich, the one who arouses anxiety in her son. That she may make herself unheimlich to him by threatening behavior cannot be discounted, but there are prior grounds for anxiety in the simple fact that, by virtue of his birth, his departure from her body, the familiar has already become strange and foreign. His greatest terror is the sight of her naked body. I would suggest, furthermore, that the uncanni-ness is greater for the male child than for the female child because his physical difference from his mother is precisely where the heimlich/unheimlich ambiv-alence is so emotionally — uncannily — powerful. Men are more likely than women to experience "home-sickness" and to express the melancholy view that "you cannot go home again." Indeed, men frequently experience them-selves as strangers and intruders in that most familiar of places, the home.

Thus, while Freud does not make an explicit connection between the un-canny and melancholia, his analysis of the uncanny suggests that they are in fact profoundly related, for melancholia, unlike mourning, is a state or condi-tion of anxiety in which one is truly ambivalent, as one laments the loss of the familiar object yet at the same time fears the object's return. The experience of its return, even if this occurs in a dream and not in real life, occasions an anxious reaction. Thus, whereas in mourning the familiar object is given up and relinquished, in melancholia there can be no final relinquishing of the object, because there is the continuing threat of its return in a new guise for the purpose of hurting or terrorizing its victim.

Thus, if "Mourning and Melancholia" alerts us to the boy's loss of the loved object and the emotions that occur as a direct result of this loss, especially his deep feelings of hatred for the one who abandoned him, "The 'Uncanny' " directs our attention to the emotions that accompany the threat of the object's return in a new, unloving guise. Together, the two essays enable us to identify the anxieties that underly the melancholic attitude to life, and also to recognize the fact that these anxieties are two sides of the same coin, for the object would not come back to haunt him unless she had discovered his hateful feelings toward her; unless, that is to say, his awful secret had been revealed to the very one from whom he most wanted to conceal it.

James

"That Shape Am I": The Bearing of Melancholy *on* The Varieties of Religious Experience

Although it was written by an American, most Americans today experience William James's *Varieties of Religious Experience* (1982, hereafter *VRE*) as foreign to them, as it seems concerned with many issues that are not now very current. The subject matter of the first chapter, "Religion and Neurology," is not likely to attract the would-be reader, as the question of whether religion is physiologically based is not one that interests us very much today. The following passage, in which James cites examples of this association of religion and physiology, seems quaint and oddly foreign to current readers: "Perhaps the commonest expression of this assumption that spiritual value is undone if lowly origin be asserted is seen in those comments which unsentimental people so often pass on their more sentimental acquaintances. Alfred believes in immortality so strongly because his temperament is so emotional. Fanny's extra-ordinary conscientiousness is merely a matter of over-instigated nerves. William's melancholy about the universe is due to bad digestion — probably his liver is torpid. Eliza's delight in her church is a symptom of her hysterical condition. Peter would be less troubled about his soul if he would take more exercise in the open air, etc." (*VRE*, 10). [27]

Although we may believe that William should improve his diet and that Peter should exercise more, we are unlikely to connect diet and melancholy, exercise and soul worries. If this particular quotation attracts our attention at all, it is very likely because the author gives his own name — William — to the one who suffers from melancholy. Perhaps James is being playful here, and we might imagine him saying: "The alert reader will recognize that I have casually but significantly introduced myself into my text. The others will miss it, but they, after all, are not the ones I would expect to convince or persuade anyway."

The foreignness of James's text continues in the second chapter, "Circumscription of the Topic," which seems so out of step with what religion in contemporary America is all about. Here James states the working definition of religion he will apply throughout the text, a definition that excludes the "institutional branch" of religion altogether (*VRE,* 28–31). This might not seem so foreign to our usual ways of thinking about the nature of religion if it meant only that he is uninterested in matters of church polity and administration, but he goes much farther than this, including in the excluded institutional branch such activities and phenomena as worship and sacrifice, ceremony and theology, as well as ideas about God. The alert reader is likely to say, "This doesn't leave very much of what I have taken religion to be." James agrees, as he emphasizes that his working definition of religion is "for the purpose of these lectures," and he asks his readers to accept its "arbitrariness" (*VRE,* 28, 31). What remains after the institutional branch is "stripped away"? "The feelings, acts, and experiences of individual men [and women] in their solitude, so far as they apprehend themselves to stand in relation to whatever they may consider the divine" (*VRE,* 31). This is the definition that he asks his reader to accept as valid for his present purposes.

To our ears, this definition of religion strikes two jarring notes. One is that religion is defined as individualistic and noncommunal ("individuals in their solitude"). The other is that the definition's author seems rather unconcerned about what these individuals may actually "apprehend," so long as they themselves consider it divine. The definition seems quite limiting on the one hand, and rather loose on the other. Anticipating that his readers may object to this "circumscription of the topic," James imagines what they may be thinking: "To some of you personal religion, thus nakedly considered, will no doubt seem too incomplete a thing to wear the general name. 'It is a part of religion,' you will say, 'but only its unorganized rudiment. . . . The name "religion" should be reserved for the fully organized system of feeling, thought, and institution, for the Church, in short, of which this personal religion so called, is but a fractional element'" (*VRE,* 29).

In response to this imagined objection, James promises to say something about "the theologies and ecclesiasticisms" in his concluding chapter, and he then notes that at least in one respect personal religion is more fundamental than either theology or ecclesiasticism, for "the *founders* of every church owed their power originally to the fact of their direct personal communion with the divine" (*VRE*, 30). However, he is not really interested in the institutionalization of these personal religious experiences, and the final chapter does not in fact make good on his promise to deal with the relation between personal religious experience and "the theologies and ecclesiasticisms." Instead, it focuses on the subconscious self, "a well-accredited psychological entity," as the field through which apprehensions of the divine occur (*VRE*, 511–13), and James's conclusions are presented not in order to initiate a dialogue between psychology of religion and systematic or doctrinal theology but as a contribution to the emerging field of "the science of religion" (*VRE*, 488–90). A concluding postscript, added after the final chapter, clarifies certain philosophical issues left hanging in the final lecture, and it too fails to make good on his promise to discuss the relationship of personal to "ecclesiastical" religion.[1]

What is the contemporary reader to make of this "circumscription of the topic," this exclusive focus on personal religion, on religion as the experiences of individuals in their solitude? In a country where being religious is usually defined as churchgoing, and where the growth and decline of religion is measured by the percentage of Americans who belong to churches, James's "circumscription of the topic" seems more than arbitrary. It appears downright perverse. He has offered a definition of religion that excludes the social, participatory aspects of religion and also excludes its theological and ethical preoccupations.[2]

The question is whether personal religion can be "thus nakedly considered." Some readers of his text have astutely pointed out that the very language individuals use to describe their experiences of "apprehending" God is itself derived from the ecclesiastical and theological traditions that James has "arbitrarily" excluded (Nørager 1995). They note that the religious experiences recorded in *The Varieties* illustrate this. For example, the conversion account by Stephen H. Bradley that introduces James's first chapter on conversion is replete with Christian theological terms (Saviour, Holy Spirit, and so forth) and is viewed by Bradley himself as similar to the experiences of the original apostles on the Day of Pentecost. Furthermore, while his experience occurred in solitude, at home, it was triggered by his having attended church earlier that evening (*VRE*, 189–93). As Proudfoot and Shaver point out in their application of attribution theory to religious experience,

> Bradley, like so many prospective devotees before and since, could not understand his feelings in naturalistic terms. Religious symbols offered him an explanation that was compatible with both his experience and his former

beliefs. He did not consider explanations involving Krishna, Zeus, or the Koran. The content of the scripture and the experience of being moved or physiologically aroused were confidently linked together. These are the two components of emotion described by [attribution theorist Stanley] Schachter. It seems likely that religious symbols and doctrines often serve as labels for experiences of arousal which initially appear to be anomalous. As in Schachter's experiments, individuals seek plausible explanations for their feelings among whatever explanations are available in the environment [1975, 323].

Thus, for Bradley, the experience derives its meaning from a specific theological and ecclesiastical context and cannot be understood apart from it. If James separates the personal and the institutional branches of religion, the Bradleys, Bunyans, Luthers, and Saint Theresas who populate his text do not. Without the institutional branch, they have no way of attributing meaning or significance to their religious experiences. There is no other way for them to authenticate their experiences.

What are we contemporary readers of James's text to make of this objection to his whole project? I suggest that we may do one of two things. On the one hand, we may take the view that what James has tried to keep separate — the personal and the institutional — cannot be treated separately from each other. In adopting this view, we may in fact claim James's own ostensible support for it, as he himself has said that his division of the two aspects of religion is an arbitrary one. On the other hand, we may take the view James seems to have adopted in his own life, that an individual may be "religious" in the purely personal sense of the term and be so without the assistance of the institutional branch of religion — and this, we should note, includes theology. When discussing the attacks of melancholy that James and his father experienced, Erikson refers to the "extreme individualism" of each man's religious "life style" (1968, 153). James himself, in challenging the view so common to the sciences of his day that the experiences of individuals are of no concern, that only the aggregate matters, points out that religion makes no such blunder: "The individual's religion may be egotistic, and those private realities which it keeps in touch with may be narrow enough; but at any rate it always remains infinitely less hollow and abstract, as far as it goes, than a science which prides itself on taking no account of anything private at all. By being religious we establish ourselves in possession of ultimate reality at the only points at which reality is given us to guard. Our responsible concern is with our private destiny, after all" (*VRE,* 500–1).

To be "privately religious" assumes that (like James) one is not a church-goer, and that therefore one's personal religious experiences will have no connection to any ecclesiastical context. It also means that one does not use theological language, or the language of any religious tradition, to describe and interpret the personal experiences that one takes to be "religious." The question, then, is whether religion may in fact be an entirely individual matter, unrelated to and disconnected from any and all religious traditions.

The illustrations James employs in *The Varieties* provide overwhelming evidence against this idea. Virtually every account of personal religious experience he includes in his book supports the counter thesis, that there is no purely personal religious experience, that all religious experiences are related in one way or another to religious traditions, drawing on their systems of ideas and beliefs, or their social and communal aspects, or both. The only experiences in *The Varieties* that *might* challenge this overwhelming evidence are James's own experiences, to which I now turn.

The Possibility of Purely Personal Religion

Two years after the publication of *The Varieties,* James in 1904 responded to a questionnaire sent out by Professor James B. Pratt of Williams College (Brown 1973, 123–25). In response to the question "Is God very real to you, as real as an earthly friend, though different?" James replied, "Dimly (real); not (as an earthly friend)." When asked "Do you feel that you have experienced his presence? If so, please describe what you mean by such an experience," James wrote simply, "Never." Addressing those respondents who answered this question in the negative, Pratt asked whether they "accept the testimony of others who claim to have felt God's presence directly." James answered affirmatively: "Yes! The whole line of testimony on this point is so strong that I am unable to pooh-pooh it away. No doubt there is a germ in me of something similar that makes response." To Pratt's open-ended question "What do you mean by a 'religious experience'?" James answered, "Any moment of life that brings the reality of spiritual things more 'home' to one."

If we take James's response to Pratt's questionnaire at face value, we must conclude that he does not feel that he has ever experienced the presence of God. However, he is sympathetic toward the testimony of others who claim to have felt God's presence directly. He elaborates on this sympathy in his response to another question in the survey: "I suppose that the chief premise for my hospitality towards the religious testimony of others is my conviction that 'normal' or 'sane' consciousness is so small a part of actual experience. . . . The other kinds of consciousness bear witness to a much wider universe of experiences, from which our belief selects and emphasizes such parts as best satisfy our needs" (Brown 1973, 124).

If he has not "experienced" God, does this mean that he does not believe in

God? In response to Pratt's question "Why do you believe in God?" — for which Pratt offers a list of possible "whys," — James indicates that his belief is not based on any rational or intellectual argument for the existence of God ("emphatically, no"), or on personal experience, or on biblical authority, or the preachings or writings of "a prophetic person." However, to his negative response to the "personal experience" option he adds that he believes "because I need it so that it 'must' be true," and to his negative response to the "biblical authority" option he adds that he does make "admiring response" to "the whole tradition of religious people."

In these responses to Pratt's questionnaire, James comes across as religiously unconventional, as a religious outsider who does not belong to the ranks of those who have experienced the presence of God and are able to articulate these experiences in the language of the religious tradition with which they identify. To say that one makes "admiring response" to those who claim experiences of God is to present oneself as a spectator, as one who watches the others but for one reason or another cannot or will not participate.

In an essay on James's brother Henry, P. J. Eakin (1985) tells of how Henry, like William, did not participate in the Civil War (their two younger brothers, Wilky and Bob, *did* serve in the Union Army) yet viewed his experience of being psychologically immobilized as a result of fighting a fire in his hometown of Newport as simultaneously an acknowledgment of his having "missed out on life" and an imaginative identification of himself as "a member of the elect company of the experienced" (p. 125).[3] A similar ambiguity occurs in the case of William James, as he cannot claim to be numbered among the truly religious, any more than Henry can claim to have served in the Union Army, and yet he can identify with the religious in an imaginative fashion because he has had experiences that are similar to religious ones. Another response to Pratt's questionnaire captures some of this ambiguity. On the one hand, he asserts that there is more to "spiritual reality" than God: "God, to me, is not the only spiritual reality to believe in. Religion means primarily a universe of spiritual relations surrounding the earthly practical ones, not merely relations of 'value,' but agencies and their activities." On the other hand, science takes a far too narrow view of what is or is not true: "What e'er be true, it is not true exclusively, as philistine scientific opinion assumes." It is true, but not exclusively true, that Henry was not an active participant in the Civil War, for he was in some true sense a casualty of it. William has not had experience of God, but he has had experience of the "spiritual" reality that surrounds the "earthly" reality. The term *religious outsider* captures the ambiguity of his association with "the elect company of the experienced."

While James had a lifelong interest in and experimented with psychic phenomena and altered states of consciousness, his most significant experiences that bordered on the religious were those of "mental disease" (James 1950, 2:416) and, specifically, his struggles with melancholia. These continued throughout his life, leading him to seek temporary relief through various practical remedies, including baths and hydrotherapy treatments, medication, diet, exercise, and hypnotism (or "mind cure"). Prior to his delivery of the Gifford Lectures, he wrote a letter to his daughter, Margaret, from the baths of Bad-Nauheim in Germany, where he was receiving treatment for his chronic melancholy. In it, he describes what it is like to suffer from melancholy: "Among other things there will be waves of terrible sadness, which sometimes lasts for days; and dissatisfactions with one's self, and irritation at others, and anger at circumstances and stoney insensibility, etc., etc., which taken together form a melancholy" (Rubin 1994, 20). He adds by way of encouragement: "Now, painful as it is, this is sent to us for an enlightenment" (p. 20).

Gerald E. Myers (1986) points out that James suffered from a variety of psychosomatic illnesses throughout his life, including angina, backaches, fatigue, and depression, and that he was willing to try any practical remedy that might alleviate the suffering. Yet while he felt that his melancholia, like his other conflicts, had psychological causes, he also believed that melancholia "is more philosophical and less medical than angina. Certain kinds of depression intensify or diminish simply in response to the ideas or beliefs which happen to occupy the mind" (p. 51). According to Myers, he seems to have reasoned that his "despondency was a state of mind that . . . would evaporate if he were somehow able to reject philosophical pessimism" (p. 51). Myers also notes that James made little effort to determine the psychological causes of his melancholy. He even points out that James was not especially good at self-analysis, and that his introspective powers were in one sense quite limited:

> James was skillful in rendering his feelings into words or in recording his habits and mannerisms, but he was oddly uninterested in self-analysis. He could be aware of his tendency to be silent in his father's presence, to feel relief when away from his wife, to dread being alone, to be assertive toward younger siblings, to dislike exact disciplines such as formal logic, to escape whenever he became a parent, to be endlessly neurotic — *yet he was not motivated even to speculate about the psychological causes of these phenomena, much less to seek those causes out introspectively.* This feature of James's personality is undoubtedly what some scholars mean when discussing his innocence of himself or his lack of interest in self-analysis [Myers 1986, 49; my emphasis].

So far as these melancholic episodes were concerned, the challenge in alleviating them was "less finding the nexus of causes underlying them than battling them as they appear. It is less important to diagnose their origins than it is to vanquish them through creating future-oriented incentives. James fought his battles largely through what he called acts of thought" (Myers 1986, 52).

I shall return to James's inability or reluctance to trace the psychological origins of his melancholy, because this has direct bearing on the argument that melancholia is rooted in a boy's loss of his mother's unconditional love. For the moment, I want to make the point that his lifelong struggle with melancholia was the primary basis for his belief that he had something in common with people of religious temperament. William Styron's (1990) account of his own devastating descent into melancholia supports James's belief, as he speaks of the "pain that crushes the soul" and the "anxiety and incipient dread that I had hidden away for so long somewhere in the dungeons of my spirit" (Styron 1990, 62, 40). Words like *soul* and *spirit* have an unmistakable religious bearing.[4]

The *Diagnostic and Statistical Manual of Mental Disorders* (1994) is helpful for determining the severity of James's melancholia. It views melancholia as a special feature of a major depressive episode that occurs in the course of a major depressive disorder. The typical features of a major depressive episode are feelings of depression, sadness, hopelessness, or discouragement, often accompanied by somatic complaints (bodily aches and pains) or increased irritability (for example, persistent anger, a tendency to respond to events with angry outbursts, or an exaggerated sense of frustration over minor matters); loss of interest or pleasure, either "not caring anymore" or not feeling any enjoyment in activities previously considered pleasurable; reduced appetite; insomnia; psychomotor changes, such as agitation or retardation in speech, thinking, and body movements; decreased energy; a sense of worthlessness or guilt; inability to think, concentrate or make decisions; and thoughts of death, suicidal ideation, or suicide attempts. If five or more of these symptoms are present, including depressed mood or loss of interest or pleasure for a two-week period, a major depressive episode is indicated. A major depressive episode *with melancholic features* adds lack of pleasure in all or almost all activities, *or* a lack of reactivity to usually pleasurable stimuli.

The individual's depressed mood does not improve, even temporarily, when something good happens (criterion A). In addition, at least three of the following symptoms are present: a distinct quality of the depressed mood; depression that is regularly worse in the morning; early morning awakening; psychomotor retardation or agitation; significant anorexia or weight loss; or excessive or inappropriate guilt (criterion B). The quality of mood characteristic of major depressive episode *with melancholic features* is experienced as qualitatively different from the sadness experienced during bereavement or a nonmelancholic depressive episode. This may be elicited by asking the person to compare the quality of the current depressed mood with that experienced after a loved one's death. If the response is merely that it seems more severe, longer-lasting, or present without a reason, this is insufficient basis for concluding that melancholia is involved, as psychomotor changes are nearly always present and, in contrast to depression after the death of a loved one, excessive or inappropriate guilt is also characteristic of melancholia (1994, 320–22, 383–84).

James's own depressive episodes appear to have had a melancholic dimension. They typically involved lack of reactivity to usually pleasurable stimuli, together with symptoms of psychomotor agitation and retardation, irritability, inability to think, and excessive guilt. Myers mentions that letters written by James's students were critical of his habit of suddenly dismissing his classes, saying, "I can't think today. We had better not go on with class" (Myers 1986, 487). James also complained of being "interrupted every moment by students come to fight about their marks," and "when money was involved and he felt unfairly treated, James could become extremely angry and aggressive" (Myers 1986, 35, 29). His feelings of guilt for behavior he seemed unable to alter are especially illustrated in his habit of leaving his wife to care for the family. According to Myers, "he was often absent, if only as far away as Newport, on holidays such as Christmas, New Year's Day, and birthdays. Although he must have appreciated the difficulties his absences caused for his family, he seems to have been powerless to alter the habit" (Myers 1986, 36–37).

His irritability and sense of guilt were characteristically related. As Myers also notes, "William often apologized to his wife for outbursts of temper before a parting, reiterated his love for her and his appreciation of her care and devotion, and expressed the hope that the trip was improving his nerves so that he would be easier to live with when he returned" (Myers 1986, 37). Thus, his melancholia went beyond mere sadness; it also included psychomotor alterations that were observable by others and cognitive changes of which he himself was painfully aware.

The DSM notes that, in the case of depressed children and adolescents, "an irritable or cranky mood may develop rather than a sad or dejected mood," and that such irritability must be distinguished from "a 'spoiled child' pattern of irritability when frustrated" (1994, 321). While Myers says that there was "something impish in his manner [that] suggested an eternal boyishness" (Myers 1986, 41), one guesses that James was irritable from childhood, not because he was "spoiled" but because he was already melancholic.

What James himself emphasizes in his accounts of his melancholic episodes is his sense of profound sadness and awareness of the reality of death. In describing a particularly distressing period in his life, a trip to the Amazon in

1865 when he was 23 years old, he wrote, "To me the peculiar feature which at all times of the day and everywhere made itself felt was the sadness and solemnity produced by the flood of sun and the inextricable variety of vegetable forms, elements which one would suspect beforehand to have a gay and cheerful effect on the observer" (Myers 1986, 48). This puts us in mind of his contention in *The Varieties* that "there must be something solemn, serious, and tender about any attitude which we denominate religious. If glad, it must not snicker; if sad, it must not scream or curse. It is precisely as being *solemn* experiences that I wish to interest you in religious experiences" (*VRE*, 38). ⌊54⌋

In his essay "Is Life Worth Living?" (1986) James notes that the question in his title would never arise if our optimistic moods could be made permanent and if the optimistic constitution that some persons exhibit all the time could be made universal: "But we are not magicians to make the optimistic temperament universal; and alongside of the deliverances of temperamental optimism concerning life, those of temperamental pessimism always exist, and oppose to them a standing refutation. In what is called 'circular insanity,' phases of melancholy succeed phases of mania, with no outward cause that we can discover; and often enough to one and the same well person life will present incarnate radiance to-day and incarnate dreariness to-morrow" (1986, 34). He then proceeds to quote a poem by James Thomson from his book *The City of Dreadful Night* that portrays a preacher speaking to a congregation gathered in a great unillumined cathedral at night. The lines from which James quotes begin "O Brothers of sad lives! they are so brief" and contain this strange word of comfort:

> But if you would not this poor life fulfil,
> Lo, you are free to end it when you will,
> Without the fear of waking after death.

In commenting on these lines, James notes that they "flow truthfully from the *melancholy* Thomson's pen, and are in truth a consolation for all to whom, as to him, the world is far more like a steady den of fear than a continual fountain of delight" (p. 37, my emphasis). Continuing, James observes "that life is not worth living the whole army of suicides declare," and "we, too, as we sit here in our comfort, must 'ponder these things' also, for we are of one substance with these suicides, and their life is the life we share" (p. 37).

Suicide is a desperately lonely act, but it is the outcome of the depressive or deeply melancholic condition if other factors do not intervene (see Styron 1990, 65–67). Thus, if James considered his melancholia the basis on which he could claim his own "imaginative identification" with the religious, we may understand why the religious experiences would have to be ones that occur in solitude, when an individual is alone and without any social supports whatever, and why such experiences would need to be solemn. His point is not that all melancholic episodes are religious or that all religious experiences are rooted in melancholia, but that there is sufficient similarity between them for the one to shed light on the other. To explore this point further, I now want to direct our attention to James's early writings on melancholy, using these as background for his discussion of "religious melancholy" in *The Varieties*.

Melancholy as Mental Pathology

James discusses melancholy in the second volume of his *Principles of Psychology* in a chapter entitled "The Perception of Reality" (1950, 2:283–384). This chapter expands on an article he wrote for the philosophical journal *Mind* when he was 27 years old. It begins with a consideration of the nature of belief and specifically with his assertion that belief is the "sense of the reality" of that which is believed. Thus, belief is "the mental state or function of cognizing reality" (p. 283). This means that doubt and inquiry, not disbelief, are the true opposites of belief, because in doubt and inquiry the "content of our mind is in unrest," as we do not yet know whether the object is real or not, whereas in disbelief we have settled the issue by declaring to ourselves that the object does not exist in the real world. He further suggests that belief, on the one hand, and doubt and inquiry, on the other, are emotions that may be "pathologically exalted." For example, belief is typically "exalted" in states of drunkenness, especially in nitrous-oxide intoxication, and doubt is pathologically exalted in what has been called "the questioning mania," in which individuals seem condemned to think about such questions as "Why is a glass a glass, a chair a chair?" and "Why are humans the size of humans, and not as big as houses?"

But then he adds that there is "another pathological state which is as far removed from doubt as from belief, and which some may prefer to consider the proper contrary of the latter state of mind. I refer to the feeling that everything is hollow, unreal, dead" (1950, 2:285). This is melancholy, and James returns to it later in the chapter, after having first discussed what makes something real *for us:* "The mere fact of appearing as an object at all is not enough to constitute reality. That may be metaphysical reality, reality for God; but what we need is practical reality, reality for ourselves; and, to have that, an object must not only appear, but it must appear both *interesting* and *important.* . . . Whenever an object so appeals to us that we turn to it, accept it, fill our mind with it, or practically take account of it, so far it is real for us, and we believe it. Whenever, on the contrary, we ignore it, fail to consider it or act upon it, despise it, reject it, forget it, so far it is unreal for us and disbelieved" (1950, 2:295). Thus, "Whatever things have intimate and continuous connection with my life are things of whose reality I cannot doubt" (p. 298).

Therefore, what happens in melancholy, or at least in certain forms of it, is that "nothing touches us intimately, rouses us, or wakens natural feeling. The consequence is the complaint so often heard from melancholic patients, that nothing is believed in by them as it used to be, and that all sense of reality is fled from life. They are sheathed in india-rubber; nothing penetrates to the quick or draws blood, as it were" (1950, 2:298).

James continues this analysis of melancholy by quoting Wilhelm Griesinger, author of a major text in the mid-nineteenth century entitled *Mental Pathology and Therapeutics,* who noted that such patients will say, "I see, I hear, but the objects do not reach me, it is as if there were a wall between me and the other world!" Griesinger continues:

> In childhood we feel ourselves to be closer to the world of sensible phenomena, we live immediately with them and in them; an intimately vital tie binds us and them together. But with the ripening of reflection this tie is loosened, the warmth of our interest cools, things look differently to us, and we act more as foreigners to the outer world, even though we know it a great deal better. Joy and expansive emotions in general draw it nearer to us again. Everything makes a more lively impression, and with the quick immediate return of this warm receptivity for sense-impressions, joy makes us feel young again. *In depressing emotions it is the other way. Outer things, whether living or inorganic, suddenly grow cold and foreign to us, and even our favorite objects of interest feel as if they belonged to us no more.* Under these circumstances, receiving no longer from anything a lively impression, we cease to turn towards outer things, and the sense of inward loneliness grows upon us. . . . Where there is no strong intelligence to control this *blasé* condition, this psychic coldness and lack of interest, the issue of these states in which all seems so cold and hollow, the heart dried up, the world grown dead and empty, is often suicide or the deeper forms of insanity [in James 1950, 2:298, my emphasis].

James does not discuss melancholy any further in his chapter "The Perception of Reality," but toward the end of the chapter he takes up the role played by imagination in making unreal things seem real: "Who does not 'realize' more the fact of a dead or distant friend's existence, at the moment when a portrait, letter, garment or other material reminder of him is found? The whole notion of him then grows pungent and speaks to us and shakes us, in a manner unknown at other times" (p. 303). This illustration implies that melancholy concerns absence and loss, and the desire to regain the lost object in some form or other, a point to which I shall return when discussing James's own melancholic episodes.[5]

In *Melancholia and Depression* (1986), Stanley W. Jackson discusses Griesinger's text, "a work that had a tremendous influence on his contemporaries and on their nineteenth-century successors" (p. 160). According to Jackson, Griesinger's basic thesis was that there are successive states of mental depression in melancholia. The initial melancholic state, which Griesinger termed "stadium melancholicum" and described as "a state of profound emotional perversion, of a depressing and sorrowful character," is "the direct continuation of some painful emotion dependent upon some objective cause [for example, grief, jealousy] and it is distinguished from the mental pain experienced by healthy persons by its excessive degree, by its more than ordinary protraction, by its becoming more and more independent of external influences" (p. 161). The next stage is hypochondriasis, in which the bodily sensations are real but somatically unfounded and the intellect functions soundly but starts from false premises. The third stage is melancholia proper, in which "the mental pain consists in a profound feeling of *ill-being,* of inability to do anything, of suppression of the physical powers, of depression and sadness, and of total abasement of self-consciousness" (p. 162). Also typical of this third stage, as summarized by Jackson, is "a tendency toward increased unhappiness and dejection, irritability, either discontent or withdrawal from others, preoccupation with self, sometimes hatred of others, and sometimes contrariness. And a tendency toward indecisiveness and inactivity [reflecting] a worsening of the disorder of the will" (p. 162). More serious manifestations of third-stage melancholy are the appearance of false ideas and judgments "corresponding to the actual disposition of the patient" (p. 162).

Griesinger states that the course of melancholia is usually chronic, with remissions. Intermissions of the disease for extended periods are rare. If the melancholia worsens, it may transform itself into mania, which in turn results in violent actions or extreme excitations of the will. So far as predisposing factors are concerned, Griesinger cites influences in one's upbringing as well as hereditary factors. Precipitating causes might include some subtle, as yet unidentified, cerebral pathology; subtle psychological changes, perhaps from simple nervous irritation or slight nutritional changes; and circulatory problems. But more important are psychological factors, especially painful emotional states:

> In individual cases these painful emotional states may vary very much in their nature and in their causes: sometimes it is sudden anger — shock or grief excited by injury, loss of fortune, a rude interference with [one's sense of]

modesty, a sudden death, etc.; sometimes it is the result of the slow gnawings of disappointed ambitions on the mind, regret on account of certain unjust actions, domestic affliction, unfortunate love, jealousy, error, forced sojourn in inadequate circumstances, or any other injured sentiment. In every case there are influences which, through intense disturbance of the mass of ideas of the *ego,* cause a mournful division in consciousness, *and we always see the most powerful effects where the wishes and hopes have been for a long time concentrated upon a certain object.* Where the individual has made certain things indispensible to his life, and when these are forcibly withdrawn, the passage of the ideas into efforts is cut off, and accordingly a gap in the *ego* and a violent internal strife results [in Jackson 1986, 164–65, my emphasis].

Griesinger also considers "mixed" causes, physical and psychological combined, and especially notes drunkenness, masturbation, and sexual deprivation (p. 165).

In his consideration of therapeutic interventions, Griesinger argues that hospitalization is called for only when the condition is at least of moderate severity and has continued unchanged for some months; otherwise, he instead recommends careful regulation of diet, rest and activity, fresh air, and exercise. He advises distracting the patient from his preoccupations by means of "mild, cheering external influences" and recommends that "the topics of melancholics' preoccupations and delusions be avoided." Also, a moderately severe manner is often more helpful than consolation (p. 166).

Except for the fact that he quotes Griesinger approvingly in *The Principles of Psychology,* we do not know the degree to which James agreed with his views on the nature of melancholia and treatment for it, but Jackson's summary of his views affords us a general idea of what James would have understood his affliction to be, what causes he might have considered responsible for it, and what he judged to be its long-term prognosis. We may assume that James would not have envisioned being cured of his affliction, that he understood he would need to learn to live with it. The very fact that Griesinger recommends various ameliorative strategies, excluding only bloodletting, underscores the sheer tenacity of melancholia. In reading Griesinger, James could not have missed this point. It would be hard to imagine James *not* coming to the conclusion that his illness had no cure, only more or less adequate short-term remedies. If he tried many different remedies, it would not have been because he was seeking some magical cure but because he was intent on keeping his affliction within the pain threshold that he felt he could endure (*VRE,* 134–35).

Let us now return to *The Varieties* and James's discussion of melancholy and its relationship to religion.

The Religious Attitude and the Melancholy Temperament

The chapter of *The Varieties* that relates most directly to melancholy is chapter 5, "The Sick Soul," which comprises the sixth and seventh Gifford Lectures (*VRE*, 127–65). This chapter is typically discussed in relation to the chapter immediately preceding it, "The Religion of Healthy-Mindedness." Of course, James invites us to view the two chapters together, as he proposes that "healthy-mindedness" and "sick-soulness" are two contrasting ways in which individuals are religious. However, much is to be gained by relating "The Sick Soul" chapter to chapter 3, "The Reality of the Unseen," which immediately precedes "The Religion of Healthy-Mindedness" chapter. This earlier chapter enables James to formulate a rather different typology, that between "the life of religion" and "the melancholic temperament."

He begins "The Reality of the Unseen" with the following statement: "Were one asked to characterize the life of religion in the broadest and most general terms possible, one might say that it consists of the belief that there is an unseen order, and that our supreme good lies in harmoniously adjusting ourselves thereto. This belief and this adjustment are the religious attitude in the soul" (*VRE,* 53). He adds that his task will be "to call attention to some of the psychological peculiarities of such an attitude as this, of belief in an object which we cannot see" (p. 53). In other words, the *religious attitude* and the *melancholic temperament* are polar opposites: The religious attitude involves *belief in an unseen order,* whereas melancholy is an inability to take interest in, or give one's attention to, *the world that is seen.* For the melancholiac, the seen world is *unreal,* as it does not appear interesting or important; it is not "believed" in. For the religious individual, the *unseen* world is real, as it is considered both interesting and important; it *is* believed in.

We may also see how the religious attitude and the melancholic temperament, while initially polar opposites, might become conjoined, and why melancholic personalities may find themselves peculiarly attracted to religion. For if the seen world loses interest and importance for them, perhaps the unseen world may assume the place the seen world previously held. Moreover, the melancholiac would find justification for this lack of interest in the seen world from many religious writings which testify to the belief that only the unseen world ultimately matters. This means that the religious attitude and melancholy temperament have a not simple but a complex relation to one another, as in one sense they are polar opposites but in another sense are the mirror image of one another. Thus, James's use of melancholia to explore religion psychologically is not as arbitrary or self-indulgent as it may first appear.

In his chapter "The Reality of the Unseen," James suggests that the "objects" in the unseen world may be present to our senses or present in our thoughts only. In either case, they "elicit from us a *reaction;* and the reaction due to things of thought is notoriously in many cases as strong as that due to sensible presences. It may even be stronger. The memory of an insult may make us angrier than the insult did when we received it. We are frequently more ashamed of our blunders afterwards than we were at the moment of making them" (*VRE,* 53). This is also the case with religion. Very few Christian believers have had a "sensible vision" of their Savior: "The whole force of the Christian religion, therefore, so far as belief in the divine personages determines the prevalent attitude of the believer, is in general exerted by the instrumentality of pure ideas, of which nothing in the individual's past experiences directly serves as a model" (*VRE,* 54).

Yet, besides the "sensible vision" and the "pure idea," there is an experience which falls somewhere in between. This is "a sense of reality, a feeling of objective presence, a perception of what we may call 'something there,' more deep and more general than any of the special and particular 'senses' by which the current psychology supposes existent realities to be originally revealed" (*VRE,* 58). He suggests that these "vague and remote" senses of "something there" may be "excited" by our senses but may also be excited by an idea. Hallucinatory experiences provide proof "of such an undifferentiated sense of reality," as it oftens happens that an hallucination is imperfectly developed: "The person affected will feel a 'presence' in the room, definitely localized, facing in one particular way, real in the most emphatic sense of the word, often coming suddenly, and as suddenly gone; and yet neither seen, heard, touched, nor cognized in any of the usual 'sensible' ways" (*VRE,* 59).

THE CASE OF THE INTIMATE FRIEND

James then offers an illustration of this hallucinatory experience, judging that this will help clarify what he has in mind before passing "to the objects with whose presence religion is more peculiarly concerned" (*VRE,* 59). This means that the experience he is about to consider has relevance for religion but is not itself a religious experience. The experience, he tells us, is that of "an intimate friend of mine, one of the keenest intellects I know" and written "in the response to my inquiries" (*VRE,* 59). [6 2]

The "intimate friend" begins his account by noting that several times in the past few years he has felt the so-called consciousness of a presence. The experience he is about to reveal occurred in September 1884. The previous night he had had "a vivid tactile hallucination of being grasped by the arm, which made me get up and search the room for an intruder" (*VRE,* 59). But the "sense of presence" occurred on the following night:

> After I had got into bed and blown out the candle, I lay awake while thinking
> on the previous night's experience, when suddenly I felt something come into
> the room and stay close to my bed. It remained only a minute or two. I did not
> recognize it by any ordinary sense, and yet there was a horrible unpleasant
> "sensation" connected with it. It stirred something more at the roots of my
> being than any ordinary perception. The feeling had something of the quality
> of a very large tearing vital pain spreading chiefly over the chest, but within
> the organism — and yet the feeling was not *pain* so much as *abhorrence*. At all
> events, something was present with me, and I knew its presence far more
> surely than I have ever known the presence of any fleshly living creature. I was
> conscious of its departure as of its coming: an almost instantaneously swift
> going though the door, and the "horrible sensation" disappeared [*VRE,* 59–
> 60].

The subsequent night, when his mind was absorbed in some lectures he was
preparing, he once again felt the presence of "the thing that was there the night
before" and was again aware of the previous night's "horrible sensation." This
time, he "mentally concentrated all my effort . . . to charge this 'thing,' if it
was evil, to depart, if it was *not* evil, to tell me who or what it was, and if
it could not explain itself, to go, and that I would compel it to go." Wordlessly,
it departed, just as "on the previous night, and my body quickly recovered its
normal state" (*VRE,* 60).

Observing that he experienced the very same "horrible sensation" on two
previous occasions, once for a full quarter of an hour, he makes particular note
of the fact that "in all three instances the certainty that there in outward space
there stood *something* was indescribably *stronger* than the ordinary certainty
of companionship when we are in the close presence of ordinary living people.
The something seemed close to me, and intensely more real than any ordinary
perception. Although I felt it to be like unto myself, so to speak, or finite,
small, and distressful, as it were, I didn't recognize it as any individual being or
person" (*VRE,* 60). James himself quickly adds this disclaimer: "Of course
such an experience as this does not connect itself with the religious sphere"
(*VRE,* 60). So far as he is concerned, this was a hallucinatory experience, not a
religious one. He says, however, that this kind of experience may "upon occasion" connect itself with the religious sphere. In fact, "the same correspondent
informs me that at more than one other conjuncture he had the sense of
presence developed with equal intensity and abruptness, only then it was filled
with a quality of joy" (*VRE,* 60). On these other occasions, he had felt "the
sure knowledge of the close presence of a sort of mighty person, and after it
went, the memory persisted as the one perception of reality. Everything else
might be a dream, but not that" (*VRE,* 60–61). Yet, James notes, "My friend,
as it oddly happens, does not interpret these latter experiences theistically, as

signifying the presence of God. But it would clearly not have been unnatural to interpret them as a revelation of the deity's existence" (*VRE*, 61), for, after all, the friend in this instance had felt "the close presence of a sort of mighty person." If this were not someone he knew, what would prohibit him from determining that this "mighty person" was in fact God?

James concludes his discussion of this case with the notation that he will have more to say later about these experiences of what his friend called "a startling awareness of some ineffable good" when he takes up the subject of mysticism (chapter 11 of *The Varieties*). The balance of his chapter "The Reality of the Unseen" is mostly taken up with accounts of similar experiences that *were* interpreted theistically.

I have centered on the case of the "intimate friend" at some length because I have a strong suspicion that it concerns James himself. We know for certain that he included an account of his own experience of "the worst kind of melancholy" in his chapter "The Sick Soul," and that he sought to disguise the fact that he was the author of that particular account by pretending that it was written by a Frenchman with whom he had been in correspondence (*VRE*, 159–61). Thus, we know that he was capable of using his own experiences to illustrate and support the points he wanted to make (he also did this in several instances in *The Principles of Psychology*), and that he was not reluctant to devise a false identity for the supposed author of the account. As there is a rather playful quality to his observation that the "Frenchman" was "evidently in a bad nervous condition at the time of which he writes" (*VRE*, 160), so there is a playful quality to his observation here that his "intimate friend" is "one of the keenest intellects I know" (*VRE*, 59).

There are various stylistic features to the account that are reflective of James's own style, such as the tendency to underline single words and phrases, to place technical words within quotation marks, and to make frequent use of semicolons and dashes. We also know that James was a strong believer in the introspective method of psychology, and this means that he was in the habit of writing detailed accounts of what was going on in his mind. As he stated in his chapter "The Methods and Sources of Psychology" in the first volume of *The Principles of Psychology*, "Introspective observation is what we have to rely on first and foremost and always. The word introspection need hardly be defined—it means, of course, the looking into our own minds and reporting what we there discover" (1950, 2:185). He emphasizes that introspection includes both feelings and thoughts, not thoughts exclusively, for the word *thought* tends to exclude physical sensations, and these he believes ought not to be omitted from the introspective process. The case of the intimate friend is replete with allusions to feelings and physical sensations.

An even more significant textual clue to the plausibility that the intimate friend is James himself is provided by the "French Sufferer" case in his chapter "The Sick Soul." In that case, James placed a significant clue to his identity in a footnote to the account, which cited "another case of fear equally sudden" in a book written by his father (*VRE*, 161). There is a similar clue in the case of the intimate friend. In the French Sufferer case, the author (whom we know to be James) states that he awoke each morning "with a horrible dread at the pit of my stomach," and then, in another footnote, James cites John Bunyan's account of a very similar experience in which Bunyan felt "such clogging and heat at my stomach." The Bunyan quote goes on to add, "By reason of this my terror, [I felt] that I was, especially at such times, as if *my breast-bone would have split asunder*" (emphasis added). In the intimate friend case, the friend reports that he had a very unpleasant sensation in the course of the second night's experience, the feeling of which "had something of the quality of *a very large tearing vital pain spreading chiefly over the chest, but within the organism*" (emphasis added). While the sensation of a "tearing" in the chest region does *not* occur in the French Sufferer account itself, it clearly does so in the intimate friend account and is responsible in part for his sense of terror. The quotation from Bunyan, alluding to the sensation of feeling that his "breast-bone would have split asunder," links the accounts of the French Sufferer and intimate friend. This physiological reaction is the "horribly unpleasant 'sensation'" connected with the intimate friend's feeling of a presence in the room.

A letter from James to his wife is also relevant. In it, he speaks of "a characteristic attitude in me" that "always involves an element of active tension, of holding my own, as it were, and trusting outward things to perform their part so as to make it a full harmony, but without any *guaranty* that they will. Make it a guaranty—and the attitude immediately becomes to my consciousness stagnant and stingless. Take away the guaranty, and I feel . . . a sort of enthusiastic bliss, of bitter willingness to do and suffer anything, which translates itself physically by a kind of *stinging pain inside my breastbone* (don't smile at this—it is to me an essential element of the whole thing!)" (Myers 1986, 49, emphasis added). In other words, strong psychological emotions typically produce equally strong physiological reactions.

While these textual clues offer much support for my view that the intimate friend account is James's own, the most telling evidence is provided by a direct comparison of the verbal content of it and the French Sufferer account. Before we turn to that, however, I want to draw some conclusions from the intimate friend account for James's understanding of himself as a religious outsider. Note that he prefaces this account with the disclaimer that it is not about a religious experience as such and then concludes the account with a similar disclaimer. His reason for including it in the chapter entitled "The Reality of the Unseen" was not that it was a religious experience but that, as a hallucinatory experience, it gave credence to the claims that are made for religious experience. Why? Because, as the intimate friend observed, his hallucinatory experiences carried "the certainty that there in outward space there stood *something* [that] was indescribably *stronger* than the ordinary certainty of companionship when we are in the close presence of ordinary living people" (*VRE*, 60). Therefore, by the same token, we should not pooh-pooh the claims of religious individuals when they testify to having experienced the presence of God or of some other divine or quasi-divine person, and to having experienced this presence as decidedly *stronger* than that of persons who belong to the "seen" world. Hallucinatory experiences should make us more receptive to the testimony of individuals who offer personal accounts of *feeling* the presence of God and of having absolutely no doubt of God's presence. If it was in fact James's own, this hallucinatory experience would therefore support his "hospitality towards the religious testimony of others" while at the same time making no claim to having had a religious experience himself.

But what, then, are we to make of the intimate friend's other experiences, those in which he had "the sure knowledge of the close presence of a sort of mighty person"? Could *these* have been religious experiences? James says no, because, for whatever reasons, his friend did "not interpret these latter experiences theistically, as signifying the presence of God," though he adds that "it would clearly not have been unnatural to interpret them as a revelation of the deity's existence" (*VRE*, 61). Evidently the intimate friend did not offer some alternative interpretation, such as that the "mighty person" was a human being he had personally experienced, perhaps his father, so the theistic interpretation was not thereby foreclosed. Yet he simply did not make the interpretive leap that religious individuals are prepared to make by saying that this "mighty person" was God or some divine or quasi-divine figure.

In response to Pratt's question about God, James hedged between two options: "Is He a person?" and "Is God an attitude of the Universe toward you?" In response to the former option, James answered, "He must be cognizant and responsive in some way," and in answer to the second, he commented, "Yes, but more conscious." These responses suggest that God was more than an "attitude" for him but something less than a "person" as normally construed, that is, as having a discernible character, personality, or selfhood. Perhaps Pratt's third option — "Or is He only a Force?" — comes closest to the mark, as James answers, "He *must* do." In this sense, the idea of God as a "mighty person" is too static, failing to capture what he might call the "restless quality" of God.

In "Is Life Worth Living?" James asks how our faith in the unseen world might be verified, and he suggests that it may in fact be *self*-verifying: "I confess that I do not see why the very existence of an invisible world may not in part depend on the personal response which any of us may make to the religious appeal. God himself, in short, may draw vital strength and increase of very being from our fidelity. For my own part, I do not know what the sweat and blood and tragedy of this life mean, if they mean anything short of this. If this life be not a real fight, in which something is eternally gained for the universe by success, it is no better than a game of private theatricals from which one may withdraw at will" (1956, 61).

Given this understanding of God, we should not be surprised that the intimate friend would be unable to ascribe a "theistic" meaning to the experience of "the close presence of a sort of mighty person," even if this person could not be recognized as any *other* individual being or person. And, if I am correct that James is the intimate friend, we should not be surprised that he has such secure knowledge that no theistic interpretation was ever made by this close "friend" of his.

Examples of Religious Melancholy

As I noted earlier, the chapter entitled "The Reality of the Unseen" sets the stage for the one entitled "The Sick Soul." However, the chapter he calls "The Religion of Healthy-Mindedness" intervenes, and the first several pages of the sick-soul chapter continue his discussion of the healthy-minded temperament. These pages center on the issue of evil and distinguish healthy-minded people and sick souls according to their views of evil. The healthy-minded do not ignore evil or pretend that it does not exist, but they define evil in such manner as to propose that it is curable. For them, evil means a "maladjustment" between the self and the external world, so that "by modifying either the self or the things, or both at once, the two terms may be made to fit" (*VRE,* 134). But sick souls experience evil differently. They are those "for whom evil is no mere relation of the subject to particular outer things, but something more radical and general, a wrongness or vice in [one's] essential nature, which no alteration of the environment, or any rearrangement of the inner self, can cure, and which requires a supernatural remedy" (p. 134). Such people have a more pessimistic nature, as they believe that the problem is internal and is very resistent to any lasting cure.

After considering two major pessimistic philosophies, Stoic insensibility and Epicurean resignation, James moves into the psychological themes of "The Sick Soul," noting that melancholy lies at the extreme end of pessimism: "There is a pitch of unhappiness so great that the goods of nature may be entirely forgotten, and all sentiment of their existence vanish from the mental field. . . . As the healthy-minded enthusiast succeeds in ignoring evil's very existence, so the subject of melancholy is forced in spite of himself to ignore that of all good whatever: *for him it may no longer have the least reality"* (*VRE*, 144–45, emphasis added).

Personal accounts of melancholy are James's primary resource for exploring the phenomenon of the sick soul, as they disclose various stages in the evolution of the perception of the universe as evil, as devoid of any ultimate good. The first stage of "pathological depression" is "mere joylessness and dreariness, discouragement, dejection, lack of taste and zest and spring" (*VRE*, 145). It is usually temporary, owing to circumstances that *may* be altered, though "some persons are affected with [it] permanently," and when prolonged, it may result in suicide (*VRE*, 147). A worse form of melancholy is a "positive and active anguish, a sort of psychical neuralgia wholly unknown to healthy life" (*VRE*, 147). It may take various forms, "having sometimes more the quality of loathing; sometimes that of irritation and exasperation; or again of self-mistrust and self-despair; or of suspicion, anxiety, trepidation, fear" (*VRE*, 147). It may involve self-accusations or accusations of others. As in the previous type, the sufferer usually considers it to have no relation to "the religious sphere of experience" (*VRE*, 148).

James provides an account of this form of melancholy in a sufferer who is actually French, and who rails against the injustice of his having been afflicted with this "horrible misery of mine." James contends that the patient's "querulous temper," his excessive complaining and self-lamentation, "keeps his mind from taking a religious direction" (*VRE*, 149), a contention that reminds us of James's observation on his Amazon trip that a religious attitude "if glad, it must not snicker; if sad, it must not scream or curse." The Frenchman cannot submit to any outside influence; instead, he continues to lament his situation and hold at distant remove any thought that there may be some relief for his condition.

Next, James takes up several examples of "religious melancholy," cases in which the perception of evil is every bit as strong as in the case of the French mental patient, but in which there *is* "a religious solution" (*VRE*, 152). His first case is Leo Tolstoy, a man whose "sense that life had any meaning whatever was for a time wholly withdrawn" (*VRE*, 151). In contrast to those who have experienced a religious conversion, where there is often "a transfiguration of the face of nature," in melancholiacs

> there is usually a similar change, only it is in the reverse direction. The world now looks remote, strange, sinister, uncanny. Its color is gone, its breath is

cold, there is no speculation in the eyes it glares with. "It is as if I lived in another century," says one asylum patient. — "I see everything through a cloud," says another, "things are not as they were, and I am changed." "I see," says a third, "I touch, but the things do not come near me, a thick veil alters the hue and look of everything." — "Persons move like shadows, and sounds seem to come from a distant world." — "There is no longer any past for me; people appear so strange; it is as if I could not see any reality, as if I were in a theatre; as if people were actors, and everything were scenery; I can no longer find myself; I walk, but why? Everything floats before my eyes, but leaves no impression." — "I weep false tears, I have unreal hands: the things I see are not real things." — Such are expressions that naturally rise to the lips of melancholy subjects describing their changed state [*VRE,* 151–52].

Life was this way for Tolstoy: "It was now flat sober, more than sober, dead. Things were meaningless whose meaning had always been self-evident" (*VRE,* 152–53). He considered suicide. Yet all the while that he was overwhelmed by the sheer meaninglessness of his existence, feeling as though he were being devoured from without and within, and asking himself how he might put an end to his misery, his heart "kept languishing with another pining emotion. I can call this by no other name than that of a thirst for God. This craving for God had nothing to do with the movement of my ideas, — in fact, it was the direct contrary of that movement, — but it came from my heart. It was like a feeling of dread that made me seem like an orphan and isolated in the midst of all these things that were so foreign. And this feeling of dread was mitigated by the hope of finding the assistance of some one" (*VRE,* 156).

As James notes, when Tolstoy came out of his state of "absolute disenchantment with ordinary life," there was not a total restitution, for Tolstoy had experienced an evil that he would never, ever forget. But he did find a new special form of happiness: "The happiness that comes, when any does come, — and often enough it fails to return in an acute form, though its form is sometimes very acute, — is not the simple ignorance of ill, but something vastly more complex, including natural evil as one of its elements, but finding natural evil no such stumbling-block and terror because it now sees it swallowed up in supernatural good. The process is one of redemption, not of mere reversion to natural health, and the sufferer, when saved, is saved by what seems to him a second birth, a deeper kind of conscious being than he could enjoy before" (*VRE,* 156–57).

James's second example is John Bunyan, who differs from Tolstoy in one important respect. Whereas Tolstoy's preoccupations were largely objective, related to the purpose and meaning of life in general, Bunyan's troubles "were over the condition of his own personal self" (*VRE,* 157). James views Bunyan as a typical case of "the psychopathic temperament, sensitive of conscience to a diseased degree, beset by doubts, fears, and insistent ideas, and a victim of verbal automatisms, both motor and sensory. These were usually texts of Scripture which, sometimes damnatory and sometimes favorable, would come in a half-hallucinatory form as if they were voices, and fasten on his mind and buffet it between them like a shuttlecock. Added to this were a fearful melancholy self-contempt and despair" (*VRE,* 157).

Because he intends to discuss Bunyan's religious recovery in the next chapter, "The Divided Self, and the Process of Its Unification," James does not present it here. Instead, he briefly cites the case of another sufferer, Henry Alline, a Nova Scotian evangelist. These accounts set the stage for his final illustration of melancholy, the case of the anonymous "French Sufferer" who, as I noted earlier, is James himself (on this point, see Lewis 1991, 202–4; also Erikson 1968, 152).

The Case of the French Sufferer

James prefaces his account of the French Sufferer with the assertion, "The worst kind of melancholy is that which takes the form of panic fear" (*VRE,* 159–60). Here is his account of the Frenchman's experience of panic fear:

> Whilst in this state of philosophical pessimism and general depression of spirits about my prospects, I went one evening into a dressing-room in the twilight to procure some article that was there; when suddenly there fell upon me without any warning, just as if it came out of the darkness, a horrible fear of my own existence. Simultaneously there arose in my mind the image of an epileptic patient whom I had seen in the asylum, a black-haired youth with greenish skin, entirely idiotic, who used to sit all day on one of the benches, or rather shelves against the wall, with his knees drawn up against his chin, and the coarse gray undershirt, which was his only garment, drawn over them inclosing his entire figure. He sat there like a sort of sculptured Egyptian cat or Peruvian mummy, moving nothing but his black eyes and looking absolutely non-human. This image and my fear entered into a species of combination with each other. *That shape am I,* I felt, potentially. Nothing that I possess can defend me against that fate, if the hour for it should strike for me as it struck for him. There was such a horror of him, and such a perception of my own merely momentary discrepancy from him, that it was as if something hitherto solid within my breast gave way entirely, and I became a mass of quivering fear. After this the universe was changed for me altogether. I awoke morning after morning with a horrible dread at the pit of my stomach, and with a sense of the insecurity of life that I never knew before, and that I have never felt

since. It was like a revelation; and although the immediate feelings passed away, the experience has made me sympathetic with the morbid feelings of others ever since. It gradually faded, but for months I was unable to go out into the dark alone. In general I dreaded to be left alone. I remember wondering how other people could live, how I myself had ever lived, so unconscious of that pit of insecurity beneath the surface of life. *My mother in particular, a very cheerful person, seemed to me a perfect paradox in her unconsciousness of danger, which you may well believe I was very careful not to disturb by revelations of my own state of mind.* I have always thought that this experience of melancholia of mine had a religious bearing (*VRE,* 160–61, my emphasis).

As author of *The Varieties,* James pretends to have asked "this correspondent to explain more fully what he meant by these last words," that is, about the experience having "a religious bearing." The reply: "I mean that the fear was so invasive and powerful that if I had not clung to scripture-texts like 'The eternal God is my refuge,' etc., 'Come unto me, all ye that labor and are heavy-laden,' etc., 'I am the resurrection and the life,' etc., I think I should have grown really insane" (*VRE,* 161). James then declares there is no need for him to give further examples of religious melancholy, as he has provided one emphasizing the vanity of mortal things (Tolstoy), another the sense of sin (Bunyan), and a third the fear of the universe (himself). Thus, he has demonstrated the *variety* of religious melancholias.

His footnote reference to his father's experience of fear "equally sudden" does not include the account itself, only the source in which it appears, but the following excerpt from this account makes his point that a melancholic episode may come upon a person without any forewarning whatsoever. It happened to his father when the Jameses were in London in 1844. William, the eldest son, was two-and-a-half; Henry, his younger brother, had just turned one. His father writes:

One day, however, towards the close of May, having eaten a comfortable dinner, I remained sitting at the table after the family had dispersed, idly gazing at the embers in the grate, thinking of nothing, and feeling only the exhilaration incident to a good digestion, when suddenly — in a lightning flash as it were — "fear came upon me, and trembling, which made all my bones to shake." To all appearance it was a perfectly insane and abject terror, without ostensible cause, and only to be accounted for, to my perplexed imagination, by some damned shape squatting invisible to me within the precincts of the room, and raying out from his fetid personality influences fatal to life. The thing had not lasted ten seconds before I felt myself a wreck; that is, reduced from a state of firm, vigorous, joyous manhood to one of almost helpless infancy. The only self-control I was capable of exerting was to keep my seat. I felt the greatest desire to run incontinently to the foot of the stairs and shout for help to my wife, — to run to the roadside even, and appeal to the public to protect me; but by an immense effort I controlled these frenzied impulses, and determined not to budge from my chair till I had recovered my lost self-possession [Lewis 1991, 51].

After a few days had passed, James's father consulted several physicians, all of whom said he had overworked his brain — he had been engaged in exegetical work on the book of Genesis — and recommended the water cure at a nearby resort (Lewis 1991, 52).

While there, he complained about having to listen to the "endless 'strife of tongues' about diet, regimen, disease, politics, etc., etc.," and imagined "how sweet it would be to find oneself no longer man, but one of those innocent and ignorant sheep pasturing upon that placid hillside, and drinking in eternal dew and freshness from Nature's lavish bosom!" (Erikson 1969, 151–52). In discussing the cases of Bunyan and Alline in *The Varieties*, James remarks that "envy of the placid beasts seems to be a very widespread affection in this type of sadness" (1982, 159). Each chose a different species to envy. For Bunyan, it was dogs and toads, for Alline the birds flying overhead, and for James's father the sheep pasturing on the placid hillside. Perhaps this attention to the placid beasts, even if born of envy, reflected some interest in the visible world, and some sense that, however bad it was for them, it could be pleasant enough for at least some of Earth's inhabitants.

But we are concerned here with James's own melancholic episode, the one attributed to a young Frenchman with whom he was ostensibly in correspondence. As his opening statement about his "general depression of spirits about my prospects" indicates, he was a young man at the time. The breakdown occurred in 1870, when he was 28 years old. He had received his medical degree the previous June but had spent the next six months reading and lying about as he considered his prospects. He had decided that he did not want to become a medical doctor. His mother complained to his younger brother Henry, who was in Europe at the time, that William was resting too much. In late December he confessed in his journal to being unfitted "for any affectionate relations with other individuals," which appears to have applied especially to young women, as he did not marry until he was 36, a match that his father had strongly promoted from the outset.

A month later, around January 10, he suffered a collapse, evidently more severe than anything previously experienced. After three weeks of agony, he wrote in his journal on February 1 that he had arrived at the moment of crisis: "Today, I about touched bottom, and perceive plainly that I must face the choice with open eyes: shall I *frankly* throw the moral business overboard, as one unsuited to my innate aptitudes, or shall I follow it, and it alone, making everything else merely stuff for it?" In the same entry he noted that he had not previously made any sustained commitment to "the moral interest" but had deployed it mainly to hold certain bad habits in check (Lewis 1991, 201). As James refers in this same passage to tendencies of "moral degradation," Lewis speculates that this was an allusion to autoeroticism. If so, he may have suspected this to be a physiological cause of his melancholic state, and perhaps also a causal factor in the fate of the "epileptic patient" described in his account of his melancholic episode, since epilepsy was commonly believed to be caused by autoerotic self-masturbatory acts. Also, his hesitancy to tell his mother the story of his melancholic episode may have been due in part to this feature of the experience, though another reason is simply that she did not demonstrate much patience for the mental sufferings of others.

The experience recounted in *The Varieties* occurred at about this time. The exact date is unknown, though we may assume that it was coincident, if not identical to, the date when he "about touched bottom." In late spring, he began to improve. The turning point occurred in late April when, in the course of reading the second in a series of philosophical essays by French philosopher Charles Renouvier, he found a basis for taking a new approach to life. Renouvier had defined free will as "the sustaining of a thought *because I choose* to when I might have other thoughts." Rather than assuming that this is the definition of an illusion, James decided he would believe Renouvier's definition of free will. In effect, "my first act of free will shall be to believe in free will. For the remainder of the year, I will abstain from the mere speculative and contemplative *Grübelei* in which my nature takes most delight, and voluntarily cultivate the feeling of moral freedom, by reading books favorable to it, as well as by acting" (Lewis 1991, 204–5). By *Grübelei* he means the "questioning mania" to which he refers in *The Principles of Psychology,* a state of interminable doubt and inquiry (1950, 2:284).

This, then, would be his new approach to life: "Hitherto, when I have felt like taking a free initiative, like daring to act originally, without carefully waiting for contemplation of the external world to determine all for me, suicide seemed the most manly form to put my daring into; now, I will go a step further with my will, not only act with it, but believe as well; believe in my individual reality and creative power. My belief, to be sure, *can't* be optimistic — but I will posit life (the real, the good) in the self-governing *resistance* of the ego to the world. Life shall [be built in] doing and suffering and creating" (Lewis 1991, 205).

According to his father, William commented sometime thereafter on the marked difference between himself then and a year earlier, attributing this positive change to the fact that he no longer believed that "all mental disorder requires to have a physical basis" (Erikson 1968, 154). Erik Erikson suggests that James's first insight, that he could exercise choice over the thoughts that he would allow himself to think, was directly related to the second insight, "the abandonment of physiological factors as fatalistic arguments against a neurotic person's continued self-determination. Together they [these two insights] are the basis of psychotherapy, which, no matter how it is described and conceptualized, aims at the restoration of the patient's power of choice" (1968, 155). Perhaps by affirming his power *not* to accept physiological factors as fatalistic arguments James severed the causal link between his habit of autoeroticism and mental disorder.

James has nothing to say in *The Varieties* about the role played by the affirmation of "will" in the resolution of a melancholic crisis like the one experienced by himself, the "French Sufferer." Perhaps he assumed that to do so would reveal the true identity of this afflicted person, for he had written a great deal about the will not only in *The Principles of Psychology* (1950, 2:486–592) but also in his well-known essays in popular philosophy published in 1896, the lead essay of which was entitled "The Will to Believe" (1956, 1–31). Another possible explanation is that, at the time of writing *The Varieties,* he no longer believed that he could lift himself from the depths by his own act of will. In the summer of 1900, writing despondently to his wife from Bad-Nauheim, he said that he had *"no strength at all"* and that though he had tried to summon up a "will to believe . . . it is no go. The Will to Believe won't work" (Lewis 1991, 511). Lewis suggests that James "was now inclined to locate the source of psychic renewal, not in a conscious act of will, but much rather in the activities of the subconscious" (p. 511). If *The Principles of Psychology* may be seen as his "autobiography into the 1880s and the hard-won victory over the 'obstructed will,' *The Varieties* carries the personal story through the breakdown of energy at the turn of the century and the new alertness to the under-consciousness" (p. 511).

Thus, in explaining why he thought "this experience of melancholia of mine had a religious bearing," the French Sufferer says that he kept from going really insane by clinging to scripture texts like "The eternal God is my refuge," "Come unto me, all ye that labor and are heavy-laden," and so forth. In other words, it was not an act of will but something working in him at the subliminal level that kept him sane. Like Bunyan, he was the yielding recipient of verbal automatisms, but unlike in Bunyan's case, the scripture texts were overwhelmingly favorable. Instead of buffeting his mind between damnatory and favorable scriptural voices, he heard only favorable ones (*VRE*, 157).[6]

The Murdered Self

Because James found himself relying on scriptural texts, he now feels that "this experience of melancholia of mine had a religious bearing." Its religious bearing is sufficient, at least, to justify placing it alongside the melancholic experiences of Tolstoy and Bunyan. He even uses religious language to describe it: "It was like a revelation" (*VRE*, 160). Still, unlike Tolstoy's experience, his does not include a thirst or craving for God, and unlike Bunyan's, there is no "relief in his salvation through the blood of Christ" (*VRE*, 156, 186). The most he may or will claim for the experience is that, as he wrote to his daughter from Bad-Nauheim, such experiences, painful as they may be, are "sent to us for an enlightenment" (Rubin 1994, 20). I take James to mean by this that through such experiences we gain insights into ourselves that we may not gain in any other way. Thus, the French Sufferer is presented with a mental image of his "potential self." He sees the epileptic patient in the asylum, "a black-haired youth with greenish skin, . . . knees drawn up against his chin," and sitting there "like a sort of sculptured Egyptian cat or Peruvian mummy, moving nothing but his black eyes and looking absolutely non-human. This image and my fear entered into a species of combination with each other. *That shape am I,* I felt potentially. Nothing that I possess can defend me against that fate. . . ." (*VRE*, 160). The moment of enlightenment: I am potentially him, and against this fate I am utterly defenseless. With this horrible moment of self-recognition the world underwent a similar change: "The universe was changed for me altogether" (*VRE*, 160). If the potential self moved "nothing but his black eyes," the universe was similarly catatonic: "The world now looks remote, strange, sinister, uncanny. Its color is gone, its breath is cold, there is no speculation in the eyes it glares with" (*VRE*, 151). The picture is one of indescribable deadness.

The intimate friend experience is similar to the French Sufferer episode in that it, too, is *self*-revelatory. The first night the intimate friend felt himself being grasped by the arm. The next night he felt something come into the room and stay close to his bed. It remained only a minute or two, but long enough to stir "something more at the roots of my being than any ordinary perception" (*VRE*, 59). As in the French Sufferer episode, "there was a horribly unpleasant 'sensation' connected with it" (*VRE*, 59). And then it left, as swiftly as it had come. The third night it returned, and James now concentrated all his mental effort on charging it to go away if it was evil and to explain itself if it was not. Wordlessly, it departed as swiftly as it had come.

What was this "something" that was "indescribably stronger" than the presence of ordinary living people? As in the French Sufferer episode, it was intimately connected with himself: "*Although I felt it to be like unto myself,* so to speak, or finite, small, and distressful, as it were, I didn't recognize it as any individual being or person" (*VRE*, 60, my emphasis). An invaluable clue to "who" this intruder was is Erikson's view that the effort to form one's identity in late adolescence and early young adulthood involves more than deciding what one will become. It also requires determining what one will *not* become, which entails relinquishing or abandoning whole "parts" of oneself. His term for this is the "negative identity" — negative not because there is necessarily anything intrinsically wrong or immoral about it but because it becomes the "self" that is eventually abandoned in favor of another "self" or other "selves" that are adopted and affirmed (Erikson 1968, 172–76).

Erikson credits James for his own emphasis on the pain and even self-violence often associated with this identity struggle (1968, 22). Writing of Freud's negative identity, Erikson says that "it is in Freud's dreams, incidentally, that we have a superb record of his suppressed (or what James called 'abandoned,' or even 'murdered') selves — for our 'negative identity' haunts us at night" (1968, 22). Later, in his discussion of identity confusion, in a subsection entitled "The Confusion Returns — Psychopathology of Every Night" (a play on the title of Freud's book *Psychopathology of Everyday Life*), Erikson analyzes a series of dreams that James reports having had in San Francisco in 1906, the effect of which was to cause him to feel that he was "losing hold of my 'self,' and making acquaintance with a quality of mental distress that I had never known before" (Erikson 1968, 206).[7]

In citing James's discussion of "abandoned" or "murdered" selves, Erikson refers to his essay "Great Men and Their Environments" in *The Will to Believe* (1956, 216–54), where James uses the analogy of a young man making a fateful vocational decision to explain how nations face at any given moment "ambiguous potentialities of development." Thus, "whether a young man enters business or the ministry may depend on a decision which has to be made before a certain day. He takes the place offered in the counting-house, and is *committed.* Little by little, the habits, the knowledges, of the other career, which once lay so near, cease to be reckoned among his possibilities. *At first, he may sometimes doubt whether the self he murdered in that decisive hour might not have been the better of the two;* but with the years such questions themselves expire, and the old alternative *ego,* once so vivid, fades into something less substantial than a dream" (1956, 227, my emphasis).

Earlier, in his essay "The Dilemma of Determinism," James argued against the determinists the case that life is filled with "alternative possibilities," that "any one of several things may come to pass," some of which do come about, and some of which do not (1956, 153). Having argued this point, he wants to reassure his audience that this does not mean that life is merely random, totally left to chance, as determinists allege is the logical outcome of his position: "For what are the alternatives which, in point of fact, offer themselves to human volition? What are those features that now seem matters of chance? . . . Are they not all of them kinds of things already here and based in the existing frame of nature? . . . Do not all the motives that assail us, all the futures that offer themselves to our choice, spring equally from the soil of the past; and would not either one of them, whether realized through chance or through necessity, the moment it was realized, seem to us to fit that past, and in the completest and most continuous manner to interdigitate with the phenomena already there?" (1956, 157). The implication is that there are genuine alternatives and we do make real choices among them, because we live in "a world in which we constantly have to make what I shall, with your permission, call judgments of regret. Hardly an hour passes in which we do not wish that something might be otherwise" (1956, 159–60).

In "Great Men and Their Environments," James seems somewhat to minimize the pain associated with the "murdered self," suggesting that the doubts one originally harbored "themselves expire, and the old alternative *ego,* once so vivid, fades into something less substantial than a dream." Yet, as Erikson's analysis of James's own dreams in 1906 reveals, dreams carry enormous power, power enough to kill. "The Dilemma of Determinism" essay is darker and more ominous in tone than "Great Men and Their Environments." James seems to have been preoccupied with abandonment and murder at the time he was writing it, and the possible precipitating event for these darker ruminations were newspaper accounts of the "self-satisfied" confession of "the murderer at Brockton the other day," an unusually violent instance of wife murder. In a footnote to his views on genuine alternatives, he anticipates the favorite argument of determinists that if free will is true, "a man's murderer may as probably be his best friend as his worst enemy, a mother may be as likely to strangle as to suckle her first-born, and all of us to be as ready to jump from fourth-story windows as to go out of the front-doors, etc." (1956, 157). But, he counters, this is a spurious argument, because " 'free-will' does not say that everything that is physically conceivable is also morally possible. It merely says that of alternatives that *really* tempt our will more than one is really possible" (1956, 157). Then he adds, "Of course, the alternatives that do thus tempt our will are vastly fewer than the physical possibilities we can coldly fancy. Persons really tempted often do murder their best friends, mothers do strangle their first-born, people do jump out of fourth-story windows, etc." (1956, 157).

The serious, almost depressing tone of these remarks in an essay concerned to advance the case for the *freedom* of the will, and especially his references to temptation (mothers murdering their firstborns, friends killing friends, persons committing suicide), give an ominous tone to the whole idea of the "murdered self." It may be, as James implies in "Great Men and Their Environments," that the murdered self eventually becomes as insubstantial as a dream. But, given the violence of the act, is it not equally likely that it will come back to haunt the killer, and do so with a vengeance?

Returning, then, to the intimate friend case in *The Varieties*, it is not at all far-fetched to view the "intruder" as James's own murdered self, the self who was "killed" when James resolved his identity struggles in his late twenties. These were struggles central to the French Sufferer episode, which, we recall, occurred when he was in "general depression of spirits about my prospects" (*VRE*, 160). This murdered self, which was "like unto myself" and "finite, small, and distressful" (*VRE*, 60), may have been the artist self that he had nourished in his late teens and early twenties before being persuaded, ostensibly by his father, to follow a more respectable career in the sciences. Myers suggests that it was William's conflicts with his father over his desire to study art that inaugurated his chronic depression. As he explains, "Because William's first neurotic symptoms, such as inexplicable eye and digestive problems and anxiety, occurred at this time, it can be argued that father-son tensions were a critical factor in making William chronically depressed" (1986, 20).

It seems important, then, that the "intruder" appeared when the intimate friend's mind was "absorbed in some lectures which I was preparing" (*VRE*, 60), an activity James would most certainly not have been engaged in had he followed his original intention to be an artist. Furthermore, if the intruder is a murdered self who has come back to "haunt" James, then there is a sense in which suicide, an act of self-murder, *did* occur. He is his own victim, which makes all the more "horrible" the sight of this "finite, small, and distressful" being, a being destroyed just as he was beginning to come into his own. Jane Kenyon's observation that melancholy is an "unholy ghost" who is "certain to come again" could not be more apt, at least as regards melancholy's sense of sadness and loss (Kenyon 1993, 25).[8]

George Cotkin (1994) uses the French psychoanalyst Jacques Lacan's analysis of Hamlet to explore James's abandonment of his artistic career. He notes that Lacan "sees Hamlet as a classic melancholic suffering from the loss of a desired object, what Lacan refers to as 'the other.' While Lacan's interpretation revolves around an Oedipal and narcissistic triangle of great complexity, for both Freud and Lacan the presence of Hamlet is marked by a lost object of desire — or at least an object incapable of possession. Moreover, Freud and Lacan likewise find guilt and animosity toward the father and a resultant form of melancholia within the figure of Hamlet" (1994, 45). The "object incapable of possession" is James's vocational desire to become an artist, a desire that Henry James, Sr., quashed "through tactics of remonstrance, manipulation, and guilt inducement. With the demise of art as the object of desire, William was forced, without other appealing options, to enter into science as a vocation. While William bowed to his father's wishes, he did so reluctantly and less than successfully at first. William's initial study of physiology was often cursory; his earning of a medical degree from Harvard in 1869 was greater testimony to the program's lax nature than to James's directed study habits" (1994, 45).

I do not challenge Cotkin's argument that James's father was involved in James's decision to abandon art as a vocation. What I find missing in his analysis, however, is the link between this lost or abandoned object and the original lost object, the mother herself. What makes the loss of art as a vocation so emotionally traumatizing for James is that it recapitulates the earlier loss. Moreover, whatever his father's overt role in his abandonment of this vocation was, the deeper (even if unconscious) attribution of responsibility for this decision would have been lodged against his mother, as she (the "good enough" or "not good enough" mother) is forever identified with the primary object loss ("the perfect mother"). While Cotkin does not consider the mother's role in James's melancholia, he comes close to recognizing it by virtue of the metaphors he uses to portray the family's influence on James's style of philosophical writing and subject matter. He speaks of "the umbilical cord" that linked James to his family and says that the family "figures as the mother lode for mining the genesis and expression of William James's mature philosophy" (1994, 20). My point, of course, is that there is more than metaphor involved in James's struggle with the maternal, as he had a real mother who, unlike his father, had very definite views about her eldest son's professional prospects. How else to explain his philosophical preoccupation with the issue of determinism and freedom of choice?

In short, if the French Sufferer episode revealed to James a "potential self" that he decidedly *did not want to become but feared was altogether possible,* the intimate friend account reveals a self that he *could have become but forsook for another identity instead.*[9] For the adult James, there was perhaps some consolation in the fact that he was able to form the science of psychology into art, both by insisting on the primacy of the individual over the aggregate (see his essay "The Importance of Individuals," 1956, 225–62) and by "illustrating" his points and arguments through individual "portraits," such as those we have been discussing; "portraiture" was the art form in which he clearly excelled (see Miller 1992, 68–73 for a discussion of the relation between illustration and text in his brother's novels: one could argue that James in *The Varieties* incorporated illustration *into* the text). But such consolation came many years later.

Before we leave the intimate friend case and the theme of the murdered self, I want to anticipate a later section of this chapter ("Metaphysical Anxiety and the Devouring Will") by noting that his father's involvement in his choosing science over art is so emphasized by James's biographers that the mother-son relationship is systematically ignored. That his father exhibited far greater interest in his son's scientific than his artistic skills there can be no doubt (Lewis 1991, 80–82). But a more subtle, subversive role was in my view played by James's mother, if only because she strongly encouraged the artistic interests of James's brother Henry, praising the stories he was writing at the time, and did nothing to encourage William's interests in painting. A possible reason why she did not foster William's painting is provided by Henry, who accompanied William to John La Farge's art studio in Newport but worked on copying plaster casts while William and La Farge worked closely together on their painting. One day Henry wandered up to the second floor where William was working. To his shock and astonishment, "he found his slender, red-headed, and much-liked young cousin Gus Barker, who was on a flying visit to Newport during a Harvard vacation, standing naked on a pedestal, modeling for William's pencil drawing of him. It was Henry's first vision of a life model, and he remembered all his days how his personal artistic ambitions collapsed in an instant: 'so forced was I to recognize . . . that I might niggle for months over plaster casts and not come within miles of any such point of attack. The bravery of my brother's own in especial dazzled me out of every presumption.' Then and there, Henry tells us, he put away his drawing pencil forever" (Lewis 1991, 110–11).

What Henry leaves the reader to infer, what goes unspoken, is that his brother's "bravery" was the very act of daring to behold and portray the naked body of another young man. As Henry was his mother's confidant, we may guess that he told her the circumstances that led to his decision not to return to the art studio. Perhaps it was this episode that "inspired" their father to write a friend of his, inquiring as to how he might find a microscope to give his son William as a Christmas gift, a none-too-subtle pressure on William to consider a scientific career instead. Yet Lewis cautions that there is no hard evidence that Henry Senior actually pressured William to abandon his artistic interests, for, as Henry Junior recalled, their father's habit was to encourage them not to make any final choices but always to keep alternatives open (Lewis 1991, 112). William's precipitous abandonment of all plans for a career in art just as he was "beginning to show real promise as a portrait painter" (Lewis 1991, 111) points, instead, to the influence of James's mother and to her concerns about the moral temptations to which her son was exposed in an artist's studio.[10] I realize that at this point in my discussion the idea that his mother was the key player in the "murder" of his artist self is suppositional, but later I shall offer evidence that gives this view considerable plausibility.

The Parable of the Prehistoric Reptiles

My suspicion that James himself is the "intimate friend" might of course be mistaken. But even if this were so, it would not affect my basic argument that his hallucinatory experiences, with their decidedly melancholic overtones, are *self*-revelatory, and genuinely so. The French Sufferer account, which we know to be his own, makes this sufficiently clear. Nor would my being mistaken about the intimate friend affect James's argument that such experiences reveal the radical evil that inheres in the universe, that, therefore, they involve a deeper apprehension of reality than the religion of healthy-mindedness affords. We may protest either against his view of the universe as possessing a radical evil or against his use of hallucinatory experiences in support of it, but in *The Principles of Psychology* James is quick to defend hallucinatory experiences, noting that they are not delusions, for a delusion is a false opinion about a matter of fact, whereas a hallucination "is a strictly sensational form of consciousness, as good and true a sensation as if there were a real object there" (1950, 2:15). In fact, hallucinations are not much different from dreams, which are "our real world whilst we are sleeping, because our attention then lapses from the sensible world. . . . But if a dream haunts us and compels our attention during the day it is very apt to remain figuring in our consciousness as a sort of subuniverse alongside of the waking world" (1950, 2:294).

If dreams are potential sources of enlightenment, then hallucinatory experiences are too, and the enlightenment in the French Sufferer case is that in this world the individual self is terribly, horribly vulnerable: "Nothing that I possess can defend me against that fate, if the hour for it should strike for me as it struck for him" (*VRE,* 160). The corollary of this enlightenment is that, as the intimate friend case reveals, we are also fated to be a danger to ourselves, that partial suicide is an inescapable feature of our life in a world in which we cannot avoid making fateful choices.

James's chapter "The Sick Soul" does not, however, end with his account of the French Sufferer. Instead, it goes on to note that James purposely avoided the examples of really insane melancholia in which there *are* "delusions about matters of fact." Had he presented such cases, "it would be a worse story still—desperation absolute and complete, the whole universe coagulating about the sufferer into a material of overwhelming horror, surrounding him without opening or end" (*VRE*, 162). Here the evil would be not a matter of "intellectual perception" (enlightenment) "but the grisly blood-freezing heart-palsying sensation of it close upon one, and no other conception or sensation able to live for a moment in its presence" (*VRE*, 162). In such cases, "how irrelevantly remote seem all our usual refined optimisms and intellectual and moral consolations in presence of a need of help like this! Here is the real core of the religious problem: Help! help! No prophet can claim to bring a final message unless he says things that will have a sound of reality in the ears of victims such as these" (*VRE*, 162). And this, James suggests, is why we may expect that the "coarser religions, revivalistic, orgiastic, with blood and miracles and supernatural operations, may possibly never be displaced. Some constitutions need them too much." The deliverance, it would appear, "must come in as strong a form as the complaints" (*VRE*, 162).

Thus, in the final paragraphs of "The Sick Soul" James is especially concerned with the melancholic temperament's true apprehension of the evil of the universe, an evil of which melancholiacs know themselves to be potential victims. The healthy-minded may dismiss this insight and argue that, even if it were true, one may avert attention from it and live "simply in the light of good" (*VRE*, 163). But while this may be a successful "religious solution," it "breaks down impotently as soon as melancholy comes; and even though one be quite free from melancholy one's self, there is no doubt that healthy-mindedness is inadequate as a philosophical doctrine, because the evil facts which it refuses positively to account for are a genuine portion of reality; and they may after all be the best key to life's significance, and possibly the only openers of our eyes to the deepest levels of truth" (*VRE*, 163). One need not be possessed by "insane melancholy" to realize that the normal process of life has moments of "radical evil." After all, "the lunatic's visions of horror are all drawn from the material of daily fact" (*VRE*, 163).

Consider, for example, the "carnivorous reptiles of geologic times." Although they are now museum specimens and no longer a threat to anything, "there is no tooth in any one of these museum skulls that did not daily through long years of the foretime hold fast to the body struggling in despair of some fated living victim" (*VRE*, 164). On a smaller scale, forms of horror just as dreadful to their victims fill our world today: "Here on our very hearths and in our gardens the infernal cat plays with the panting mouse, or holds the hot bird fluttering in her jaws. Crocodiles and rattlesnakes and pythons are at this moment vessels of life as real as we are; their loathsome existence fills every minute of every day that drags its length along; and whenever they or other wild beasts clutch their living prey, *the deadly horror which an agitated melancholic feels is the literally right reaction on the situation"* (VRE, 164, my emphasis).

These are no placid beasts. His father, frustrated by talk about diet, regimen, and politics, could envision himself a sheep grazing on a quiet hillside, Bunyan could envy the dog and toad because they have no fear for the fate of their souls, and Alline could imagine himself a bird flying away from danger and distress. But James uses the image of prehistoric reptiles and modern-day cats, crocodiles, rattlesnakes, and pythons to make the sober point that there is no escaping from the evil that the melancholiac sees with unusual clarity. And perhaps the most horrific of all is the randomness of evil, the way it selects one victim and lets the other temporarily escape. In a footnote to this passage, James cites the case of a group of travelers who suddenly hear a cracking sound in the bushes, and the next instant a tiger has pounced on one of their party and carried him off (VRE, 164). The French Sufferer knows that he is potentially the black-haired youth with greenish skin, entirely idiotic: *"That shape am I,* I felt, potentially. Nothing that I possess can defend me against that fate, if the hour for it should strike for me as it struck for him." It makes one wonder "how other people could live, how I myself had ever lived, so unconscious of that pit of insecurity beneath the surface of life" (VRE, 160–61).[11]

Exploration of James's recommendations for combating a world in which radical evil is an everyday fact would be the next logical step for us to take. His essay "Is Life Worth Living?" (1956, 32–62) is perhaps his most deeply personal reflection on this struggle and may be viewed as his own "confession of faith." This is not the time, however, to introduce new issues and themes but to return to the issue left in abeyance earlier, the role of James's mother in the vicissitudes of his melancholic temperament. For this exploration, the text I shall turn to is Erik H. Erikson's *Young Man Luther* (1958), specifically Erikson's analysis of the last several paragraphs of James's chapter "The Sick Soul," especially James's parable of the prehistoric reptiles.

Metaphysical Anxiety and the Devouring Will

Just prior to introducing these paragraphs, Erikson has been discussing the role that religion plays in reaffirming the basic trust that must develop if infants are to survive in the world into which they have recently been cast: "In situations in which such basic trust cannot develop in early infancy because of a defect in the child or in the maternal environment, children die mentally. They do not respond nor learn; they do not assimilate their food and fail to defend themselves against infection, and often they die physically as well as mentally" (1958, 118). Even in the most fortunate of situations, however, there will take root "a life-long mistrustful remembrance of that truly metaphysical anxiety; meta — 'behind,' 'beyond' — here means 'before,' 'way back,' 'at the beginning'" (1958, 119). The task of religion is to address such anxiety.

But Erikson asks: What caused this anxiety to take root? What made it happen? "All religions and most philosophers agree it is *will* — the mere will to live, thoughtless and cruel self-will" (1958, 120). Then he quotes the passage in "The Sick Soul" chapter where James describes the prehistoric reptiles, specifically James's assertion that "there is no tooth in any of these museum-skulls that did not daily . . . hold fast to the body struggling in despair of some fated living victim." Erikson comments that "the tenor of this mood is immediately convincing. It is the mood of severe melancholy, intensified tristitia, one would almost say tristitia with teeth in it." He then observes that "James is clinically and genetically correct, when he connects the horror of the *devouring* will to live with the content and the disposition of melancholia. For in melancholia, it is the human being's horror of his own avaricious and sadistic orality which he tires of, withdraws from, wishes often to end even by putting an end to himself. This is not the orality of the first, the toothless and dependent, stage; it is the orality of the tooth-stage and all that develops within it, especially the prestages of what later becomes 'biting' human conscience" (1958, 121).

Erikson notes that Luther reversed the picture and saw "God himself as a devourer, as if the wilful sinner could expect to find in God's demeanor a mirror of his own avarice, just as the uplifted face of the believer [also] finds a countenance inclined and full of grace" (1958, 121). Such images of the devouring deity are mirror images of "man's own rapacious orality which destroys the innocent trust of that first symbiotic orality when mouth and breast, glance and face, are one" (1958, 122).

Here Erikson traces the desire for a will of one's own to the *penultimate* stage of infancy — the tooth stage, as it were — and links this desire to James's account of the deadly fight for survival that characterizes all sentient life on this planet. Melancholy, at least melancholy with teeth in it, is about the threat of losing that which has made life so palpably worthwhile. We feel we are losing it, or have already lost it, and must somehow gain it back, using whatever means we possess. The one with whom this struggle is originally carried out and forever remembered as our first combatant is the very one who embodies the "maternal environment," which is to say that our original fight for life is with and against the very one who gave us life in the first place. No wonder there is so much feeling of mutual betrayal, or mutual victimization, in melancholia.

"Armed" with Erikson's view of melancholy as having "teeth in it," I want to take a second look at the French Sufferer episode and to explore the suspicions Erikson's view raises about the role of the mother-son relationship in James's fears for his own sanity. I have argued that his mother had a hand in the "murder" of the self James imagined he could be, and I now want to propose that she was the key player in his fear that he might become a self whom he truly dreaded becoming but knew to be a genuine possibility. Surely there is more behind the story of the French Sufferer than James has been able or willing to tell. Conceivably, as Myers suggests, he was simply not very self-analytical (1986, 49), and the French Sufferer case as we have it in *The Varieties* is an illustration either of this fact or of the limits of introspection as a method of self-analysis. Perhaps. But I think it has more to do with reserve, a reluctance to speak negatively about his parents, especially his mother, and with the fact that he has been asked to give a series of lectures, not a personal life history. To engage in any more personal disclosure than he has already done would be self-indulgent, an affront to his audience, who came for something else.

Yet, as we have seen, James offers a clue that all was not well in his relationship with his mother when, in the French Sufferer account, he represents her as being strangely oblivious to what he was going through: "My mother in particular, a very cheerful person, seemed to me a perfect paradox in her unconsciousness of danger, which you may well believe I was very careful not to disturb by revelations of my own state of mind" (*VRE*, 161). Commentators on this passage have drawn the conclusion that James's intent here was to present his mother as a perfect example of the healthy-minded temperament, and therefore as one who was constitutionally unable to appreciate what horrible pain and suffering her son was experiencing. As Erikson observes, James's assurance "that he did not want to disturb his unaccountably cheerful mother makes one wonder how much anxiety it took for the self-made man of that day to turn to the refuge of woman" (1968, 153).

This may be true so far as it goes. But we need to remember that the story of the French Sufferer is the reconstruction of the experience by a man in his late fifties, for whom his mother is no longer objectively present. For a truer account of the feelings of the young man of 28, for whom his mother is very much alive, I suggest that the story of the *real* French sufferer, also in James's chapter "The Sick Soul," hits much closer to the mark. This is the young French mental patient who has been hospitalized against his will, and whose cursings and self-pity demonstrate that his melancholia has not taken a religious turn (*VRE*, 148–49). Why does James choose to make himself a "French" sufferer if not to draw a parallel to the first French sufferer presented in the chapter, a man who is in every respect like himself: young, philosophically minded (and thus also subject to "philosophical pessimism"), and able to speak of his mother and "abuse of power" in one and the same breath? Moreover, the *real* French sufferer is also suffering from the "worst kind of melancholy," that of panic fear. As the real French sufferer writes to his real correspondent, "Besides the burnings and the sleeplessness, fear, atrocious fear, presses me down, holds me without respite, never lets me go" (*VRE,* 148). Then the accusation, the biting sarcasm, directed against his own mother: "Eat, drink, lie awake all night, suffer without interruption — such is the fine legacy I have received from my mother!" (*VRE,* 148). After this, the note of incomprehension: Why is this happening to me? "What I fail to understand is this abuse of power. There are limits to everything, there is a middle way. But God knows neither middle way nor limits. I say God, but why? All I have known so far has been the devil. After all, I am afraid of God as much as of the devil, so I drift along, thinking of nothing but suicide, but with neither courage nor means here to execute the act" (*VRE,* 148).

Finally, he gives vent to a towering self-pity and consuming rage when he goes back in thought to the beginning of his life: "But I stop. I have raved to you long enough. I say raved, for I can write no otherwise, having neither brain nor thoughts left. O God! What a misfortune to be born! Born, like a mushroom, doubtless between an evening and a morning; and how true and right I was when in our philosophy-year in college I chewed the cud of bitterness with the pessimists. Yes, indeed, there is more pain in life than gladness — it is one long agony until the grave. Think how gay it makes me to remember that this horrible misery of mine, coupled with this unspeakable fear, may last fifty, one hundred, who knows how many more years!" (*VRE,* 149).

Conceivably, James's own panic fear for his very existence was not as severe as that of the real Frenchman. Yet James too was contemplating suicide, and he too felt "defenseless against the invisible enemy who is tightening his coils around me" (*VRE,* 148). I believe he was no less angry at his mother, the one whom the real French sufferer wants to blame, ultimately, for his hopeless condition, for even thirty years after the French Sufferer experience, James at least allows himself a criticism of his mother's "cheerful" demeanor and her "unconsciousness of danger," which is to say that he believes that she was living in denial.

He was not the only family member who was experiencing deep psychological anguish at the time, and whose condition was similarly unacknowledged by their mother. Just prior to his breakdown, while he was in Germany, his younger sister Alice was also stricken and, as Lewis points out, their mother's analysis of Alice's difficulties (in her letter to their younger brother Wilky) "reflected a wistful incomprehension: Alice's mind was untouched by the disturbance; she did not dread the attacks in advance, was 'perfectly happy when they are over,' and was patient and affectionate throughout" (Lewis 1991, 196–97). In her commentary on James's essay "The Hidden Self," published in 1890, in which James refers to the "abandoned" self, Alice recalls that when she was having her attacks "the only difference between me and the insane was that I had not only all the horrors and suffering of insanity but the duties of doctor, nurse, and straitjacket imposed upon me, too" (Lewis 1991, 197). What she means is that she had to "hold herself together" because insanity was forbidden in the James household. The problem with their mother's "healthy-mindedness" is that it reflected a refusal to acknowledge that something was desperately wrong with the James family.

Carol Holly (1995) suggests that the very fact William was in Germany at this time was viewed by one of William's friends as motivated by difficulties in the family. On hearing this, his mother wrote an indignant letter to William, complaining that his friend had dared to suggest in her presence that "some dreadful family rupture had driven you to place the ocean between you and your family." Holly comments: "In this letter, Mary James's snide and wounded tone expresses her indignation at the possibility of a 'rupture' within the James family, or at the possibility that people might imagine such a rupture had occurred. Thus she indirectly echoes her husband's belief that 'domestic discord' is the most 'frightful of all discords' and reveals her sense of responsibility not only for maintaining harmony but *for reminding her children of their responsibility as well*" (1995, 32, my emphasis).

Holly also contends that James's mother was "impatient with William's frequent expressions of weakness and anxiety" but "explicitly endorsed the patient, non-complaining posture of her second son Henry" (1995, 30). When William was undergoing his emotional crisis, she wrote to Henry that his older brother was "still very morbid, and much more given than he used to be to talking about himself. . . . If, dear Harry, you could have imparted to him a few grains of your hopefulness, he would have been well long ago." In a letter to William she "demonstrates not only how appreciative she was of what William called Henry's 'angelic patience' but also how critical she was of William for 'talking about himself.' 'Of course,' she writes to William, 'his "angelic patience" shows forth, as you say, but happily that side of his character is always in relief, and does not need great occasions (*as it does with some of us*) to bring it into view' " (Holly 1995, 46, my emphasis). Holly does not believe that Henry was actually hopeful or optimistic. Rather, he developed an "as-if personality" or "false self" in order to win or maintain parental approval. William, on the other hand, was visibly melancholic, to the obvious irritation and vexation of his mother.

Lewis traces the family dysfunctions to the fact that Henry Senior had considered marrying both Walsh sisters, finally settling on Mary, who was the older. Yet the younger sister, Catherine (Aunt Kate), accompanied the young James family to England, serving as the nurse for little William and Henry (Lewis 1991, 77). For his part, William seemed to take especially well to Aunt Kate, as he was her favorite of the two boys. By contrast, Henry Junior "felt a special bond with his mother" (Kaplan 1992, 16). Lewis describes Aunt Kate as "a more troubled personality than her older sister Mary. The two sisters resembled one another in height, bearing, and facial features, to judge from the available photographs; but Kate's face lacked the serene, faintly smiling, almost masklike composure of Mary's. Its mouth and eyes spoke of discontent, of failed or repressed hopes, perhaps of suffering" (Lewis 1991, 75). Though James himself praised Aunt Kate for "the energy of her active will" (Lewis 1991, 175), he also commented on the "sort of sub-antagonism" that prevailed between her and his father, owing, Lewis suspects, to the fact that she was spurned by Henry Senior in favor of her older sister (Lewis 1991, 75).

In any event, there were certainly ample reasons for tension and conflict in this arrangement, and one would not be surprised if Henry Senior's breakdown were more the result of this domestic situation than of his having overworked himself in his exegetical labors.[12] Of special interest to us here, however, is the fact that William was much in the care of his aunt while his mother was occupied with Henry Junior, and that this emotional separation from his mother occurred when William was developing a will of his own (that is, two to three years old). In an emotional sense, he was talking about himself when in his lecture "The Dilemma of Determinism" (1956, 157) he said that some mothers *do* strangle their firstborns. And no doubt Aunt Kate, the spurned sister, would not have protested if her sister's firstborn had a desire to "bite" his mother back for having spurned *him* in favor of her beloved second-born son. An early short story by Henry Junior, "The Romance of Certain Old Clothes," is about an incestuous triangle involving a rivalry between sisters. Of Henry's early stories, Fred Kaplan says that although it is unclear what the James family made of them, their "autobiographical resonances probably flickered fully enough in their consciousness to allow them to see that he had drawn on shared family experience" (1992, 70).

These family problems were never really resolved. Aunt Kate eventually married, when William was 13, but her marriage lasted only three years, and then she was back with the Jameses for good. When she left, Henry Senior wrote to a friend that Aunt Kate had been "a most loving and provident husband to Mary, a most considerate and devoted wife to me, and an incomparable father and mother to our children" (Lewis 1991, 76). He was of course using these familial terms — wife, husband, father, mother — in jest, but, just the same, he expresses the fact that Aunt Kate had made herself indispensable and, especially so far as William was concerned, had assumed a status that more rightfully belonged to his mother.

But does this mean that William's mother was weak and impotent, her power usurped by her younger sister? This is not how a young female visitor to the James family home experienced it. She found it "stiff and stupid . . . its 'pokey banality' ruled over by Mrs. James, while Mr. James came and went." He, the visitor observed, "never seemed to 'belong' to his wife or Miss Walsh, large stupid-looking ladies, or to his clever but coldly self-absorbed daughter [Alice]" (Lewis 1991, 199). If this account is to be believed, it was Mr. James who was without much power or influence in the family, no match, it seems, for his wife, who, as Kaplan points out, "remained stolidly, uncomplainingly healthy" when her five children and her husband succumbed to various illnesses (Kaplan 1992, 83).

Concerning the illnesses of the children, Leon Edel notes that "the young Jameses seemed to use their symptoms intuitively to manipulate their contradictory and demanding parents" (Edel 1974, 1). Edel suggests that, if the children used their illnesses to manipulate their parents, this was in retaliation against their mother's own manipulations. Thus, he advises us to study Henry Junior's letters as we would the text of a poem: "How does [Henry] James deal with his seemingly penny-pinching mother — who in turn reveals a great deal about herself in her letters and the manner in which she attempts to manipulate her children? We must be careful when we use the word 'manipulate' — but I use it in full awareness: for when there are a great many letters, it is possible to study stance and strategy behind the veiled politeness, and even lovingness, of a letter. In the case of James's mother we find her concerned with the funds he has drawn from his letters of credit. She shows her money worries. Sometimes she complains he is spending too much; at other times she wonders what he is living on" (Edel 1974, xviii–xix).

In his biography of Henry James, Kaplan makes similar comments on the power that Mrs. James wielded over her children. Henry Senior was "a great noisemaker, an actor who could be heard in the back row," whereas she "was dominant to her children and her husband, 'by the mere force of her complete availability'" (Kaplan 1992, 16). Henry Junior remarked, "She lived in ourselves so exclusively, with such a want of use for anything in her consciousness that was not about us, that I think we almost contested her being separate enough to be proud of us — it was too like being proud of ourselves" (Kaplan 1992, 16–17). Then, even more pointedly, he noted further: "She *was* he," meaning their father, and "*was* each of us." Commenting on these descriptions of James's mother, Carrie O. Kasten suggests that she was "an expert at what one might call selfless or evacuated selfhood," and Kasten likens her to a character in Henry James's novel *The Spoils of Poynton* who manifests "a perverse sort of self-gratification or egoism in her desire, while getting nothing for herself, to take charge of the affairs of others. Leon Edel sensitively discusses the way Mrs. James could be self-sacrificial, and yet 'all-encompassing,' even 'gubernatorial' " (Kasten 1987, 254–55).

I suspect, then, that William James, like the real French sufferer, held his mother more accountable than his father for his troubles. Living in the house over which his mother ruled, he was a victim, as the real French sufferer put it, of "an abuse of power." This was the power not of coercion and threat but of denial (and *self*-denial), the refusal to see reality for what it is, and the determination to see only what she wanted to see. Of the two forms of healthy-mindedness set forth in James's chapter "The Religion of Healthy-Mindedness," hers was not the involuntary but the systematic type: "In its involuntary variety, healthy-mindedness is a way of feeling happy about things immediately. In its systematical variety, it is an abstract way of conceiving things as good. Every abstract way of conceiving things selects some one aspect of them as their essence for the time being, and disregards the other aspects. Systematic healthy-mindedness, conceiving good as the essential and universal aspect of being, deliberately excludes evil from its field of vision" (*VRE,* 87–88). The systematic type is, of course, the most maddening, precisely because it *is* a refusal to acknowledge that a problem exists, that something is wrong, that someone else may be suffering, and, most important, that one just *may* be implicated somehow in the suffering of the other.

In short, James understood that his mother was indeed capable of driving him into insanity, of making him "that Shape" which he so much dreaded becoming. If she had a hand in the "murder" of his artistic self — as I suspect she did — she played a controlling role in the panic fear he suffered several years later, when he came face to face with his "potential" self, the self that he knew was horribly possible. With her, he was always locked in a struggle for survival, and the result was a melancholy with teeth in it. She could not or would not give what he wanted and needed — a mother's unconditional love — and so he fought back. He wrote home from Germany, saying that he had fallen in love with an actress of Bohemian origin, knowing that this would cause *her* to *fear* for the worst, as her first-born son was threatening to marry a disreputable woman (Lewis 1991, 187).[13] Also, he exhibited little interest in actually pursuing the medical career for which he had been training, again causing *her* to *fear* that he might never find himself, might never amount to anything much. If he was indeed lacking in any self-analytical skills, as Myers suggests, this was probably where his deficiencies lay. He was depressed about his prospects, but his indecision was serving deeper psychological interests: to get back at his mother for failing to meet *his* need for a mother who could assuage a *child's* fears.

Yet James's parable of the "carnivorous reptiles of geologic times" is the older man's effort to arrive at a more balanced perspective, and it represents a significant step toward a more "religious" view of his lifelong affliction. The "evil," he suggests, is not in the one individual or the other but in the situation. All are fighting for their lives, and in this fight all will play both roles — now victim, now victimizer; there is no way for *this* "perfect paradox" to be avoided. To come to this enlightenment, however modest its consolations, is to take a major step beyond what James calls the "querulous temper" of the real French sufferer, a temper that "keeps his mind from taking a religious direction," that "tends in fact rather toward irreligion" (*VRE*, 149). The point, finally, is not to assign blame, to attribute one's troubles to this or that person, but rather to recognize that the universe is so constructed that all of us are engaged in a struggle for our very own existence. We are all endangered selves, and this was no less true for his mother than it was, and is, for himself.

If James parts company with the real French sufferer, it is in deciding that there is finally nothing to be gained by assigning blame, for to do so locks us into the very deterministic thinking that will eventually undermine the struggle for life itself. Moreover, when we engage in the struggle for life, we see the real world and its evil — for there is no denying it — but we also see another world, the "more" that the religious temperament enables us to see (*VRE*, 512–14). As he declares in "Is Life Worth Living?" (the essay I have called his "confession of faith"),

> I confess that I do not see why the very existence of an invisible world may not in part depend on the personal response which any one of us may make to the religious appeal. God himself, in short, may draw vital strength and increase of very being from our fidelity. For my own part, I do not know what the sweat and blood and tragedy of this life mean, if they mean anything short of this. If this life be not a real fight, in which something is eternally gained for the universe by success, it is no better than a game of private theatricals from which one may withdraw at will. But it *feels* like a real fight, — as if there were something really wild in the universe which we, with all our idealities and faithfulnesses are needed to redeem; and first of all to redeem our own hearts

from atheisms and fears. *For such a half-wild, half-saved universe our nature is adapted* [1956, 61, my emphasis].

In his psychobiographical study, Cushing Strout refers to James as a "twice-born sick soul" (see 1968, 1062–81). I would rather say that he is "half-wild, half-saved." Pratt asks in his questionnaire whether the respondent believes in personal immortality and if so why. James replies, "Never keenly, but more strongly as I grow older." Why? "Because I am just getting fit to live" (Brown 1973, 125). Six years later (on August 26, 1910), he went out into the dark alone, to face the final religious experience that awaits us all when the fight has gone out of us and our part in the battle is over. This experience is all the evidence we need, and perhaps more than we want, that religious experiences are ultimately — *meta*-physically, if you will — a solitary, solemn affair. They are finally between ourselves and whatever we may consider the divine.

Melancholia and the Refusal to Interpret Experiences Religiously

I began this chapter with the question of whether religion may in fact be an entirely individual matter, unrelated to and disconnected from any and all religious traditions. By focusing on the intimate friend and French Sufferer cases and comparing them with other cases in *The Varieties,* I have shown that James himself believed that religious experiences are experiences that the experiencer interprets in the language and symbols of a religious tradition. Therefore, James does not believe that his own experiences qualify as religious experiences, as he does not so interpret them.

But we have also seen that these experiences reveal the degree to which his own self was endangered, with the intimate friend episode revealing that he was haunted throughout his life by remorse over his own "self-murder" (or "murdered self"), and the French Sufferer episode disclosing how he struggled with, and gained a victory over, the "potential self" that he was in danger of becoming. It was a victory, however, that left him permanently wounded, a lifelong melancholiac. He did not claim that either experience was religious. Instead of interpreting them in light of any religious tradition, he preferred to see them as powerful psychical experiences, as visual hallucination in the case of the intimate friend and verbal automatism in the case of the French Sufferer. The most he will claim is that the French Sufferer case had a "religious bearing" because the automatisms were consoling scripture texts.

James's reluctance to interpret these experiences as religious leaves *us,* his readers, with an interesting dilemma. We *could,* if we chose to, declare that in our own judgment they *were* religious experiences, as they may readily be so interpreted. We might call this the Pfister argument, after Oskar Pfister, the Lutheran pastor who was fond of telling Freud, a self-proclaimed atheist, that Freud was more religious than his believer friends. Or, alternatively, we *may* decide that James is the one who must judge whether or not his experiences are religious ones. If we take this approach, then we also take a giant step toward the view that religious experience is, ultimately, a personal matter, that only the experiencer can say, finally, whether the experience is religious or not.

My own inclination is to take the second position, even if it means that James's own experiences cannot then be used in support of the thesis that there may be purely personal religious experiences this side of death itself. But, then, we may also imagine that James himself would not have been content to conclude the investigation on this ironic note but would have wanted to probe further into why he himself was so reticent about interpreting his experiences religiously when others, in similar circumstances, had little or no difficulty in doing so.[14] A possible explanation for this reticence is that, had he interpreted these experiences religiously, he would have given others certain satisfactions of which he wished to deprive them, beginning, I would suppose, with his anxious mother. Thus, to refuse to interpret his experiences as religious was his revenge for the fact that as a young man he was compelled to believe that he had no choice but to commit an act of self-murder. The "teeth" in James's melancholy is that he will *not* give the religious community what it wants, that is, the right to call him one of their own, a situation it is likely to find the more frustrating in light of the fact that, for his own personal reasons — as a lifelong sufferer from melancholia — he vigorously defended religion against the philistine scientific opinion of his day.[15]

Putting a Face on the World

I believe that I have provided considerable evidence that James's melancholy is attributable first and foremost to his loss of his mother's unconditional love. In my judgment, the single most important piece of evidence in this regard is the fact that there was a special affinity between his mother and his younger brother Henry. Harold Bloom suggests that "the student of [Henry] James eventually knows that James and his fiction seem to lack the 'narcissistic scar' that Freud saw as marking all of us, being a memento of our first failure in love, the loss of our parent of the sex opposite to ours to our parent of the same sex as ours" (Bloom 1987, 12). While Bloom here fails adequately to differentiate Henry James's life from his fiction, and thus to recognize that the fiction may compensate for the loss in real life, his statement indirectly supports my argument that William, the son who was *not* his mother's favorite, when he had every right to be, *did* suffer the "narcissistic scar" of a boy's "first failure in love," namely, the "loss" of his mother's love to his only slightly younger brother, Henry.

But my concern in this chapter has not been so much to identify the specific root cause of James's loss of his mother's unconditional love as to make the general case that his melancholy may be attributed to this loss. I believe I have shown that there was much in his relations to his mother, especially as a young man, that is revealing of this deep sense of loss, and of the psychic connections between the loss and his melancholy. What I have *not* discussed, however, are the ways in which he sought compensations for this loss. One obvious compensation was his wife, Alice, who, while she did not constitute a "cure" for his melancholy, did a great deal to assuage it, especially by her fidelity to James in spite of his occasional projections onto her of his rage against his mother. Also important was Alice's mother, to whom he dedicated *The Varieties of Religious Experience,* as she, through her interest in mind cure, was sympathetic (as his own mother was not) to his "sick-soulness" (see Hutch 1995). Yet, in the final analysis, I believe it was James's sublimation of his melancholia through his affinities for the natural world that was ultimately the source of his consolation and refuge from debilitating self-hatred. To say that he sought the beneficent face of the mother in the world of nature is entirely consistent with the fact of his lifelong struggle with melancholy, especially as it involved the frustration of his desire to become an artist.

In "Mirror-Role of Mother and Family in Child Development" (1991a), D. W. Winnicott suggests that the infant's sense of being a self is dependent on a mother's capacity to "mirror" back to the infant the very emotions that the infant is expressing toward her. If the infant smiles and the mother returns his smile, he learns that he is a smiling self. If, on the other hand, his smile evokes a scowl or mere impassivity, the infant's selfhood is jeopardized, as it depends for its existence on an accurate mirroring of itself. Also, Winnicott points out that an infant's own "object constancy" is secured in a relationship in which the other's constancy is secure enough not to succumb to the infant's efforts to destroy the other.

Winnicott's essay on mirroring is directly relevant to James's discussion of animistic religion in the concluding chapters of *The Varieties.* In his chapter on "other characteristics" of religion, James is especially concerned with prayer, which he declares to be the "very soul and essence of religion," for it helps us to cultivate the appropriate attitude toward the world around us, particularly the natural world (*VRE,* 463ff.). He is especially sympathetic toward the prayerful attitude that is not based on belief that "particular events are tempered more towardly to us by a superintending providence as a reward for our reliance" but instead cultivates "the continuous sense of our connection with the power that made things as they are, [so that] we are tempered more towardly for their reception" (*VRE*, 474).[16] In other words, the change is essentially subjective:

> The outward face of nature need not alter, but the expressions of meaning in it alter. It was dead and is alive again. *It is like the difference between looking on a person without love, or upon the same person with love.* In the latter case intercourse springs into new vitality. So when one's affections keep in touch with the divinity of the world's authorship, fear and egotism fall away; and in the equanimity that follows, one finds in the hours, as they succeed each other, a series of purely benignant opportunities. It is as if all doors were opened, and all paths freshly smoothed. We meet a new world when we meet the old world in the spirit which this kind of prayer infuses [*VRE*, 474, my emphasis].

Here James reintroduces an issue that was central to his earlier lectures on the healthy-minded and the sick-soul temperaments, namely, the individual's sense of the natural world or "the mundane order of things," especially as to whether the individual regarded this world as hostile or benignly disposed toward him. In a footnote, he quotes at some length a passage from the writings of the Greek stoic Epictetus, who discerns the providence of God in all the seemingly mundane processes of nature. In the contemporary scene, however, James associates this spirit of "cultivating the continuous sense of our connection with the power that made things as they are" with the healthy-minded temperament, for it is also the spirit of "mind-curers, of the transcendentalists, and of the so-called 'liberal' Christians" (*VRE*, 474).

This spirit is expressed in James Martineau's sermon entitled "Help Thou Mine Unbelief," in which Martineau proclaims: "Depend upon it, it is not the want of greater miracles, but of the soul to perceive such as are allowed us still, that make us push all the sanctities into the far spaces we cannot reach. The devout feel that wherever God's hand is, *there* is miracle; and it is simply an indevoutness which imagines that only where miracle is, can there be the real hand of God. . . . It is no outward change, no shifting in time or place; but only the loving meditation of the pure in heart, that can reawaken the Eternal from the sleep within our souls; that can render him a reality again, and reassert for him once more his ancient name of 'the living God' " (*VRE*, 475). James himself concludes: "When we see all things in God, and refer all things to him, we read in common matters superior expressions of meaning. *The deadness with which custom invests the familiar vanishes, and existence as a whole appears transfigured*" (*VRE*, 475–76, my emphasis).

Mind-curers, transcendentalists, and liberal Christians are all healthy-minded types. Perhaps, then, we are not surprised that they would find themselves disposed, as Martineau puts it, to "discern beneath the sun, as he rises any morning, the supporting finger of the Almighty" (*VRE*, 475). But what of the sick soul, the melancholiac for whom the world that surrounds him is either indifferent or hostile? That Martineau's sermon is entitled "Help Thou Mine Unbelief" suggests that it may be addressed precisely to those who do not experience this world as reflective of the "supporting finger of the Almighty," for he goes on to describe the one who now discerns the Almighty behind the rising sun as *recovering* "the sweet and reverent surprise with which Adam gazed on the first dawn in Paradise" (*VRE*, 475). In effect, he is speaking to those who have lost the perception of the world as disclosing the reality of God. The world has not changed, for "the universe, open to the eye today, looks as it did a thousand years ago" (*VRE*, 475). The perceiver has changed, and the perceiver can change again. As James puts it, "The deadness with which custom invests the familiar vanishes, and existence as a whole *appears* transfigured" (*VRE*, 476). What we are witnessing in this case is "the state of a mind thus awakened from torpor" (*VRE*, 476).

Thus, the melancholic soul may also have experience of the world as transfigured. The difference between the healthy-minded and the sick soul may be in the fact that for the former the sense of the world being upheld by the supporting arms of God is more habitual, whereas for the latter this perception is more occasional. In support of this distinction between the habitual and the occasional, James cites the following illustration from the autobiographical recollections of the Catholic philosopher Fr. A. Gratry. According to James, the experience occurred in Fr. Gratry's "youthful melancholy period":

> One day I had a moment of consolation, because I met with something which seemed to me ideally perfect. It was a poor drummer beating the tattoo in the streets of Paris. I walked behind him in returning to the school on the evening of a holiday. His drum gave out the tattoo in such a way that, at that moment at least, however peevish I were, I could find no pretext for fault-finding. It was impossible to conceive more nerve or spirit, better time or measure, more clearness or richness, than were in this drumming. Ideal desire could go no farther in that direction. I was enchanted and consoled; the perfection of this wretched act did me good. Good is at least possible, I said, since the ideal can thus sometimes get embodied [*VRE*, 476].

If for Gratry his melancholic mood was lifted by the drummer beating the tattoo in the streets of Paris, the main character in a novel by Senancour had a similar experience, also in the Paris streets, when he came across a yellow jonquil blooming on a March day: "It was the strongest expression of desire: it was the first perfume of the year. I felt all the happiness destined for man. This unutterable harmony of souls, the phantom of the ideal world, arose in me complete. I never felt anything so great or so instantaneous. I know not what shape, what analogy, what secret of relation it was that made me see in this flower a limitless beauty. . . . I shall never inclose in a conception this power, this immensity that nothing will express; this form that nothing will contain; this ideal of a better world which one feels, but which, it seems, nature has not made actual" (*VRE*, 477).

These illustrations indicate that the sick soul is the one for whom such epiphanies are especially powerful, for through them the world suddenly appears transfigured. The "ideal" world that seemed so impossible of realization, so transcendentally removed, is suddenly present, so close that it may be seen and felt.

James reminds his listeners that he had already drawn attention to this experience of "the vivified face of the world" in his lectures on conversion, and he cites a passage in them that contrasted the experiences of the convert with those of the melancholiac: "A third peculiarity of the assurance state [in conversion] is the objective change which the world often appears to undergo. 'An appearance of newness beautifies every object,' the precise opposite of that other sort of newness, that dreadful unreality and strangeness in the appearance of the world, which is experienced by melancholy patients, and of which you may recall my relating some examples" (*VRE*, 248). In both instances, in the earlier lectures on conversion and now in his discussion of prayer, he footnotes the passage in his chapter "The Sick Soul" in which he alluded to "transformations in the whole expression of reality." In this passage he anticipates his chapter on conversion with a preliminary contrast of the experiences of the convert and the melancholiac: "When we come to study the phenomenon of conversion or religious regeneration, we shall see that a not infrequent consequence of the change operated in the subject is *a transfiguration of the face of nature in his eyes.* A new heaven seems to shine upon a new earth. In melancholiacs, there is usually a similar change, only it is in the reverse direction. *The world now looks remote, strange, sinister, uncanny.* Its color is gone, its breath is cold, there is no speculation in the eyes it glares with" (*VRE*, 151, my emphases).

Thus, the world may be experienced in both forms — now with vivified face and shining, now remote, strange, and eyes glaring — which causes one to wonder: "If the natural world is so double-faced and *unhomelike,* what world, what thing is real? An urgent wondering and questioning is set up, a poring theoretic activity, and in the desperate effort to get into right relations with the matter, the sufferer is often led to what becomes for him a satisfying religious solution" (*VRE*, 152, my emphasis).

In his lecture on prayer, however, James implies that the effort is much less theoretic, much less a matter of conscious thought or active will, and far more a matter of yielding to the sights and sounds around oneself. The energy, so to speak, comes from without, not from within:

> As a rule, religious persons generally assume that whatever natural facts connect themselves in any way with their destiny are significant of the divine purposes with them. Through prayer the purpose, often far from obvious, *comes home to them,* and if it be "trial," strength to endure the trial is given. Thus at all stages of the prayerful life we find the persuasion that in the process of communion energy from on high flows in to meet demand, and becomes operative within the phenomenal world. So long as this operativeness is admitted to be real, it makes no essential difference whether its immediate effects be subjective or objective. The fundamental religious point is that in prayer, spiritual energy, which otherwise would slumber, does become active, and spiritual work of some kind is effected really [*VRE,* 477, my emphasis].

Whatever the ultimate source of the energy may be, it will be experienced in prayer as originating outside the individual and as occurring in direct relation to the prayerful one's receptivity and yielding.

In his final chapter, "Conclusions," James asserts that the scientific attitude of the day is the greatest threat to religion because it takes the view that prayer is merely a survival from more primitive times when our ancestors believed that they could "coerce the spiritual powers" to "get them on our side," especially in "our dealings with the natural world" (*VRE,* 495). While James shares the scientific community's critique of human efforts to coerce the spiritual powers, he distances himself from its insistence on replacing animistic views of the natural world as found in religion with science's "mathematical and mechanical modes of conception" (*VRE,* 496–97). If science claims that such views of the natural world are mere "survivals" of a more primitive way of thinking, James cautions that the natural world possesses such "picturesquely striking" features that our ancestors would surely have viewed these "as the more promising avenue to the knowledge of Nature's life" than "the thin, pallid, uninteresting ideas" that guide science's approach to nature, such as considerations of weight, movement, velocity, direction, and position. "It is still in these richer animistic and dramatic aspects that religion delights to dwell. It is the terror and beauty of phenomena, the 'promise' of the dawn and of the rainbow, the 'voice' of the thunder, the 'gentleness' of the summer rain, the 'sublimity' of the stars, and not the physical laws which these things follow, by which the religious mind still continues to be most impressed" (*VRE,* 497–98).

In effect, science and the melancholic mood share in common the sense that the natural world is dead and lifeless, while the religious temperament experiences the world as dramatically, animistically alive. The fact that science shares the melancholic perception of the world as indifferent does not invalidate science, but it surely calls into question science's superior attitude toward religion. Thus, prayer, which is critically important to the perception of the natural world as transfigured, is not only the core of religion but also the basis for its rejection of the scientific view that religion is a mere survival of more primitive ways of thinking. One's perception of the phenomenal world is very much a subjective matter; for some the world is warm and inviting, for others cold and sinister. But there is an objective factor as well, in that the world "out there" is not an undifferentiated gray mass but has certain features that stand out from the rest, that are, as it were, more "animated" than its other features. For those who are religious, these are the very features of the world that have the feel of divine presence. The reality of God *is,* for them, perceptible in the promise of the dawn, the voice of the thunder, the gentleness of the summer rain, the sublimity of the stars.

These contrasts between the religious and scientific attitudes are reminiscent of James's early chapter "The Reality of the Unseen," where he laments the fact that " 'Science' in many minds is genuinely taking the place of a religion" and notes that "laws of nature" are replacing the "feeling of objective presence" in the world, a presence that is only half-metaphoric, for "even now we may speak of the smile of the morning, the kiss of the breeze, or the bite of the cold, without really meaning that these phenomena of nature actually wear a human face" (*VRE,* 57–58). In a footnote to this passage, he quotes B. de St. Pierre's observation that "nature is always so interesting, under whatever aspect she shows herself, that when it rains, I seem to see a beautiful woman weeping. She appears the more beautiful, the more afflicted she is" (*VRE,* 58). For religion, there is a certain "objective" truth in this view of nature as a beautiful woman weeping, a view that is not so much imposed upon nature as excited by it: "*Nature* is always so interesting, under whatever aspect *she* shows herself."

I suggest that for James nature becomes the mother he lost in early childhood. Nature is the mother who, by virtue of her own object constancy, vouchsafes his own. Having suggested in *The Principles of Psychology* that belief is what we take interest in, James implies in his defense of animistic religion that nature is a woman who is always capable of evoking belief, whatever the guise in which she manifests herself to us. And because this is true, we are able to believe in ourselves as well. As he writes in *The Principles of Psychology* (1950, 1:319): "To have a self that I can *care for,* nature must first present me with some *object* interesting enough to make me instinctively wish to appropriate it for its *own* sake." Thus, she enables James to believe that he has a self, one that is evocative of his own desire to care for it.

The great irony in James's mother's objection to his desire to become an artist and her encouragement instead of a career in science is that it was through art that he had hoped to recover the lost object, an object in which science takes no interest in its own address to nature. Thus, the real mother frustrated her eldest son's desire for the restoration of the original mother who had long since lost her "homelike" quality and become sinister, uncanny, and cold, a melancholiac's worst nightmare. Yet, in a very real sense, the artist in James was victorious in the end, precisely because, through *The Varieties of Religious Experience,* he was able to defend animistic religion against the philistine science of his day. Such a defense would be almost unthinkable had he not suffered throughout his life from melancholia.

why not connect w/ Al. Univ.
psychic pheaum

① - intimacy

② need for self-agency

Otto

"A Thrill of Fear": The Melancholic Sources of The Idea of the Holy

Many of us were introduced to Rudolf Otto's *Idea of the Holy* during undergraduate or graduate courses in world religions. As a result, we have formed a somewhat skewed view of both the book and the author. Otto wrote it as a Christian theologian, and although there are many references to Buddhist, Hindu, and Islamic beliefs, the book has a decidedly Christian orientation, with key chapters on the numinous in the Old and New Testaments and in the theology of Martin Luther. By situating the text in a course, and now as a book in the psychology of religion, I shall challenge the traditional reading of *The Idea of the Holy* as a text in world religions and restore it to its original home, which is Western religious consciousness and, more focally, the issue of melancholia.

When he wrote *The Idea of the Holy* in 1917, Otto's intention was to counter the tendency of the theologians of his day to focus exclusively on *concepts* of God. This implied to him their strong bias toward "rational religion." It disturbed him that the true "mother of rationalism" was theological orthodoxy, which "found in the construction of dogma and doctrine no way to do justice to the non-rational aspects of its subject" (1958, 3; hereafter *IH*). Otto is careful to emphasize in the foreword to the first English edition that he does not have a bias against the "rational" and that he certainly does not want "to promote in any way the tendency of our time towards an extravagant and fantastic 'irrationalism'" (*IH*, xxi). Indeed, he notes that the "irrational" is today "a favorite theme of all who are too lazy to think or too ready to evade the arduous duty of clarifying their ideas and grounding their convictions on a basis of coherent thought" (*IH*, xxi). At the same time, he believes that the "non-rational" has not received the attention it deserves in contemporary theology, and that understanding of the Christian tradition itself has suffered as a result.

In writing *The Idea of the Holy,* he proposes to center on the "non-rational" aspect of religion by exploring the experience of the "Holy." Recognizing that the holy has a moral connotation (Kant, for example, spoke of the "holy will"), which has led to its acquisition of a rational aspect as well (that is, as "absolute goodness"), he proposes to set aside these moral and rational aspects so that the nonrational features of the holy may be brought clearly into focus. His term for this is the *numinous,* from the Latin word *numen,* which is the "mental state" that prevails in the encounter with the holy. He argues that this "mental state is perfectly *sui generis* and irreducible to any other" (*IH*, 7), that other "states of mind" may resemble it, and may be alluded to in order to help us elucidate it, but are not of the same order as the numinous, and the numinous in turn cannot be reduced to these other states of mind.

In a brief footnote, Otto acknowledges somewhat grudgingly his debt to William James. Against Schleiermacher's view that we can "come upon the very fact of God" as a way of accounting for our "feeling of dependence," which Schleiermacher himself takes to be a numinous feeling, Otto says that the sense of the holy is not a matter of inferring from an inner feeling, for in this case we have an "immediate and primary" experience of the "object outside the self." To this assertion he adds that its truth "is so manifestly borne out by experience that it must be about the first thing to force itself upon the notice of psychologists analyzing the facts of religion" (*IH*, 10). He then quotes the following passage from James's *Varieties:* "As regards the origin of the Greek gods, we need not at present seek an opinion. But the whole array of our instances leads to a conclusion something like this: It is as if there were in the human consciousness *a sense of reality, a feeling of objective presence,* a *perception* of what we may call '*something there,*' more deep and more general than any of the special and particular 'senses' by which the current psychology supposes existent realities to be originally revealed" (quoted in *IH*, 10).

Otto concludes that "James is debarred by his empiricist and pragmatist standpoint from coming to a recognition of faculties of knowledge and potentialities of thought in the spirit itself, and he is therefore obliged to have recourse to somewhat singular and mysterious hypotheses to explain this fact" (*IH*, 10–11). Nonetheless, "he grasps the fact itself clearly enough and is sufficient of a realist not to explain it away" (*IH,* 11). Thus, while claiming that James's empiricist and pragmatist position limits his ability to explore the state of mind that prevails in the experience of the numinous, Otto finds the psychologist James to be more astute than the theologian Schleiermacher, for James at least begins with the actual experience of the holy and not, as Schleiermacher does, with a general feeling (of dependence) that invites one to infer the existence of the holy.

However, Otto later criticizes James for failing to notice "the non-rational element that thrills" in the great number of autobiographical testimonies included in *The Varieties.* He follows this general indictment with several quotations from these autobiographical accounts, all illustrations of the "blissful excitement, rapture, and exaltation verging often on the bizarre and the abnormal" found in "all truly felt states of religious beatitude" (*IH,* 37). As Otto's only other direct reference to James is a footnote consisting of a quotation from a testimony by Theodore Parker found in *The Varieties,* a testimony Otto considers illustrative of rationalism's superficial understanding of sin, we may assume that Otto believes that James himself is somewhat deaf to the deeper levels of "numinous unworthiness" below the surface of "mere morality" (*IH,* 53).

From these references and citations we must conclude that Otto considers James's treatment of the experience of the numinous superficial. Yet *The Idea of the Holy* may be viewed as a sequel to *The Varieties* since, by implication at least, Otto accepts the essential validity of James's delineation of his subject as "the feelings, acts, and experiences of individuals in their solitude so far as they apprehend themselves to stand in relation to" the divine (*VRE,* 31). He also agrees with James that, for an experience to qualify as religious, it must be solemn. Thus, in his discussion of the element of fascination in the numinous experience, he speaks of its solemnity: "It is not only in the religious feeling of longing that the moment of fascination is a living factor. It is already alive and present in the moment of 'solemnity,' both in the gathered concentration and humble submergence of private devotion, when the mind is exalted to the holy, and in the common worship of the congregation, where this is practiced with earnestness and deep sincerity, as, it is to be feared, is with us a thing rather desired than realized. It is this and nothing else that in the solemn moment can fill the soul so full and keep it so inexpressibly tranquil" (*IH,* 35–36).

If Otto differs here from James, it is in the fact that for him a solemn experience may occur in common worship as well as in solitude (though even here the difference is only relative, as Otto has in mind the experience an individual may have in the *context* of common worship). Also, the fact that James speaks of "feelings" while Otto refers to "mental states" is only an apparent difference between them, for as James makes clear in *The Principles of Psychology*, the object of his investigations is "states of consciousness." For James, the problem is how to refer to these states of consciousness. "Feeling" has the advantage that it connotes a "subjective condition" but has the disadvantage that it is often considered a synonym for "sensation" as opposed to "thought," whereas the word *thought* seems to exclude "sensations," and these are very important components of states of consciousness (1950, 1:185–86). As we have seen, James concludes that both words — "feeling" *and* "thought" — are necessary to avoid the limitations and attendant misunderstandings resulting from the use of only one of them. Otto's criticisms of the rationalists and their tendency to focus only on "concepts," and his emphasis on the sensations that accompany the experience of the holy, indicate that he shares, by implication, James's expanded view of "mental states" or "states of consciousness."

Another important similarity between Otto and James is that both advocate the use of the method of introspection for investigating these states of consciousness. For James, this means that the psychologist takes his own "states of consciousness" as his object of investigation, and that introspection is essentially a "reflection" on a "state of consciousness" which has already taken place. As he describes the process,

> No one has emphasized more sharply than [Franz] Brentano himself the difference between the immediate *feltness* of a feeling, and its perception by a subsequent reflective act. But which mode of consciousness of it is that which the psychologist must depend on? If to *have* feelings or thoughts in their immediacy were enough, babies in the cradle would be psychologists, and infallible ones. But the psychologist must not only *have* his mental states in their absolute veritableness, he must report them and write about them, name them, classify and compare them and trace their relations to other things. Whilst alive they are their own property; it is only *post-mortem* that they become his prey [1950, 1:189].

In a footnote to this passage, James cites Wilhelm Wundt's assertion that "the first rule for utilizing inward observation consists in taking, as far as possible, experiences that are accidental, unexpected, and not intentionally brought about" (1950, 1:189). Thus, the unexpected, unpremeditated experiences of the holy that interest Otto are precisely the kinds of experiences that best lend themselves to introspective investigation. While alive, these experiences "are their own property," so immediate and so unintentional that one has no opportunity at the time they are occurring to think about what is taking place. The sensation is the primary thing. But, once over, they may become the experiencer's "prey" as he considers what happened to himself and why.

For James, the psychologist uses his own "states of consciousness" for investigation. Unlike psychologists who study the experiences of others, and light years away from those who concern themselves with the beliefs and opinions held by others, the introspectionist psychologist is his own subject, and his states of consciousness are his focus of interest. As David Bakan points out, this requires considerable personal courage, especially if the psychologist intends to make a public report of his introspective observations (Bakan 1967, 99). As James readily acknowledges, there is also the problem of the fallibility of one's memory or observation of the conscious state (1950, 1:189), and as Bakan points out, problems of repression and rationalization may arise as well. However, both emphasize that if one is aware of these sources of error and distortion, one may take precautions against them. I shall return to the problem of repression later, as I believe it plays an important role in Otto's introspective investigations into his own experience of the holy.

Like James, Otto was a strong proponent of the introspective method. In challenging the argument of "naturalistic psychologists" that numinous experiences merely testify to the power of tradition in a given culture and merely reflect the remarkable ability of the culture's own collective memory to survive over time in spite of the culture's modernizing tendencies, Otto contends that this argument ignores "a fact which might be thought at least to have a psychological interest, and which they could notice in themselves by careful introspection, namely, the *self-attestation* of religious ideas in one's own mind. This is, to be sure, more certain in the case of the naive than in that of the more blasé mind; but many people would identify it in their own consciousness if they would only recall deliberately and impartially their hours of preparation for the ceremony of Confirmation. But what the mind 'attests' it can also under favorable circumstances evince and elicit from itself in premonitory stirring and felt surmise" (*IH*, 130–31). Of course, experiences of the holy reflect the ability of cultural traditions to survive modernizing tendencies, but this does not mean that those who continue to experience the holy are merely experiencing the survivability of cultural traditions. The rite of confirmation is a cultural survival, but it may evoke an experience of the holy that is direct, not culturally mediated, and therefore most powerfully felt.

If Otto argues in favor of the introspective method against the "naturalistic psychologists" who view religious experiences as mere cultural survivals rather than as "anticipations" and "presentiments" of the holy, does he, like James, include examples of his own religious experiences in *The Idea of the Holy*? Not directly. Like James, he cites the religious experiences of others to support his argument, but he does not refer directly to any of his own experiences of the holy. Like James's disguise of his identity as the "French Sufferer" and "intimate friend," Otto's indirection supports Bakan's view that a problem with making oneself the object of investigation is that public report of one's investigations is less likely.

However, Otto *did* have several personal experiences that qualify as numinous experiences. Philip C. Almond (1983) notes that Otto had "two separate experiences of the grandeur, sublimity and mystery of the universe" on a journey to Egypt, Palestine, and Greece in 1895.[1] He was 26 years old at the time. The first experience, during a visit to the Sphinx, was mentioned in a footnote in his *The Philosophy of Religion* (published in English in 1931). "The general feeling of 'the unfathomable depth and mystery of existence and universe,' he writes, 'was most vividly present to the writer, in the evening silence of the sandy desert, that faces the huge Sphinx of Giza and its eyes gazing into the infinite'" (Almond 1983, 309). Almond directs our attention to the following statement by Otto in *The Idea of the Holy*: "It is indeed beyond question that the builders of these temples, and of the Sphinx of Gizeh, which set the feeling of the sublime, and together with and through it that of the numinous, throbbing in the soul almost like a mechanical reflex, must themselves have been conscious of this effect and have intended it" (*IH, 66*).

The other experience occurred as Otto was approaching Jerusalem. He described it in an unpublished travel letter:

> I had let my friends ride ahead while another section of the party remained further behind me. Evening was coming. We had said goodbye to the gracious old monks of St. John's monastery, the bells of which, echoing as if in greeting, were becoming quieter and quieter, gradually dying away. Now the sun was sinking and the shadows continued to extend over the plain. The long chain and the high peaks of the mountains of Judea loomed before us, sharply outlined in the golden Western sky; to the left, in the distance, lay the surface of the Dead Sea. In the background, however, the mountains of Moab presented an indescribably beautiful sight. Dark and immense masses of clouds had collected over them, illuminated here and there by reflections of the setting sun. There, right next to one of the highest peaks, there begins to emerge a rainbow of wonderful brilliance with the most delicate colors, sparkling more and more and silhouetted against the darkest clouds. And directly next to it, another with the colors inverted, and finally around both of these a third, woven quite finely and delicately. This sparkles until the sun is quite gone, and then it fades away slowly and disappears. In front of us, however, towards the West, the vault of Heaven is wonderfully blue and infinitely deep for a long time, until growing dark, out of its depths the stars light up. At such moments, the fragmented self is integrated and becomes aware of its place within the whole [Almond 1983, 309, his translation].

Common to both of these experiences was the feeling of the sublime, which Kant distinguished from the beautiful: "The sublime *moves,* the beautiful *charms.* The mien of a man who is undergoing the full feeling of the sublime is earnest, sometimes rigid and astonished. On the other hand the lively sensation of the beautiful proclaims itself through shining cheerfulness in the eyes, through smiling features, and often through audible mirth. . . . The sublime must always be great; the beautiful can also be small. The sublime must be simple; the beautiful can be adorned and ornamented" (Kant 1960, 26–27). In his own discussion of the holy, however, Otto suggests that the experience of the numinous involves more than the sublime, as it also has a "mystical" effect that joins with the sublime, an effect attributable to the fact that the numinous is usually felt when "negative" factors are present, these being darkness, or semidarkness, and silence (*IH,* 68). Thus, his account of his experience of the Sphinx emphasizes the "evening silence" of the desert, while his description of his entry into Jerusalem emphasizes the semidarkness.

Several years later (in 1911 or 1912, when Otto was in his early forties), he had another experience while traveling, one to which Almond attributes his "conviction of the centrality of 'the Holy'" (1983, 313). It occurred in the synagogue at Mogador (now Essaouria) in Morocco and is recounted in a travel letter:

> It is Sabbath, and already in the dark and inconceivably grimy passage of the house we hear that sing-song of prayers and reading of scriptures, that nasal half-singing half-speaking sound which Church and Mosque have taken over from the Synagogue. The sound is pleasant, one can soon distinguish certain modulations and cadences that follow one another at regular intervals like *Leitmotive.* The ear tries to grasp individual words but it is scarcely possible and one has almost given up the attempt when suddenly out of the babel of voices, causing a thrill of fear, there it begins, united, clear and unmistakeable: *Kadosh, Kadosh, Kadosh Elohim Adonai Zebaoth Male'u hashamayim wahaarets kebodo!* (Holy, Holy, Holy, Lord God of Hosts, the heaven and the earth are full of thy glory).
>
> I have heard the *Sanctus Sanctus Sanctus* of the cardinals in St. Peter's, the *Swiat Swiat Swiat* in the Cathedral of the Kremlin and the Holy Holy Holy of the Patriarch in Jerusalem. In whatever language they resound, these most exalted words that have ever come from human lips always grip one in the depths of the soul, with a mighty shudder exciting and calling into play the mystery of the other world latent therein. And this more than anywhere else here in this modest place, where they resound in the same tongue in which Isaiah first received them and from the lips of the people whose first inheritance they were [Almond 1983, 313, his translation].

Almond directs the reader's attention to the following statement of Otto's in *The Idea of the Holy.* The context is Otto's discussion of the "mystery" that often accompanies the experience of the numinous: "There are other manifestations of this tendency of the feeling of the 'mysterious' to be attracted to objects and aspects of experience analogous to it in being 'uncomprehended.' It finds its most unqualified expression in the spell exercised by the only half intelligible or wholly unintelligible language of devotion, and in the unquestionably real enhancement of the awe of the worshipper which this produces" (*IH*, 64). Continuing, Otto criticizes the efforts of "recent practical reformers" of the Christian liturgy. In these carefully arranged schemes, we find "nothing unaccountable, and for that very reason suggestive; nothing accidental, and for that very reason pregnant in meaning; nothing that rises from the deeps below consciousness to break the rounded unity of the wonted disposition, and thereby point to a unity of a higher order" — in a word, little that is really spiritual (*IH*, 65). In contrast, he cites "the ancient traditional expressions, still retained despite their obscurity, in our Bible and hymnals" and notes "the special emotional virtue attaching to words like 'Hallelujah,' *Kyrie eleison,* 'Selah,' just because they are 'wholly other' and convey no clear meaning" (*IH*, 65).

Thus, while Otto does not include accounts of his own numinous experiences in *The Idea of the Holy,* these examples reveal that he had several such experiences, usually in places where he was a stranger. The second of these experiences — on his entry into Jerusalem — is especially significant for its reference to the sense of inner wholeness and unity with the universe that he experienced: "At such moments, the fragmented self is integrated and becomes aware of its place within the whole." But the third experience especially interests me, as it does Almond, because unlike the other two experiences that occurred in nature, this one happened in a setting of common worship and evoked in Otto "a thrill of fear" and "a mighty shudder exciting and calling into play the mystery of the other world latent therein." Almond suggests that the earlier experience of approaching Jerusalem in early evening "reflects quite clearly the romantic vision of nature, and is reminiscent of Schleiermacher's notion of the intuition of the infinite in the finite and the eternal in the temporal," while the later experience enabled Otto to come to a recognition of the central place of the holy in religion. This indicates that for Otto there was something uniquely powerful about the experience in the synagogue, and that its power was somehow connected to its evocation of an inner "thrill of fear," of "a mighty shudder."

The Place of Fear in Religious Experience

This experience involving an inner "thrill of fear" enables us to make another important connection between Otto and James, which is that both tend to associate religion and fear. James's own experience, the French Sufferer account in *The Varieties,* was one of "panic fear," the "worst kind of melancholy" (*VRE,* 159–60). When he entered the dressing room, "suddenly there fell upon me without any warning, just as if it came out of the darkness, *a horrible fear of my existence*" (*VRE,* 160). As the image of the epileptic patient simultaneously crossed his mind, "there was such a horror of him, and such a perception of my own merely momentary discrepancy from him, that it was as if something hitherto solid within my breast gave way entirely, and *I became a mass of quivering fear*" (*VRE,* 160).

Fear is also a state of consciousness to which James frequently alludes in *The Principles of Psychology,* as when he cites the effect of animals on children: "Animals, for example, awaken in a child the opposite impulses of fearing and fondling. But if a child, in his first attempts to pat a dog, gets snapped at or bitten, so that the impulse of fear is strongly aroused, it may be that for years to come no dog will excite in him the impulse to fondle again" (1950, 2:395). He also discusses a form of fear that is not provoked by an external object (for example, a threatening dog) but has a "purely bodily cause": "Thus, to take one special instance, if inability to draw deep breath, fluttering of the heart, and that peculiar epigastric change felt as 'precordial anxiety,' with an irresistible tendency to take a somewhat crouching attitude and to sit still, and with perhaps other visceral processes not now known, all spontaneously occur together in a certain person; his feeling of their combination *is* the emotion of dread, and he is the victim of what is known as morbid fear" (1950, 2:459).

He cites in this regard a friend (whom I suspect to be James himself): "A friend who has had occasional attacks of this most distressing of all maladies tells me that in his case the whole drama seems to center about the region of the heart and respiratory apparatus, that his main effort during the attacks is to get control of his inspirations and to slow his heart, and that the moment he attains to breathing deeply and to holding himself erect, the dread, *ipso facto,* seems to depart" (1950, 2:459).

These examples of fear, presented in James's chapter on the emotions in *The Principles,* indicates that the intensity of the fear is related in part to whether or not the "object" or causative agent, whether outside or inside the body, is identifiable. In general, the more elusive the cause, the greater the fear. Another factor, however, has considerable bearing on the experience of fear, and this is whether, and to what extent, the present experience brings to mind earlier experiences that have in the meantime been forgotten or repressed. James's own experience of panic fear in the French Sufferer episode is illustrative, for he reports that as this "horrible fear" of his own existence came over him, there arose in his mind "the image of an epileptic patient whom I had seen in the asylum. . . . This image and my fear entered into a species of combination with each other" (*VRE*, 100). In *The Principles,* he claims that such "combinations" are responsible for "the emotion of dread." Prior to this experience, he was unconscious of his similarity to the epileptic patient. But now, in the moment of fear, he suddenly sees the connection, which causes him to feel "a horrible dread at the pit of my stomach" and "a sense of the insecurity of life that I never knew before, and that I have never felt since" (*VRE*, 160).

Freud's essay "The 'Uncanny'" is precisely concerned with the fears that arise with the return of the repressed. *Das Unheimliche,* which manifests itself in feelings of uneasiness, fear, shuddering, or dread, has to do with the familiar, *das Heimliche,* with earlier experiences that have since been concealed and kept from the conscious mind. The uncanny, then, is anything "that ought to have remained hidden and secret, and yet comes to light." Freud says the fact that it has remained hidden and secret is attributable to the capacity of the mind to repress earlier experiences, especially childhood experiences that had unusual emotional force. He also suggests that many of the fears of childhood appear in religion, such as fears associated with uncertainty as to whether "an apparently animate being is really alive; or conversely, whether a lifeless object might not be in fact animate" (1958, 132). He notes that moderns experience the uncanny when phenomena they consider "incredible" are experienced as altogether possible. Beliefs associated with animistic religion, such as the existence of spirits, typically evoke a "conflict of judgment" as to what is possible and what is not. Thus, "an uncanny experience occurs either when repressed infantile complexes have been revived by some impression, or when the primitive beliefs we have surmounted seem once more to be confirmed" (1958, 157).

While Otto's *Idea of the Holy* is concerned with the strange experience of having "the primitive beliefs we have surmounted seem once more to be confirmed," I want to give attention for the moment to the other cause of the uncanny—"when repressed infantile complexes have been revived by some impression"—because in Otto's own case such repressed infantile complexes are directly related to the more ostensibly religious form of his own experience of the numinous experience. Freud's suggestion that the uncanny is often associated with one's mother, and especially her body, is particularly relevant. While we may look a bit askance at Freud's association of das Heimliche with the mother's genitals, and even as we may question his effort to trace all childhood fears ultimately to castration anxiety, it is harder to argue against his suggestion that the mother represents what is heimlich for the child, and that therefore our most powerful experiences of das Unheimliche are those that bring repressed memories of our mothers to mind. I would add to Freud's claim James's observation that the first impulse another person or object evokes in us is apt to keep us from ever awakening the opposite impulse in us. But what about situations in which the same individual evokes both impulses in us simultaneously? I suggest that the mother is most likely to be this person, and that her ability to evoke opposite impulses in us accounts in part for the fact that she can be both heimlich and unheimlich, often confusedly so, in the very same experience. This may explain why she may be experienced by the child as mysterious or unfathomable.

The Synagogue as Uncanny Enclosure

Consider, in this light, Otto's experience of the holy in the Moroccan synagogue. An example Freud cites of das Heimliche is the cradle song, with its dreamlike quality and its replication of the "in and outflowing waves of the current" (1958, 126). Otto refers in his account of his experience of the synagogue worship to "that sing-song of prayers and reading of scriptures, that nasal half-singing half-saying sound." He describes it as a "pleasant" sound, and as one listens, "one can soon distinguish certain modulations and cadences that follow one another at regular intervals like *Leitmotive*." But then the "sound" grows more powerful as "suddenly, out of the babel of voices," it becomes "unified, clear and unmistakable," causing in Otto, the stranger, "a thrill of fear." Whenever such powerful cadences are heard, one is always gripped "in the depths of the soul, with a mighty shudder exciting and calling into play the mystery of the other world latent therein." What began as rather heimlich, a pleasant lullabylike singsong of prayers and readings, culminates in something that is very unheimlich, causing "a thrill of fear" and "a mighty shudder."

Thus, this whole experience was, for Otto, profoundly uncanny. This was partly because primitive beliefs he had previously "surmounted seem[ed] once more to be confirmed," for a modern critical scholar like Otto was likely to experience a "conflict of judgment" between his own disbelief in the spirit world (or animism) and what he sensed to be going on in "this modest place," where the words resounded "in the same tongue in which Isaiah first received them and from the lips of the people whose first inheritance they were." But no less important was the other source of the uncanny, "when repressed infantile complexes have been revived by some impression" — in this case, something having to do with Otto's childhood experience of his mother. What this experience in the synagogue in Morocco recalls from his childhood is not self-evident, yet the basic form of the experience is that das Heimliche becomes unheimlich: the familiar is de-familiarized, and with this de-familiarization comes a "thrill of fear" and a "mighty shudder exciting and calling into play the *mystery* of the other world latent therein" (my emphasis).

Thus, our task is to seek to penetrate the mystery of Otto's childhood. That it concerned his mother is suggested by the fact that the experience in the synagogue began with cadences reminiscent of a mother's lullaby. But what accounts for the change from das Heimliche to das Unheimliche, the shift from the familiar to the un-familiar, and thus the need to repress all memory of the childhood experience?

An initial clue derives from the fact that, unlike his experiences at the Sphinx and during his approach to Jerusalem, this experience occurred in an enclosed space. In his discussion of the means by which the numinous is expressed in art, Otto argues that artists' representations of the sublime and the magical are only indirect means of representing the numinous. The more direct methods in Western art are darkness and silence, and in Asian art there is a third direct means for producing a strongly numinous impression, which is by using emptiness and empty distances. Regarding darkness, he suggests that "the darkness must be such as is enhanced and made all the more perceptible by contrast with some last vestige of brightness, which it is, as it were, on the point of extinguishing; hence, the 'mystical' effect begins with semi-darkness" (*IH*, 68). Silence corresponds to the semidarkness in the language of musical sound. If silence originated in "the fear of using words of evil omen," it now appears as "a spontaneous reaction to the feeling of the actual *numen praesens*" (*IH*, 68–69). Emptiness is found in Chinese architecture, which achieves the impression of solemnity not by lofty vaulted halls or imposing altitudes but by enclosed spaces, courtyards, and vestibules. In Chinese art, emptiness is found in pictures in which "almost nothing" is painted, so that what is evoked in the viewer is "the feeling that the void itself is depicted as a subject, is indeed the main subject of the picture" (*IH*, 70). This void, like darkness and silence, is "a negation, but a negation that does away with every 'this' and 'here,' in order that the 'wholly other' may become actual" (*IH*, 70).

Otto's discussion of these three artistic means of directly representing the numinous, especially the Asian use of emptiness, brings to mind Erik H. Erikson's essay "Womanhood and the Inner Space," particularly his description of "the inner space" as a low enclosure that is, however, typically experienced as empty: "No doubt the very existence of the inner productive space exposes women early to a specific sense of loneliness, to a fear of being left empty . . . , of remaining unfulfilled" (Erikson 1968, 277; I shall return to Erikson's essay in chapter 5). But this is to view the matter from the mother's own perspective.

What of the small boy for whom his mother is the very representation of the inner space? To him, her task is to render heimlich the house in which he lives, lest he experience it as empty and void.

Given that Otto was the twelfth of thirteen children, we should perhaps give attention less to the circumstance that concerns Erikson — the mother's fear of being left empty — and more to the possibility that Otto experienced his childhood home as the very antithesis of the numinous, because it was anything but silent and empty. No doubt he yearned for times when he could experience the "inner space" as peaceful, when he might have his mother all to himself. And perhaps his low position in the birth order made him feel small in the company of bigger and older children, a feeling reflected, if also momentarily transcended, in his experience of approaching Jerusalem in the semidarkness of evening: "In front of us, however, towards the West, the vault of Heaven is wonderfully blue and infinitely deep for a long time, until growing dark, out of its depths the stars light up. *At such moments, the fragmented self is integrated and becomes aware of its place within the whole*" (my emphasis). I would guess that Otto, low in the birth order in a very large family, would have experienced such fragmentation a great deal of the time and thus have cherished those rare moments when he felt integrated and aware of his significance within the whole. In such moments, perhaps ones in which he felt the "exaltation" of his mother's presence, he would no longer feel fragmented but whole. Yet these moments would also underscore how alienated he felt most of the time, how much he felt he was *not* an integral part of the whole.

By viewing Otto's relative insignificance in the family in light of his discussion of methods artists employ to represent the numinous, we assume that for him the numinous was largely conspicuous by its absence. This of course is a paradox, because the Chinese painters assist the observer in the experience of the numinous precisely via their representations of "emptiness." Yet the paradox of the matter is precisely what Otto wishes to emphasize, and his discussion of the numinous in Luther's religious life is significant in this regard, as he argues that Luther's appreciation for the uncanny is reflected in his insistence on the "paradoxical" nature of God. Moreover, he recalls that Luther's own expressions of the numinous, especially in *De servo arbitrio,* had "rung in my ears" long before "I identified it in the *gadosh* of the Old Testament and in the elements of 'religious awe' in the history of religion in general" (*IH,* 97–101).

However, we have so far only scratched the surface of Otto's "repressed infantile complex" that was revived by the experience in the synagogue, as we have not yet considered what may have transpired between his mother and himself in the earliest years of his life, especially her own direct implication in making his childhood world unheimlich. That he was the twelfth of thirteen children allows us to draw certain conclusions, but it does not tell us much about how his mother and he got along; it gives more of a glimpse into what he would have valued in their relationship than what he would have needed to repress. Almond's intuition that the two earlier experiences of the Sphinx and the approach to Jerusalem are more "romantic" than the experience in the synagogue, where Otto was gripped "in the depths of [his] soul," suggests that there was something deeper in Otto's childhood experiences — ominously so — than the moments when he felt his fragmented self to be integrated, when he was aware of his place within the family as a whole.

Otto's Attempts to Take His Own Life

Facts, as such, are difficult to come by, as there is no full-length biography of Rudolf Otto. There are, however, these brief statements in Almond's essay on Otto's life and work:

> Louis Karl Rudolf Otto was born in Peine (Hanover) on 25 September 1869. His father, Wilhelm, was a manufacturer and owned factories in Peine and later in nearby Hildesheim. His mother, Katherine Karoline Henriette, *née* Reupke, was eighteen years younger than her husband *and was very much responsible for the rearing of Rudolf,* the twelfth of thirteen children. When Rudolf was twelve years old, his father died. As one would expect, the family was left well provided for and, in the year 1880, Otto was enrolled in the *Andreanum,* a grammar school in Hildesheim where the family had moved shortly before his father's death [1983, 306, my emphasis].

Almond describes the Otto household as very religious, and very strict. The atmosphere

> into which Rudolf Otto was born was very religious. Certainly it was a religiously conservative household and he himself describes the evangelical-Lutheran piety with which he was imbued as very strict. It strongly influenced his own religious views from an early age: "I couldn't read any history calmly," he later remarks, "unless I was convinced beforehand that the people in it were also devout and not 'catholic,' or Jews or heathens." Moreover, from his earliest school days, the desire to be a pastor had developed and he took an avid interest in everything connected with theology and the church [1983, 306–7].

Almond notes that Otto's conservatism continued throughout his early formal schooling, and that his decision to attend Friedrich Alexander University in Erlangen "was motivated by his desire to avoid the University of Göttingen for fear of being forced into too liberal a theological position. And at Erlangen, he hoped to be provided with the means to defend the theological orthodoxy to which he was committed" (1983, 307).

Subsequent life experiences and friendships, however, led to his becoming increasingly liberal, so much so that throughout his thirties and early forties he was "excluded from a full professorial position by the Lutheran church" (Almond 1983, 311). Only when the church's veto was lifted in 1915, when he was 46, was a full professorship made possible. Prior to the rescinding of the veto, Otto "considered giving up theology and contemplated becoming a pastor at a German church in Paris, or a missionary in China" (1983, 311). He "came close to a nervous breakdown" but was helped in part by the encouragement he received from Ernst Troeltsch, who responded to one of Otto's letters during the period of his greatest despair: "You must now above all, *pull yourself together,* and call to mind the views which you hold for yourself as a man, quite apart from any and every theology. You must have views which are for your own personal use. What you do with theology, we will want to look further into. . . . If it doesn't go well, then you will just have to begin something different. For the moment attend in general only to peace of mind and the strength of the inner man" (Almond 1983, 311–12, his translation, my emphasis).

Two years after he became a full professor at Breslau, *The Idea of the Holy* was published, and that very year he became a professor at the University of Marburg, where he was to remain until his retirement in 1929. Almond describes his career at Marburg as difficult and unhappy, noting that "for the major part of Otto's time at the University of Marburg, Dialectical Theology overshadowed all else. Ernst Benz reports that Otto's lectures were ridiculed by students committed to the existentialist theology of Rudolf Bultmann, and that the religious collection founded by Otto was referred to as the 'heathen temple' by those students for whom Dialectical Theology implied the unnecessariness and superfluity of the history and comparison of religions. And the polemical situation that resulted was, along with Otto's increasing ill-health, an influence on his decision to retire early, in March 1929" (1983, 319).

Otto died eight years later (on March 6, 1937, at the age of 67), in what Almond describes as "somewhat tragic and mysterious circumstances." The immediate cause of death was pneumonia, which he contracted eight days after entering the psychiatric hospital in Marburg, as a result of his having wandered away from the hospital.

> He had entered the psychiatric hospital in order to overcome an addiction to morphine. He had been treated with this in order to alleviate the pain which

had arisen as the result of an accident five months before. In early October 1936, Otto had hiked — alone uncharacteristically — to Staufenberg near Marburg. Here, having made a strenuous climb to the top of the tower of a manor house, he fell some sixty feet. There is much uncertainty as to the cause of this event. But I [Almond] believe that the cumulative weight of the evidence points to his having attempted to take his own life.

In the first place, the nature of the injuries that Otto received — a broken leg and foot — are not indicative of his having either accidentally fallen or, as has been suggested, of his having suffered a heart attack. Moreover, while it is not impossible to fall from the tower, it was nonetheless highly improbable [1983, 320–21].

In Almond's view, suicide would not have been inconsistent with Otto's lifelong tendency toward "deep depression." According to his niece, he was "depressive by nature," and as Almond notes, "he was in a state of depression at this time and remained so after the event." In December 1936, two months after the fall, his sister wrote, "Rudolf complains much about his head, so that he cannot often think coherently; also depressions have set in again. . . . He cries more often" (1983, 321, Almond's translation). Almond adds, "And while in the psychiatric hospital, he tried to leave in order to throw himself under a train" (p. 321).

Otto was described by people who knew him as stiff and formal. Noting that he had few student followers, Almond suspects that this was "a function of Otto's personality." He cites this recollection of Joachim Wach:

Rudolf Otto was an imposing figure. He held himself very straight. His movements were measured. His sharply-cut features remained serious and scarcely altered even when joking. The color of his skin was yellowish-white and testified to past illness. . . . His hair was white and cut short. A small white moustache covered his upper lip. Most fascinating of all were his steel-blue eyes. They had a certain rigidity about them, and it was often as if, when he spoke, he saw something to which others had no access. . . . Something mysterious surrounded him. Familiarity was the last thing a visitor would have expected of him or he himself would have encouraged. The students, who followed his lectures spellbound, called him "der Heilege" (the Saint) [Almond 1983, 319].

Thus, there was a certain "uncanniness" about his physical presence. He "saw something to which others had no access"; "something mysterious surrounded him"; "familiarity was the last thing . . . expected . . . or . . . encouraged."

John W. Harvey, the translator of *Das Heilege* into English, had a similar impression of Otto, though he also indicates that an "unaffected friendliness" came over Otto once the ice was broken:

> I well remember my own first meeting with Otto, sometime in the very early twenties. It was an impression so surprising as almost to be daunting. This, whatever he was, was almost the opposite of the German *Gelehrter* as one commonly found him, and far removed indeed from the traditional figure of caricature (if indeed the latter was ever typical of the German professor at all), bearded and bespectacled, dreamy and pedantic. Otto's figure was tall and erect and suggested the soldier rather than the scholar, with his Kaiser moustaches and his tight, light, military-looking jacket fastened high at the neck. Nor was a diffident foreigner reassured by the touch of formality in his address, which later one came to recognize as merely the scrupulous respect he paid to the strict grammar of courtesy. But in a very short time the thin film of ice was effectively broken, and his, and his household's, unaffected friendliness had quite won his visitor's heart, aided by the dry humor that played about persons as well as things, shrewdly yet without malice, and was one of his most endearing qualities [*IH*, xii].[2]

As described here by Harvey, Otto's unheimlich demeanor began to shade over into das Heimliche, eventually setting the visitor at ease. One could not forget, though, even in these moments of ease, the sense of das Unheimliche that preceded them. As Wach indicates, the visitor would not be likely to initiate familiarity with Otto for fear of being rebuffed or perhaps even chastised.

Much could be made of these biographical facts, in particular Otto's attempts at suicide and eyewitness accounts of his personal demeanor, but I shall keep my observations brief and to the point. Especially striking to me about these accounts of Otto's personality is what they reveal about his relationship to his own body. That he was given to deep depression — or melancholy — is perhaps not as surprising as the fact that his attempted suicides were so violent, so abusive of his body. Instead of suicide by means of an overdose of morphine, he contrived to fall to his death from a sixty-foot tower or to throw himself under a moving train. Are these suicide attempts not in some degree at least reminiscent of the "thrill of fear" that he felt in the synagogue in Morocco? Together with personal accounts of his physical rigidity — his militaristic bearing, his jacket tightened at the neck — these attempted suicides suggest that he had come to despise his own body, perhaps even to blame it, for his difficulty in relating to others. Even his eyes, as Wach points out, "had a certain rigidity about them," and if they also seemed to bear witness to the fact that "he saw something to which others had no access," how was he any different from the Sphinx at Giza, "its eyes gazing into the infinite"? One feels that the uncanniness of Otto's encounter with the Sphinx was that in it he recognized himself.

I suggest that this attitude toward his own body had its origins in very early childhood, when such attitudes are typically formed, and that it points to his having been indoctrinated in the art of self-control, his body being the external manifestation of such inner control, reflected preeminently in his ability to hold his emotions and desires in check. While we do not know the particulars of his upbringing, we *are* informed by Almond that he grew up in a very strict religious household, and that his mother, eighteen years younger than his father, "was very much responsible for the rearing of Rudolf." We are also informed that his father died when Rudolf was twelve, an event that often causes young boys to curtail whatever rebellious feelings they may have toward their mothers for fear of causing them even greater grief.

Child-rearing Practices in Nineteenth-Century Germany

The missing particulars may perhaps be inferred from the child-rearing manuals that would have been available to Otto's mother, manuals that Alice Miller in *For Your Own Good: Hidden Cruelty in Child-rearing and the Roots of Violence* (1984) aptly describes as "poisonous pedagogy." Miller suggests we may find in these texts the "breeding grounds of the hatred" that children felt for their parents (1984, 8).

As Rudolf was born in 1869, and was the twelfth of thirteen children, it is reasonable to assume that his mother either read or was familiar with the ideas contained in recently published child-rearing manuals, such as the one published in 1858 by D. G. M. Schreber, a German expert on child-rearing (and the father of the paranoid patient whom Freud treated). Miller takes the following statement by Schreber from Katherina Rutschky's *Schwarze Pädogogik*. Schreber writes:

> Another rule with very important consequences: Even the child's permissible desires should always be satisfied *only* if the child is in an amiable or at least calm mood but *never* while he is crying or behaving in an unruly fashion. First he must have regained his composure even if his previous behavior has been caused, for example, by his legitimate and periodic need to be fed—only then, after a brief pause, should one grant the child's wish. This interval is necessary because the child must not be given even the slightest impression that anything can be won by crying or by unruly behavior. On the contrary, the child perceives very quickly that he will reach his goal only by means of the opposite sort of behavior, by self-control (albeit still unconscious) [Miller 1984, 27].

If Otto was disposed to cry, and to cry often, in the closing months of his life, is it possible that he was making up for the suppression of his urge to cry in the beginning years of his life? In any case, the issue was self-control, the ability to maintain one's composure even when entirely legitimate needs were being frustrated.

Continuing, Schreber emphasizes that the parent must maintain perfect consistency. Otherwise, one will merely prolong the training:

> The training just described will give the child a substantial head start in the art of waiting and will prepare him for another, more important one: the art of self-denial. After what has been said, it can be taken almost for granted that every impermissible desire, be it to the child's disadvantage or not, must be met with an unfailingly consistent and absolute refusal. Refusal alone, however, is not enough. One must at the same time see to it that the child accepts the refusal calmly; one must take care that this calm acceptance becomes a sound habit, if need be by making use of a harsh word, a threatening gesture, and the like. Be sure not to make any exceptions! — then this too will take place much more easily and quickly than one thinks possible. Every exception of course invalidates the rule, both prolonging the training and making it more difficult. — On the other hand, accede to the child's every permissible desire lovingly and gladly. . . .
>
> A very good exercise in the art of self-denial, appropriate for this age, is to give the child frequent opportunity to learn to watch other people in his immediate vicinity eating and drinking without desiring the same for himself [Miller 1984, 28].

Here Schreber emphasizes that mere external compliance with the frustration of one's desires is not enough; there must be a heartfelt acceptance of the deprivation, so that the child forms a genuine spirit of self-denial. The practice of requiring the child to watch others eating and drinking without desiring the same for himself must have been quite widespread, for biographers of Ralph Waldo Emerson note that his parents often ate their dinners while their children hungrily watched.

A quotation from another German expert in child-rearing at the time, K. A. Schmid, indicates that biblical support for these practices was commonly put forward, including such texts as "Thou shalt beat him [the child] with the rod, and shalt deliver his soul from hell" (Proverbs 23:14). Commenting on this proverb, Schmid writes: "With these words, Solomon reveals to us that true love can also be severe. This is not the kind of stoic or narrowly legalistic severity that is full of self-satisfaction and would rather sacrifice its charge than ever deviate from its principles; no, however severe, it lets its tender concern shine through, like the sun through the clouds, in a spirit of friendliness, compassion, and patient hope" (Miller 1984, 29). Schmid's exegesis of the proverb suggests that the parent will be able somehow to communicate her love for her child even as she is beating him. The child should perceive her love shining through the beating, like the sun through the clouds. This is no "stoic or narrowly legalistic severity." Rather, the pain is inflicted "in a spirit of friendliness, compassion, and patient hope."

Schmid also makes the point that the severe love of the parent is a manifestation, in its way, of the love of God. The following passage begins with an affirmation of the love that emanates from the Trinitarian God and concludes with an analogy drawn from the work of surgeons:

> True love flows from the heart of God, the source and image of all fatherhood (Ephesians 3:15), is revealed and prefigured in the love of the Redeemer, and is engendered, nourished, and preserved in man by the Spirit of Christ. This love emanating from above purifies, sanctifies, transfigures, and strengthens natural parental love. This hallowed love has as its primary goal the growth of the child's interior self, his spiritual life, his liberation from the power of the flesh, his elevation above the demands of the merely natural life of the senses, his inner independence from the world threatening to engulf him. Therefore, this love is concerned that the child learn at an early age to renounce, control, and master himself, that he not blindly follow the promptings of the flesh and the senses but rather the higher will and the promptings of the spirit. This hallowed love can thus be severe even as it can be mild, can deny even as it can bestow, each according to its time; it also knows how to bring good by causing hurt, it can impose harsh renunciation like a physician who prescribes bitter medicine, like a surgeon who knows very well that the cut of his knife will cause pain and yet cuts in order to save a life [Miller 1984, 29].

Schmid also cites Schleiermacher's view of discipline as "life-inhibiting," because discipline "is at the very least curtailment of vital activity insofar as the latter cannot develop as it wishes but is confined within specific limits and subjected to specific rules." Schmid asserts that this view of discipline is much too limited, for discipline "can also mean restraint; in other words, partial suppression of enjoyment, of the joy of living." Moreover, "a consideration of the idea of punishment reveals that, in the task of education, healthy discipline must always include corporal punishment. Its early and firm but sparing application is the very basis of all genuine discipline because it is the power of the flesh that needs most to be broken" (Miller 1984, 31).

Schmid then adds this dire warning: "Where human authorities are no longer capable of maintaining discipline, divine authority steps in forcibly and bows down both individuals and nations under the insufferable yoke of their own wickedness" (Miller 1984, 31). He concludes: "Even truly Christian pedagogy, which takes a person as he is, not as he should be, cannot in principle renounce every form of corporal chastisement, for it is exactly the proper punishment for certain kinds of delinquency: it humiliates and upsets the child, affirms the necessity of bowing to a higher order and at the same time reveals paternal love in all its vigor" (Miller 1984, 44).

Schmid's reference here to "paternal love" may imply that the disciplining of children was primarily the father's task, not the mother's. But another author, writing in 1896, suggests otherwise: "Mothers, who are ordinarily entrusted with their children's education, very rarely know how to deal with unruly behavior successfully" (Miller 1984, 31). This statement is consistent with Almond's observation that Otto's mother "was very much responsible for the rearing of Rudolf."

Much of the literature that Miller cites in *For Your Own Good* focuses on the frustration of desires and corporal punishment as primary methods of discipline. In *Breaking Down the Wall of Silence* (1991), however, Miller notes that she was slow to realize that she had been abused as a child because her mother's method of maintaining power over her daughter was by means of silence. Miller says of her mother's "silent treatment,"

> For days my mother would ignore me in order to demonstrate her total power over me and reduce me to subservience. She needed this power to disguise her own insecurities to others and to herself. She also wished to deny her responsibility toward the child that she had not wanted in the first place. The needs and questions of this little girl simply ricocheted off this wall [of silence]. For her part, my mother felt no need to feel responsible for her sadism. As far as she was concerned, her behavior was justifiable punishment for my wrongdoing. She was, as they say, "teaching me a lesson."
>
> For a child who for many years had no brothers or sisters and whose father, on the rare occasions that he was at home, never offered his protection, this long, unremitting silence was an agony [Miller 1991, 19].

As Miller's quotations from German child-rearing manuals in *For Your Own Good* do not identify the "silent treatment" as a method of punishment, we can only guess that it, too, was part of the parent's arsenal of disciplinary techniques in the period of Otto's childhood. There is, however, considerable emphasis on the *child's* maintenance of silence as a form of *self*-control. In any event, the general point of these manuals is that the parent is justified in using any technique that works in the guerrilla warfare between parent and child, because the parent's cause is right and just. After all, the parent is acting not in self-interest but in the child's own best interests.

One could quote this child-rearing material at much greater length, as Miller does, but the quotations I have given suffice to make the case that in her role as disciplinarian the mother "de-familiarizes" herself in the eyes of her child, thus undermining whatever assumptions he held that they might live together in a spirit of easy familiarity, of *Heimlichkeit*. Originally a contented, secure insider in the "inner space" that she embodies, he finds himself now estranged, no longer a certified insider but an alienated outsider, looking from the margins on a scene from which he has suddenly and unexpectedly become defamiliarized. His eyes often tell the story as they reveal his incomprehension, his new and sad awareness that there is another side to his mother that, before this, he simply did not know existed. She, of course, following the "wisdom" of the experts, will console herself with the thought that her child will not perceive her as two different persons, but will recognize the love in her severity, the tenderness in actions that make him fearful and afraid, if not also hateful and vengeful. However, to see it this way — to see it from her point of view — is to expect a greater capacity for critical reflection than a child, especially one who is frightened, is likely to possess. There is no sun in the clouds however desperately he himself wants to believe there is.

While we may confidently assume that Otto *was* disciplined (the very fact that he exhibited throughout his life the self-control that discipline was designed to effect being proof enough), we do not know how it was characteristically carried out. So let me now present two plausible scenarios. Scenario *one* would take the view that Otto was at least occasionally beaten, while scenario *two* would opt for the view that his mother at least occasionally used the silent treatment. Of course, other scenarios are possible, but these two allow us to explore the potential connections between his "repressed infantile complexes" and his adult experiences of the holy. That his mother employed *none* of these methods is not outside the realm of possibility, but this would not square very well with Otto's own attestation to the fact that he was brought up in a home that was very religious and very strict. If it was not strict in the area of child discipline, it would be hard to imagine that it was strict at all.

The Thrill of Fear That Accompanies Being Beaten

One of the anomalies attending the fact that being beaten is physically painful is the related fact that children often persist in the behavior which prompts the beating. If being beaten is so painful, why does the child persist in misbehavior? Why is a single beating not sufficient to extinguish all expressions of misbehavior?

The "experts" cited above attribute this anomaly to the child's willfulness (or "natural will"). In their view, the child possesses a powerful natural will which is so strong that it requires numerous inflictions of physical pain before it is successfully broken. But there is a more plausible explanation, one based on Erik Erikson's view that from the very beginning of life child and mother "activate" one another (1964, 165). What a child cannot stand, what is in fact a prescription for emotional if not actual physical death, is the *absence* of such activation. If we assume that a child growing up in the late nineteenth century was, as the child-rearing manuals recommend, emotionally *de*-activated much of the time, it would follow that the beatings he received, especially if they were only occasional, as the literature stipulates, would be highly stimulating. Of course, they would cause the boy to feel estranged from his mother, rejected, the object of her severe displeasure. On the other hand, these beatings might also be strangely exhilarating, perhaps sexually stimulating, particularly if they were the only occasions on which his mother became emotionally involved in what transpired between them. This scenario suggests that he would repress such experiences, whereas he would be likely to remember beatings received from his father—not, however, because the pain was so excruciating, but because his mother's beatings were emotionally, even sexually, stimulating, so much so that he would risk the same act of misbehavior in order to "suffer" the same act of punishment.

These experiences, in Otto's own apt phrase, would have "the thrill of fear" about them. Though painful indications of what the child once had but has since lost—the peace of the inner space—these episodes would also be capable, in another of his apt phrases, of evoking "a mighty shudder *exciting and calling into play* the mystery of the other world latent therein" (my emphasis), the "mystery," that is to say, of sexuality itself. For the male child, beatings by his mother are, as it were, expressions of "latent sexuality," literally, "rough sex." For a boy whose "goodness" would attract little attention and receive little reward from a mother burdened with the task of raising so many children, including one even younger than himself, it may well have seemed that the best way to attract her attention, to excite her and call her into play, was by misbehaving. The very fact that he *sought* religious experiences as an adult, going to considerable pains and personal hardship to increase the likelihood that he might indeed have them, suggests that there may have been several such experiences in his childhood, each more "thrilling" than the previous one, until one day they ceased altogether.

The Unbearable Silence That Evokes Unspeakable Dread

The second scenario is at the opposite extreme of the first. Here the boy's mother has begun to tire of the usual methods of discipline (for example, frustrating her son's desires by withholding food or proscribing play) and has decided on a more dangerous course of action, a more extreme withholding. She will withhold her very self, making herself as if dead to him. She will refuse to use the organ, her voice, that had been the primary means by which she first activated him with lullabies and cradle songs. If a mother wanted to make herself unheimlich to her son, there would be no better method than to refuse to speak to him and to rebuff his own efforts to gain a hearing, however minimal, however grudging. He will plead that she end this unbearable silence and then, accepting failure, will become silent himself, and sullen.

Otto's discussion of artists' direct methods of representing the numinous takes on new meaning in light of the mother's refusal to speak, as now the silence is the feeling *not* of the actual *numen praesens* but of the *numen absentia,* what Freud refers to as the dread that one who is believed to be alive is actually dead. The "inner space" too has become palpably empty. Unlike in the work of Asian architects and artists, this is a scene not of enchantment, spell, and "real sublimity" but of something overpowering that feels sadistic, hateful, and mean, a punishment out of all proportion to the seriousness of the child's wrongdoing and thus seemingly motivated by some unexplainable and unaccountable wrath. It is as if the silence the mother was forced to develop as a child as a mark of her own goodness has now been unleashed on her own boy child in a powerful reversal of status and control.

Should she choose to add further insult to injury, she may contrive to listen and respond with a light-hearted cheerfulness to the other children, who have not incurred her wrath, underscoring her contempt for the little boy who has wronged her. From the child's point of view, this is a wrath that makes the wrath of a beating pale in comparison, because there is no conceivable end to it. As Miller writes, this "long, unremitting silence" could last for days. If she tried to discover the cause of it, she "was denied any clarification as to the nature of her offenses" (Miller 1991, 19). In fact, the child's inability to understand how he could have provoked such a long and unremitting silence testifies loudly to the child's utter lack of conscience: "Can't you understand how you have wronged me? Are you so blind, so obtuse, so morally depraved, that you cannot even see it?"

Giving the lie to the assumption that the silence embodies a meaningful punishment is the fact that it typically ends for no apparent reason. Suddenly, mother speaks, and, as speech is restored, light returns. The inner space is restored to its normal hubbub of routine activity. What made the silence end? If the child knew, he could try to replicate the magic when it happens again, as it surely will. But the child does not know and can only rejoice in the fact that he and his mother are once again on speaking terms. The unbearable silence ended as abruptly as it began, and all that the child knows is that his unspeakable dread has lifted too.

Child Punishment: Losing His Mother the Hard Way

I realize, of course, that these two scenarios are merely imaginative recreations of what may have occurred between Rudolf and his mother when he was a little boy. They assume that she was more-or-less faithful to the child-rearing conventions of the day, and that he was a sensitive child who could not lightly pass off any sign or indication that she was unhappy with him, or that he was somehow implicated in her own unhappiness. I do not think that these are far-fetched assumptions. On the contrary, we need to invoke one or the other of these two scenarios, or possibly both, if we are to account for his adult experiences as well as for the impressions that he made on others. The fact that he was "depressive by nature" throughout his life and suicidal near the end of it is especially relevant. His depression may be attributed to his loss of his earliest love object in the natural and inevitable process of de-familiarization, but its severity, culminating in attempted suicide, indicates that he blamed himself for the loss. As Freud describes the melancholiac, "the patient represents his ego to us as worthless, incapable of any effort and morally despicable; he reproaches himself, vilifies himself and expects to be cast out and chastised. He abases himself before everyone and commiserates [with] his own relatives for being connected with someone so unworthy. He does not realize that any change has taken place in him, but extends his self-criticism back over the past and declares that he was never any better" (Freud 1963, 167).

Why is he unable to mourn the loss of his mother and move on, perhaps now free to relate to someone else? Because

> in melancholia the relation to the object is no simple one; it is complicated by *the conflict of ambivalence.* This latter is either constitutional, i.e., it is an element of every love-relation formed by this particular ego, or else it proceeds from *precisely those experiences that involved a threat of losing the object.* For this reason *the exciting causes of melancholia are of a much wider range than those of grief,* which is for the most part occasioned only by a real loss of the object, by its death. In melancholia, *countless single conflicts in which love and hate wrestle together are fought for the object;* the one seeks to detach the libido from the object, the other to uphold this libido-position against assault. These single conflicts cannot be located in any system but the unconscious, *the region of memory traces of things.* [Freud 1963, 177–78, my emphases].

Either of the two scenarios presented above, the one based on the excitation of sexual feelings, the other on the dread of an unbearable silence, may account for a son's "conflict of ambivalence" toward his mother. They also point to the fact that "the exciting causes of melancholia are of a much wider range than those of grief," for in melancholia "countless single conflicts in which love and hate wrestle together are fought for the object." Each time the son goes through the process of de-familiarization and re-familiarization with his mother, such wrestling occurs. Also, as I have suggested, for a small boy this process typically occurs under the aegis of discipline and punishment. In a strict religious family, the conflict is magnified, because the mother and son are wrestling over the fate of his eternal soul.

How does suicide fit into all this? Freud suggests that suicide has long been known to be an expression of "murderous impulses against others re-directed upon" the self, but that it is even better understood when viewed in light of melancholia. In melancholia, one's attacks against oneself are actually displaced attacks on the object that has since been lost, though not, as in grief, through physical death. In suicide, the sadism against the internalized object is so strong that the ego's own self is unable to prevail against it. In effect, "the ego is overwhelmed by the object" (Freud 1963, 173). In Otto's case, this means that the internalized object of his mother evoked such strong sadistic urges (counter-sadistic, no doubt) that his own ego was helpless to intervene.

But perhaps his ego would not have been so vulnerable were it not already diminished and demeaned by religious experiences that confirmed its essential lack of worth in the face of the holy. To explore this possibility, we need to turn to Otto's analysis of the experience of the holy with both his "repressed infantile complexes" and his late attempts at suicide in mind.

Otto's Analysis of the Mysterium Tremendum

I suggest that Otto's religious experiences, especially the experience in the Moroccan synagogue that aroused "his conviction of the centrality of 'the Holy'" (Almond 1983, 313), are revisitings of "precisely those experiences that involved a threat of losing the object" (Freud 1963, 177), experiences that were destined to be "exciting causes of melancholia" and in which his mother became the object of fear or dread. To give this suggestion the substantiation it requires, we need to return to *The Idea of the Holy,* specifically to Otto's discussion of "the numinous state of mind," which he characterizes as the awareness of one's "submergence into nothingness before an overpowering absolute might of some kind" (*IH*, 10). Our discussion of German child-rearing practices when he was a child enables us to recognize in Otto's characterization of the "numinous state of mind" the child's experience of finding himself confronted with the incontrovertible fact that, as Schreber puts it, nothing "can be won by crying or by unruly behavior" (Miller 1984, 27).

After identifying the numinous as the state of mind that prevails in the encounter with the holy, Otto introduces the phrase *mysterium tremendum* to identify the primary emotional tone of the numinous experience. He then discusses the tremendum and the mysterium somewhat separately. In his chapter "The Analysis of 'Tremendum,'" he identifies three elements typically comprising the feeling of tremendum. First is the element of what Otto calls *awefulness* or *dreadfulness*. To convey this, he uses words like tremor, trembling, shuddering, the sense of the uncanny (as in "my blood ran cold" or "my flesh crept"), all of which indicate that the emotion of awefulness has a powerful physiological component.[3] While all emotions have physiological associations, when we experience awe and dread our awareness of our bodies is heightened and intensified, and we become uncommonly conscious of things happening to our bodies that are unusual or extraordinary. Otto also indicates that when we experience the tremendum, we feel that we are experiencing God's wrathfulness. However, he cautions that "wrath," at least as represented in the Old Testament, has "no concern whatever with moral qualities" but is like a hidden force of nature, "like stored-up electricity, discharging itself upon any one who comes too near." It is "incalculable," "arbitrary," "daunting" (*IH*, 18–19).

The second element is the *overpoweringness* or "aweful majesty" of the holy. The holy is like no other overpoweringness we ever experience, because it leaves the self feeling totally annihilated: "In contrast to 'the overpowering' of which we are conscious as an object over against the self, there is the feeling of one's own submergence, of being but 'dust and ashes' and nothingness. And this forms the numinous raw material for the feeling of religious humility" (*IH*, 20). Thus, in the numinous experience we are conscious of our creaturehood, feeling our impotence and "nothingness" against the holy's overpowering might.

Mysticism has made of this experience its most central affirmation: "For one of the chiefest and most general features of mysticism is just this *self-depreciation* . . . , the estimation of the self, of the personal 'I,' as something not perfectly or essentially real, or even as mere nullity, a self-depreciation which comes to demand its own fulfillment in practice in rejecting the delusion of selfhood, and so makes for the annihilation of the self" (*IH*, 21). Mysticism therefore directly opposes Schleiermacher's view that speculation about God originates in our consciousness of our absolute dependence, for this would mean that we begin with ourselves, whereas mysticism argues that such speculation "starts from a consciousness of the absolute superiority or supremacy of a power other than myself" (*IH*, 21).

The third element is *energy* or *urgency*. Especially in its wrathfulness, the numinous object impresses upon us its vitality, passion, emotional temper, will, force, and excitability. This feature of the mysterium tremendum is central to the idea of God as a "living God," not a "philosophic" God of mere rational speculation (*IH*, 23). While philosophers have condemned these expressions of the energy of the *numen* as "sheer anthropomorphism," Otto contends that these terms stand for a genuine aspect of the divine nature (that is, its nonrational aspect) and serve to protect religion itself from being rationalized away (*IH,* 23). Otto laments the fact that Luther's emphasis on the "willfulness" of God has been lost in modern Lutheranism (*IH,* 107–8).

These three elements comprise the core features of the tremendum. Given our interest in Freud's essay "The 'Uncanny,'" published two years after Otto's book, Otto's attention to the uncanny in his discussion of the tremendum is especially significant. Several years earlier, Otto had written an article on Wilhelm Wundt's *Völkerpsychologie,* in which he argued that the numinous has a quality of "awe" that distinguishes it from "dread" in the ordinary sense. On the other hand, the numinous experience's "pedigree," these other experiences of dread, is often apparent. Thus, the real distinction is not between the uncanny experience in the encounter of the holy and, say, in the experience of a "ghost" but in the fact that the uncanny is "not found in the case of any 'natural' fear or terror," as when we are confronted by a wild animal (*IH,* 16). Otto writes:

> The "cold blood" feeling may be a symptom of ordinary, natural fear, but there is something non-natural or supernatural about the symptom of "creeping flesh." And anyone who is capable of more precise introspection must recognize that the distinction between such a "dread" and natural fear is not simply one of degree and intensity. The awe or "dread" *may* indeed be so overwhelmingly great that it seems to penetrate to the very marrow, making the man's hair bristle and his limbs quake. But it may also steal upon him almost unobserved as the gentlest of agitations, a mere fleeting shadow passing across his mood. It has therefore nothing to do with intensity, and no natural fear passes over into it merely by being intensified. I may be beyond all measure afraid and terrified without there being even a trace of the uncanniness in my emotion [*IH,* 16].

In the experience of the numinous, even the "shudder" that often accompanies the uncanny may be replaced with a "mystical aura." The issue, then, is not the emotional intensity, whether of pleasure or pain, but one's consciousness of being a creature, which, as I noted, Otto describes "as the feeling of personal nothingness and submergence before the awe-inspiring object directly experienced" (*IH,* 17). The overwhelming quality of the holy accounts for its uncanniness, and the immediacy of the holy is felt especially in its incalculable and arbitrary wrath. He freely acknowledges that to claim that wrath is "the 'ideogram' of a unique emotional moment in religious experience" must be "gravely disturbing to those persons who will recognize nothing in the divine nature but goodness, gentleness, love, and a sort of confidential intimacy, in a word, only those aspects of God which turn towards the world of men" (*IH,* 19). The uncanniness of the experience of the holy is attributable to the fact that the holy has an aspect that turns away from the world of humanity, that withholds love and confidential intimacy.

In his chapter "The Analysis of 'Mysterium,' " Otto takes up the first major element of the mysterium, identifying it as the fourth element of the mysterium tremendum. This is the "wholly other," or the experience of the holy as a mystery "which is quite beyond the sphere of the usual, the intelligible, and the familiar" (*IH,* 26). If the word *tremor* comes closest to articulating what the tremendum evokes, the word *stupor* captures the sense of the mysterium, as it "signifies blank wonder, an astonishment that strikes us dumb, amazement absolute" (*IH,* 26). This experience of being utterly astounded has no parallels in normal human experience, for even if we acknowledge that, say, a piece of complicated technology is a "mystery" to us, the holy is absolutely "beyond our apprehension and comprehension, not only because our knowledge has certain irremovable limits, but because in it we come upon something inherently 'wholly other,' whose kind and character are incommensurable with our own, and before which we therefore recoil in a wonder that strikes us chill and numb" (*IH,* 28).

In a footnote to this statement about being struck "chill and numb," Otto quotes the following from Augustine's *Confessions:* "What is the light which shines right through me and strikes my heart without hurting? It fills me with terror and burning love: With terror inasmuch as I am utterly other than it, with burning love in that I am akin to it" (Augustine 1992, 229). In Henry Chadwick's translation of this passage, the chapter from which the quotation is taken bears the heading "Terror and Love." Otto suggests that in this passage Augustine "very strikingly" depicts the "stiffening, benumbing element of the 'wholly other' " (*IH,* 28). Augustine also, of course, captures the paradox of the numinous experience, that it simultaneously evokes fear and love. I shall return to this point later, as the same paradox occurs in the punishment scenarios of early childhood.

Following his chapter on the mysterium, Otto takes up the element of *fascination,* the fifth element of the experience of the numinous. Fascination is the counterpart to the stupor felt in the presence of the mysterium, and thus the mysterium consists of two conflicting elements: stupefaction on the one hand and entrancement on the other. Fascination also expresses the fact that the numinous not only repels but is also "the object of search and desire and yearning" (*IH,* 32). In the encounter with the holy, one feels a bliss and rapture unlike any bliss or rapture ever before experienced. Also, "just as 'wrath,' taken in a purely rational or a purely ethical sense, does not exhaust that profound element of *awefulness* which is locked in the mystery of deity, so neither does 'graciousness' exhaust the profound element of *wonderfulness* and rapture which lies in the mysterious beatific experience of deity" (*IH, 3 2*). Although the blessings suggested by "doctrines of salvation" are implied here, the mysterium "bestows upon man a beatitude beyond compare, but one whose real nature he can neither proclaim in speech nor conceive in thought. . . . It gives the peace that passes understanding, and of which the tongue can only stammer brokenly" (*IH, 3 3–34*). In the experience of the numinous as *fascinans,* one senses the soul being transported upward, virtually bursting with its own emotion.

Thus, in addition to the three elements of the tremendum, Otto identifies two elements more closely linked to the mysterium, and these round out the total experience of the numinous. If the three features of the tremendum point to the fact that the encounter with the holy is an overwhelming experience, the two elements associated with the mysterium indicate that it is also a wondrous, transporting experience, causing one to seek the experience again and again. It may be a painful, threatening experience, but it is also attractive, as it fills one with terror and love, and a kind of numbing, stupefying bliss. If the numinous experience were only terrifying and repelling, few would seek to experience it a second time. Yet, Otto emphasizes, this is an experience that many want to have repeated, as all other experiences of bliss are poor substitutes for that experienced in the encounter with the holy.

Following these analyses of the mysterium tremendum, Otto takes up several issues that are best understood as theological in nature. Some years after the publication of *The Idea of the Holy,* he sought to correct misunderstandings about what kind of book he had written: "Our line of inquiry in *Das Heilege* was directed towards Christian theology and not towards religious history or the psychology of religion" (Almond 1983, 317). I shall comment briefly on the two theological issues that have direct bearing on our explorations. The first is raised in his chapter "The Holy as a Category of Value." He discusses here how theology, under the influence of rationalism, has reduced the experience of the holy to a category of ethical and moral value. The "creature-feeling" that is at the center of the numinous experience and denotes "numinous unworthiness" has been "transformed to and centered in *moral delinquency*" (*IH, 52*). The Old Testament view of the creature as profane and thus unworthy to stand before the holy is all but lost in this reduction of the profane to moral and ethical considerations. Otto is especially critical of the fact that sin in the sense of creatureliness is being replaced by sin understood as moral delinquency, and he contends that "the theory of certain dogmatists, that the demand of morality as such urged man on to an inner collapse and then obliged him to look around for some deliverance, is palpably incorrect"

(*IH,* 52–53). Dogmatic theology has mistakenly transferred the language of "atonement" and "covering"—so that one may stand before the holy and not defile it or be destroyed by it—from the mystical sphere where it belongs into the realm of rational ethics, attenuating this language into moral concepts (*IH,* 53–54).

The second issue is his contention, in the same chapter, that the God of the New Testament is not less but more holy than the God of the Old Testament, and that in Christianity "the unworthiness of the profane in contrast to Him is not extenuated but enhanced" (*IH,* 56). The paradox in Christianity, however, is that the holy allows greater access to and intimacy with himself. Thus, in his chapters on the numinous in the Bible, Otto contrasts Job's encounter with the holy and his self-abasement as he "repented in dust and ashes" with Jesus's teaching that the "Holy One" is a "heavenly Father." The story of Jesus's agony at Gethsemane is a powerful example of "the awe of the creature before the *mysterium tremendum,* before the shuddering secret of the numen," as the paradox in this case is that the God of wrath and fury is yet "my Father" (*IH,* 85). He notes, further, that Jesus's teachings enhance the awe and shuddering dread with which the Old Testament associates the numinous experience, and that the Epistle to the Hebrews makes an especially strong association of the holy with the day of judgment (*IH,* 84–85). Thus, contrary to popular theological opinion, the New Testament continues to emphasize the mysterium tremendum and especially affirms the self-loathing of the creature before the august majesty of the Holy One. Most important, Christianity makes a fateful association of the "heavenly Father" with the "Holy."

The Holy: A Priori *Category or Repressed Personal Prehistory?*

Having reviewed Otto's analysis of the mysterium tremendum and identified certain key theological concerns, let us return to the question of the relationship of the experience of the holy to early childhood experiences of parental punishment. Unintentionally, Otto himself sets the stage for the asking of this question in his chapter "The Numinous in Luther." Here he accounts for Luther's attacks on the rationalists of his day by noting that Luther's sense of the tremendum was not a residuum of his scholastic training but derived from "the mysterious background of his religious life, obscure and 'uncanny' " (*IH,* 97). He suggests that "it matters not from what source" Luther's religious "consciousness was first stirred," whether "nominalism" or "the traditional teaching of his Order." What matters is that we have "in Luther the numinous consciousness at first hand, stirred and agitated through its typical 'moments,' as we have come to know them" (*IH*, 97). What he does not consider is the possibility that Luther's "numinous consciousness" was first stirred in his experience of the uncanny in his early childhood, in episodes involving estrangements (de-familiarizations) between himself and his mother.

That Otto would not consider *this* possibility is not surprising, as it would raise questions about the sui generis nature of the experience of the Holy or, at the very least, would mean that its "pedigree" may be traced to origins he would find humiliating, both personally and for his professional status as a "Christian theologian." However, as I noted earlier, he credits Luther with having inspired his own understanding of "the numinous and its difference from the rational long before I identified it in the *gadosh* of the Old Testament," adding that Luther's eloquent intonations of the numinous "have rung in my ears from the time of my earliest study of Luther" (*IH*, 99–100). What he does not say is that this personal resonance with the words of Luther is an *echo* of his own personal past. Otherwise, how to account for the fact that Luther's "eloquent intonations" were so attractive to him?

In his chapter "The Holy as an *A Priori* Category," Otto claims that the method of introspection, supported by Kantian critical examination of reason, affords the conclusion that the numinous "issues from the deepest foundation of cognitive apprehension that the soul possesses, and, through it of course comes into being in and amid the sensory data and empirical material of the natural world and cannot anticipate or dispose with those, yet it does not arise *out* of them, but only *by their means*" (*IH*, 113). Thus, introspection is the method by which the "a priori" nature of the "Holy" is known. Yet, as we have seen, the method of introspection is not infallible, and one of the major reasons for this is that we may repress certain experiences and so not even realize that our introspections are partial and incomplete. In light of this fact, the philosopher's "a priori" is the psychologist's "personal pre-history." Therefore what seems to the theologian to be "a priori" because it "issues from the deepest foundation of cognitive apprehension" is for the psychologist "a posteriori," as it is reminiscent of an originative experience long since repressed.

The emotional power in an experience like Otto's in the synagogue in Morocco may be attributed to the fact that it was evocative of a state of consciousness he had experienced years before, having its own ambivalent mixture of fear and ecstasy, terror and love. If it was reminiscent of an episode in which he was punished by his mother, this would explain why it had such an aura of mystery about it, for the one with whom he had been on such familiar terms suddenly took on the face and demeanor of wrath itself and became to him the "wholly other." Who else but the mother, the very embodiment of familiarity, of immediate and fully recognizable presence, would become, suddenly and without warning, so "wholly" other? Surely not the father, for he was always the figure who hovered in the background and then, when Rudolf was twelve, departed forever.[4]

In daring to explore the "irrational" side of religion, Otto took an important first step toward identifying the source of his experience of the numinous. Had he gone farther in his introspections, he might also have become aware of the sources of his melancholia, and his attempts to end his life with uncommon violence against himself would perhaps have been averted. His whole point in *The Idea of the Holy* is that the Object — the "Holy" — is stronger than the ego's self, for the experience of the numinous confirms one's creaturehood. Before the holy, one is nothing, or less than nothing. If, as Freud suggests, suicide is an attack against the internalized other that the ego's own self is powerless to challenge because it is so impoverished, we may readily appreciate the difference it would have made had Otto been able to make the association between his later experiences of the numinous and his early childhood experiences of being the object of his mother's overwhelming wrath or her excruciating withdrawal into silence.

The Mysterium Tremendum and Child Abuse: An Unholy Alliance

If thus far I have been critical of Otto for failing to see any connection between the experience of the holy and early childhood traumas, I now want to consider the potentially positive uses of his theological analyses for the exploration of the relationship between Christian theology and the abuse of children. The tendency of Christian theology to introduce a "moral delinquency" element to the experience of the holy and its identification of the "Holy" as a "heavenly Father" have had the effect of creating a powerful — and tragic — relationship between the mysterium tremendum and child abuse. When the mysterium tremendum is linked to moral delinquency, the child's misbehavior may be viewed as an offense against God, and by identifying the "Holy" as a "heavenly Father," the child's father (or parent) could more easily be viewed as standing in for God or as acting in God's behalf when punishing the child for misbehavior.

The biblical letter to the Hebrews, which in Otto's judgment is among the strongest affirmations in the New Testament of God as mysterium tremendum, makes these connections explicit. According to Philip Greven, this is the most cited biblical text among Christians in support of the "harsh physical discipline of children" (Greven 1991, 52). The anonymous author of Hebrews acknowledges that he himself was the victim of child abuse (12:10), as he says that "our earthly fathers disciplined us . . . at their pleasure" (or "at their own discretion"), whereas God, "the Father of spirits," "disciplines us for our good." He implies, in other words, that God's discipline is more purely motivated than is the discipline meted out by earthly fathers. After all, earthly fathers did not always discipline for the good of the child. Yet, as Alice Miller points out, the adult's claim to be acting for the good of the child has been used to rationalize all sorts of abusive actions toward children (1984). As Greven concludes, "Although no one actually knows who wrote Hebrews, this unknown author has had, and continues to have, an incalculable impact upon the lives of children" (1991, 52; see also Capps 1995, 58–77).

While Greven challenges use of the Bible to support harsh physical punishment of children, on the grounds that Jesus "never advocated such punishment" (1991, 51), he does not address the possibility that the physical punishment of children may be responsible for the very idea of God as mysterium tremendum. Would the mysterium tremendum view of God have been so compelling to the author of Hebrews if he had not been treated so harshly and capriciously by his own father? Is his belief in God as mysterium tremendum the outcome of beatings he sustained at the hands of his earthly father?

Affirmative answers to these questions find support in an article by Leo Ferrari on the beatings that Augustine sustained as a young boy (Ferrari 1990, 55–67). In this case, the beatings were inflicted by teachers. Yet when young Augustine complained to his parents about having been beaten in school, his parents mocked him and did nothing to intervene. When he called upon God to save him from these beatings, he says that God also laughed at him and did nothing to stop them. In recounting these beatings in his *Confessions,* however, he takes the side of his parents and of God against the suffering boy, viewing the abuse as deserved and even beneficial. Ferrari argues that Augustine's image of God throughout the *Confessions* bears a remarkable likeness to the "irate schoolmaster" of his childhood and, through a series of direct quotations from the *Confessions,* demonstrates that a prominent theme in the text is the "scourging God."

Ferrari also claims that Augustine's God resembles more "the stern Jehovah" of the Old Testament than the merciful and loving God of the New Testament. As we have seen, Otto would challenge this assertion that the New Testament God is less "wrathful" than the Old Testament God, but Ferrari is certainly correct in his contention that Augustine's God is one who evokes fear and even terror yet in the process demonstrates his love. The following is a typical passage in the *Confessions* in which God is experienced as simultaneously frightening and loving: "But you, Lord, 'abide for eternity and you will not be angry with us for ever' (Ecclesiasticus 18:1; Psalm 84:6). You have mercy on dust and ashes, and it has pleased you to restore my deformities in your sight (Psalm 18:15). By inward goads you stirred me to make me find it unendurable until, through my inward perception, you were a certainty to me. My swelling was reduced by your hidden healing hand, and my mind's troubled and darkened eye, under the hot dressing of salutary sorrows, was from 'day to day' (Psalm 60:9) brought back to health" (Augustine 1992, 120–21).

If God is the agent of the healing, the same hand with which he beat Augustine becomes the healing hand that reduces the swelling. And if God is the one who blackened his eye, God is also the one who dresses the wound. Relevant to the latter act of parental violence is Freud's observation in "The 'Uncanny'" that "we know from psycho-analytic experience . . . that this fear of damaging or losing one's eyes is a terrible fear of children. Many adults still retain their apprehensiveness in this respect, and no bodily injury is so much dreaded by them as an injury to the eye" (Freud 1958, 137). Of course, Freud goes on to argue that this dread of losing "so precious an organ as the eye" is a "mitigated form" of the deeper and greater dread of castration.

In my view, Ferrari makes a persuasive case for the relationship between the beatings that Augustine suffered as a child and his belief in God as the holy, as mysterium tremendum. The psychological term for this is "identification with one's aggressors," indications of which are evident in Augustine's tendency as an adult to excuse his parents and God for failing to intervene against his attackers (Augustine 1992, 11–13; see also Capps 1995, 21–36).

Admittedly, my argument that the child's experience of being abused at the hands of an adult is reflected in the mysterium tremendum experience appears reductionistic, as it not only explains an idea of God by means of an all-too-common human experience but also seems to offer a unicausal explanation of a religious idea that may have multiple causes. While I do not believe that I am being reductionistic here, as I do not challenge claims for the reality of God in some form, the risk of being accused of reductionism is well worth taking when there are such serious moral issues involved. That the child's experience of being terrorized by an adult lies behind the mysterium tremendum is supported by Otto's own analysis of the five elements of the experience of mysterium tremendum: (1) the dread that includes physical responses of trembling and shuddering in the face of the other's wrath; (2) the experience of being overpowered to the extent that one also experiences self-annihilation; (3) the activation of the numinous object's passion, force, emotional temper, and excitability against its recipient; (4) the confrontation with the unusual and unfamiliar, which leaves one astounded, chilled, and numbed; and (5) the fascination, yearning, and bliss with which one associates the very one who also fills one with holy dread. Regarding this last point, various experts on child abuse have noted that children typically have strong feelings of love for the very adult who also fills them with terror (Shengold 1989; Greven 1991, 148–68).

The Mysterium Tremendum in the Psychology of Religion

Because Otto was a theologian and not a psychologist of religion, it is understandable, though regrettable, that he could not recognize the repressed infantile complex that lies behind the numinous experience he portrays. We might have expected, however, that psychologists of religion would have made the connection that I am now making between the mysterium tremendum and the experience of childhood trauma. That they have not done so testifies to their own desire to believe that Otto is right, that the numinous state of consciousness found in religion *is* sui generis — that is, incomparable, finally, to any other human experience. Let us consider in this light two important figures in the psychology of religion, Paul W. Pruyser and C. G. Jung, both of whom failed to make the connection between the mysterium tremendum and the experience of childhood trauma. While symptomatic of the failure of psychologists of religion to make this connection, they *do* set the stage for the argument that I am making here: Pruyser because he suggests that the mysterium tremendum has *some* basis in early childhood experience, and Jung because he invites us to question the God of the mysterium tremendum on moral grounds and thus, in effect, to accuse the mysterium tremendum itself of moral delinquency.

PRUYSER: MYSTERIUM TREMENDUM AND THE
TRANSITIONAL SPHERE

In every book and many of the articles he wrote on the psychology of religion, Pruyser made reference to Otto's *The Idea of the Holy*. In his first book, *A Dynamic Psychology of Religion* (1968), he praises Otto's phcnomcnological approach as "a convincing answer to the fallacious assumption that the psychology of religion deals only with man — it must deal with God, for religion is the establishing, experiencing, and nurturing of a relation between man and his gods" (1968, 17). He also praises Otto for having "rescued the numinous from being invested only by pleasant, positive affect. The numinous mystery is, qua mystery, both a *tremendum* and a *fascinans*. It always invokes both shuddering and admiration. It attracts and repels at once. It elicits devotion and fear. It instills dread and trust. It is dangerous and comforting. It inspires awe and bliss" (1968, 336). Pruyser notes as well Otto's inference that the tremendum aspect is more conspicuous at the beginning of religion, that the scales are only gradually tipped in favor of the fascinans, and that quite a step occurs from awe to trust, from a God of wrath to a God of love. Moreover, "the dynamic core of awe persists, no matter what else is added in latter refinements. As long as the Holy remains a mystery, it is a *tremendum*. The moment it loses its mysterious features it ceases to be holy; it is then a concept or a rational insight. Power is always of its essence, for the Holy is not a concept but a symbol, charged with energy" (1968, 336).

In *Between Belief and Unbelief* (1974), Pruyser discusses Otto in his chapter "Coming to Terms with Mystery." He centers here on the power of the holy to attract and repel, noting that its "mystery is *tremendum* in the sense that it evokes tremor, shuddering, or shaking, the typical accompaniments of dread," but that "the mystery of the holy is also *fascinosum:* it attracts, it intrigues, it fascinates — and it also elicits a special feeling: *bliss.*" He concludes: "The most important features of Otto's phenomenology of the holy are its dynamic ambiguity, its combination of contrasts, and its capacity to induce complex cognitive and emotional states" (1974, 105).

Pruyser suggests that psychoanalytic object-relations theory may help to explain why some individuals have a greater disposition toward experiencing the holy, and he introduces D. W. Winnicott's views on the transitional sphere and transitional object, suggesting that infants who were encouraged to develop the transitional sphere are more likely to have such a disposition. Critical to Winnicott's theory of the transitional sphere is the view that the subjective and the objective are interactive and coexistent. Thus, Pruyser suggests, the holy arises in the transitional sphere where subject and object interact: "The transcendent, the holy, and mystery are not recognizable in the external world by plain realistic viewing and hearing, nor do they arise directly in the mind as pleasurable fictions. They arise from an intermediate zone of reality that is also an intermediate human activity — neither purely subjective nor purely objective" (1974, 113).

In *The Play of the Imagination: Toward a Psychoanalysis of Culture* (1983), Pruyser discusses Otto in his chapters on the visual arts and on religion. He notes that the fascinans inherent in the sacred may also be ascribed to art objects: "However difficult it may be to define art and art objects to everyone's satisfaction, they are distinguishable from ordinary objects by their arresting quality, their drawing power, their appeal" (1983, 74). A special relation occurs between the work of art and the beholder: "Being arrested, the beholder becomes somewhat reverential, momentarily quiet, rather ceremonial in conduct. He assumes an attitude of surrender" (1983, 74–75). Pruyser does not discuss the other aspect of the holy in relation to art, its capacity to repel, horrify, or terrify. However, in his earlier essay on the lessons of art theory for psychology of religion (1976), he suggests that a phenomenology of the arts patterned after Otto's phenomenology of numinous experience would pry art loose "from its coupling with the idea of beauty, with which it may have only a remote or accidental connection." Art "need not be enjoyable at all" but "may produce ugly or horrifying images and stir up painful affects. If a particular work of art is found to be arresting, persuasive, compelling, or shocking, and if it succeeds in transforming people's minds or attitudes, it may become a classic that belies the very idea of satisfaction or pleasure. It is simply there, in all its awesomeness; possibly in its awfulness" (1976, 10). Here Pruyser captures the dynamic ambiguity of art, its *tremendum* as well as *fascinosum* elements. His discussion recalls Otto's own employment of the Kantian distinction between the sublime and the beautiful in art.

Pruyser's comment on Otto in his chapter on religion in *The Play of the Imagination* is uncharacteristically brief. It consists of a single paragraph located in a larger discussion of transcendence and mystery, his point being that the religious person experiences a subject-reversal when confronted by the holy. While previously engaged in reflecting on the object, one is now held in the object's thrall and is compelled to acknowledge "the prior existence, the greater power, the august presence, and the overwhelming dynamic self-affirmation whereby the Holy poses itself and reduces man to its object—which now undergoes an ambiguous emotional state in which awe and bliss commingle. The crucial feature is the Holy's dynamism, which cannot be matched by anything human; or so it is felt by the believing soul" (1983, 157).

In what proved to be his final writing on the psychology of religion, an essay on future scenarios for it (1987), Pruyser again alludes to Otto's concept of the mysterium tremendum, noting that it, together with Freud's concept of the dynamic unconscious, "should serve the psychology of religion for at least another fifty years" (1987, 180). He does not discuss these two concepts in any detail. But he does allude to Erwin R. Goodenough's *Psychology of Religious Experiences* (1965), a text that had great influence in the formation of his own dynamic psychology of religion and was the stimulus for his views of Otto's importance for the psychology of religion. Thus, in *A Dynamic Psychology of Religion,* Pruyser notes that Goodenough found a way to link Otto's mysterium tremendum and Freud's dynamic unconscious by recognizing that the tremendum "is not just an external or all-encompassing reality," but that there "is also a *tremendum* within man, namely the dynamic unconscious which contains some very important forces of nature which must be controlled. The *tremendum* consists of 'all the sources of terror,' all the threats which exist or are sensed. From this inner *tremendum* too we shield ourselves by throwing a curtain before it, a curtain of repression" (1968, 337).

In *Between Belief and Unbelief,* Pruyser observes that Goodenough stressed the mysterium tremendum feature of Otto's idea of the holy and then, edified by Freud's thoughts, "saw the *tremendum* not only as the external and cosmic *x*, chaotic in appearance, which controls the universe, but also as the internal and personal *x,* also chaotic, of our motives, childhood fixations, and sense of guilt. Both are equally mysterious and powerful—awe-inspiring in a very potent sense" (1974, 62–63). Thus, for Goodenough the internal tremendum is the "id," that within us which remains unsocialized, and of which we are afraid, because we cannot deny its power, its mystery, its capacity both to allure and repel us (1974, 230–31). Pruyser does not discuss the interconnections between the internal and external tremendums, but he does emphasize that we seek ways to defend ourselves against both: against the *external* tremendum by means of the curtain of religion, which helps us to placate or domesticate the holy, and against the *internal* tremendum by means of repression, forgetting, or denial.

While Pruyser's uses of Winnicott and Goodenough give Otto's phenomenological approach to the numinous a psychodynamic dimension it otherwise lacks, Pruyser fails to offer an account of the childhood origins of an adult's disposition to respond to the mysterium tremendum. Nor does he attempt to explain the psychodynamic connection between the mysterium tremendum and repression, forgetting, or denial.

Regarding his proposal that the mysterium tremendum may be traced developmentally to the emergence of the transitional sphere and its objects, I would certainly agree that the transitional sphere is implicated in the sense of the sacred, especially as represented in sacred rituals (Pruyser 1974, 205–8). But Winnicott's theory of the transitional sphere does not adequately account for the fear and even terror of the numinous experience. As Winnicott indicates in his famous essay on transitional objects and transitional phenomena (1971), the theoretical issue raised by the transitional sphere concept is that of illusion and disillusionment, and the whole question of the "real" and the "not real." But, as Pruyser himself notes, the mysterium tremendum is far more threatening than that. The transitional sphere, with its inception in the mother-infant relationship at feeding time, is at worst a frustrating, potentially disillusioning experience, whereas the experience of the mysterium tremendum involves trembling, shuddering, and dread. At best, Winnicott's concept may account for the *fascinans* aspect of the holy, its element of attraction, devotion, and bliss, which is in fact very much how Pruyser construes the transitional object (for example, as "a center of ceremonial engagement," an object of veneration, and so forth [1974, 207]). This is much the way that Winnicott himself views the transitional object, for he suggests that a patient's allusion to an angel standing by her bed which she did not "really believe" was there is an example of a transitional object (1971b, 27).

None of this, however, accounts for the intensity of feeling, the highly charged emotions, associated with the mysterium tremendum. Some other childhood experience, one more dreadful and frightening, is needed to account for the full range of elements associated with the mysterium tremendum. Only the experience of being severely punished by one's mother, whether by beating or by prolonged silence, manifests such intensity of feeling.

One reason Pruyser nominated Winnicott's theory of the transitional sphere and not the more emotionally charged punishment scenario (with its "uncanniness") as the experiential basis for the mysterium tremendum is that it accords better with his interpretation of the role of religion in his own childhood. In *The Play of the Imagination,* he relates that his father died when he was a young boy and that his primary experience of his father was via a large portrait on the mantelpiece (1983, 169). This portrait was more conducive to humor than fear, for when it was Paul's turn to pray "the Lord's Prayer" aloud at the dinner table, he would intone the words "Our Father who art in heaven" while simultaneously casting a sideways glance at his father's portrait, a mocking act "supported by the stifled laughter of my siblings, checked instantly by my mother's glances of dismay" (1983, 160).

From kindergarten through the ninth grade, he attended a Calvinist school that was "strict, somber, and punitive," but it was counterbalanced by a home, presided over by his mother, that was "mellow, optimistic, and forgiving." The choice between them was not difficult to make: "Home won over school, undoubtedly because the former had deeper roots in my childhood practicing of the transitional sphere. The hands of God, much talked about in school, seemed more like my mother's tender-and-firm hand than the threatening and often slapping extremities of my teachers. Small wonder, too, that I have always found the highlight of worship services in the benevolently outstretched hands of the pastoral blessing, and that one of my dearest pictures is Rembrandt's etching of the father blessing his prodigal son upon his return" (1983, 170).

There is little of the tremendum in this childhood scenario. But there is much of the fascinosum of the holy, its power to attract, to elicit devotion, even to comfort and create a sense of overwhelming bliss. Of course, Pruyser does not suggest that he led a charmed life as a child, that he never experienced anguish or fear. Yet he notes that as a child he made a self-conscious choice to associate religion with the kindness he received at home and not with the punitive actions of his teachers at school. Perhaps his adult recollection creates a division of school and home that is neater and more absolute than he actually experienced as a child, but in any event this explains why he identified with the mellower, fascinans aspect of the holy and not with its terrifying aspects. If art reflects both aspects of the holy, he preferred, so far as *religious* art is concerned, a painting that emphasizes the beatitude, not the awfulness, of the holy.

Pruyser's failure to relate the idea of the holy to childhood trauma may also be attributed to Goodenough's characterization of the "inner tremendum" as the id and, more specifically, as that aspect of the human self that resists socialization (Pruyser 1974, 230–31). This suggests that if there is something "wrong" with us, even demonic or evil, it is not because of the way we were socialized but rather because there is something within us that has successfully *resisted* socialization. It does not occur either to Goodenough or to Pruyser that socialization in the form of child abuse may be responsible for creating the child's sense of inner tremendum. Nor does it occur to them that the repression connected with the inner tremendum might be repression of memories associated with the socialization process; in this case, one's experience of abuse as a child. While neither Pruyser nor Goodenough directly identify the id with the theologians' notion of the "natural will" that is inherently sinful, they come dangerously close to such identification, especially in Goodenough's suggestion that the tremendum within the person "contains some very important forces of nature which must be controlled" (Pruyser 1968, 337). How are they to be controlled except through the sorts of punishments that alienate child and mother from each other?

JUNG: JOB ENCOUNTERS THE MYSTERIUM TREMENDUM

Jung, too, fails to make a direct connection between the mysterium tremendum and childhood trauma, but he goes much farther than Otto in inviting this connection. He does so by raising questions about the morality of the mysterium tremendum, and raising them in such a way that we are put in mind of the punishment scenario that occurs between the child and his mother. Otto was quite clear that the holy, while not reducible to the moral or ethical, is surely not amoral. In discussing Luther's view of the numinous, he alludes to the "perplexed endeavor" of theology to find "a name for the elements of the non-rational and the mysterious in the repulsive doctrine that God is *exlex* (outside the law), that good is good because God wills it, instead of that God wills it because it is good, a doctrine that results in attributing to God an absolute fortuitous will, which would in fact turn Him into a 'capricious despot'" (*IH*, 101). Otto notes that such pernicious ideas are to be found in Luther himself, but he accounts for these lapses on the part of Luther and others on the grounds that "they are caricatures prompted by a deficient psychology and a mistaken choice of expressions and not by any disregard of the absoluteness of moral values" (*IH,* 102). As we shall see, Jung questions the morality of God, at least as he is represented in the Book of Job and other biblical writings.

We recall that Otto himself viewed the Book of Job, with its brilliant account of God's appearance to Job in the thunderstorm, as a powerful example of the numinous experience. Especially revealing is Otto's observation that when Job confesses "Therefore I abhor myself and *repent* in dust and ashes," he "avows himself to be overpowered, truly and rightly overpowered, not merely silenced by superior strength" (*IH,* 78). Job's confession is "an admission of inward *convincement* and conviction, not of impotent collapse and submission to merely superior power" (*IH,* 78). This distinction, between confessing because one accedes to the superior power of one's adversary and confessing because one is convinced inwardly of one's depravity, is reminiscent of the view of the authors of the child-rearing texts cited by Miller that the whole purpose of the punishment is to effect an inward change, not a mere compliance based on fear of the parent's superior physical strength. Otto also notes that there is a nonrational quality to illustrations drawn from nature, and he specifically cites the example of the ostrich (Job 39:13–18), which as depicted in Job is anything but a rational creature and offers no evidence in support of a purposive teleology in nature. The ostrich "leaveth her eggs in the earth, and warmeth them in the dust, and forgetteth that the foot may crush them or that the wild beast may break them. She is hardened against her young ones as though they were not hers: her labor is in vain without fear; because God hath *deprived her of wisdom,* neither hath he imparted to her *understanding*" (Job 39:14–18, Otto's emphasis).

I wonder if Otto's use of the mother-ostrich parable to illustrate that the natural world is not rationally ordered may be an indirect allusion to the human world, where human mothers' treatment of their young is no less irrational, lacking true wisdom and understanding. Is he on the verge of a genuine insight into how it is with human mothers and their human offspring? Or does the phrase "her labor is in vain without fear" (meaning the child's fear?) reflect his acceptance of the views promulgated in the child-rearing manuals that unless the mother creates fear in her child, her labor in the child's behalf is in vain? The translator here uses the King James Version; the Revised Standard Version renders it "Though her labor be in vain, yet she has no fear," resolving the ambiguity.

Despite these potential resonances between his discussion of Job's repentence and similar episodes in childhood, Otto presents these Joban materials simply as powerful accounts of the experience of the holy. In *Answer to Job*

(1969), however, Jung comes at this biblical text from a psychologist's point of view, one quite different from Otto's because Jung believes there is something not right, something suspicious and questionable, about the biblical account of Job's encounter with the mysterium tremendum.

Jung notes that, even at the time Job was written, "there were already many testimonies which had given a contradictory picture of Yahweh—the picture of a God who knew no moderation in his emotions and suffered precisely from this lack of moderation" (1969, 3). He points out that Yahweh "admitted that he was eaten up with rage and jealousy and that this knowledge was painful to him" (1969, 3). Yet insights like this existed alongside obtuseness, loving-kindness alongside cruelty, creative power alongside destructiveness: "Everything was there, and none of these qualities was an obstacle to the other. Such a condition is only conceivable either when no reflecting consciousness is present at all, or when the capacity for reflection is very feeble and a more or less adventitious phenomenon. A condition of this sort can only be described as *amoral*" (1969, 3).

Jung acknowledges that his own view of this "dark" side of God may not accurately reflect how the people of the Old Testament felt about their God, but this, he says, is beside the point. What he wants to do in *Answer to Job* is to set forth how

> a modern man with a Christian education and background comes to terms with the divine darkness which is unveiled in the Book of Job, and what effect it has on him. . . . In this way I hope to act for many who feel the same way I do, and to give expression to the shattering emotion which the unvarnished spectacle of divine savagery and ruthlessness produces in us. . . . The Book of Job serves as a paradigm for a certain experience of God which has a special significance for us today. These experiences come upon man from inside as well as from outside, and it is useless to interpret them rationalistically. . . . It is far better to admit the affect and *submit to its violence* than to try to escape it by all sorts of intellectual tricks or by emotional value-judgments [1969, 4, my emphasis].

Jung is saying here that there is no point in trying to rationalize away the "dark side" of God, for in doing so we merely deny "the shattering emotion which the unvarnished spectacle of divine savagery and ruthlessness produces in us." Better to accept these emotions as real and "submit" to the emotional violence that is being done to us. On the point of the inadequacy of the rationalistic view of God, and on the emotional effects of the holy, he and Otto are in agreement.

Yet in these initial paragraphs of *Answer to Job*, Jung already indicates that his view of the mysterium tremendum will not be as neutral or as purely phenomenological as Otto's. His use of the word *violence* is especially telling, because it indicates that while he shares Otto's concern that we not view the "wrath" of God from a narrow ethical or moral point of view, we *should* be prepared to say that there are certain moral issues involved, especially insofar as *God's* behavior is concerned. Citing Job's answer to Yahweh, "Behold, I am of small account; what shall I answer thee?" (Job 40:4), Jung observes that "in the immediate presence of the infinite power of creation, this is the only possible answer for a witness who is still trembling in every limb with the terror of almost total annihilation" (1969, 5). That is to say, Job is in no position to offer any moral reflections about what has been going on, and he would certainly be well advised *not* to say anything about the "moral requirements which might be expected to apply to a god" (1969, 5). He has no choice but to praise Yahweh's "justice" and affirm his belief that Yahweh will in fact act justly toward him.

Yet, in Jung's view, Job's own ambivalent conflicts are evident here, for Job knows that morally speaking Yahweh is seriously flawed. In making a bargain with Satan, causing Job to lose his possessions, family, and personal health, Yahweh revealed himself to be unreflective, jealous of his power but deficient in wisdom (like the mother ostrich?), and therefore proved himself to be Job's moral inferior. Hence, "in spite of his doubt as to whether man can be just before God," Job "still finds it difficult to relinquish the idea of meeting God on the basis of justice and therefore of morality" (1969, 7). On the other hand, "he has to admit that no one except Yahweh is doing him injustice and violence. He cannot deny that he is up against a God who does not care a rap for any moral opinion and does not recognize any form of ethics as binding" (1969, 7). Job does not doubt the essential unity of God, but he

> clearly sees that God is at odds with himself — so totally at odds that he, Job, is quite certain of finding in God a helper and an "advocate" against God. As certain as he is of the evil in Yahweh, he is equally certain of the good. In a human being who renders us evil we cannot expect at the same time to find a helper. But Yahweh is not a human being: he is both a persecutor and a helper in one, and the one aspect is as real as the other. Yahweh is not split but is an *antinomy* — a totality of inner opposites — and this is the indispensable condition for his tremendous dynamism, his omniscience and omnipotence. Because of this knowledge Job holds on to his intention of "defending his ways to his face," i.e., of making his point of view clear to him, since notwithstanding his wrath, Yahweh is also man's advocate *against himself* when man puts forth his complaint [1969, 7].

Jung exaggerates the differences between Yahweh and humans, as the fact that a single human being may be both a helper and one who does evil is very common. This is my whole point about the de-familiarization that occurs between the mother and her son in the punishment scenario. However, Jung's point that the conflict with Job has placed God in a very difficult position is most insightful: If from Job's perspective the issue is how he can continue to have faith in a God who is a totality of inner opposites, the issue for God is that he has been forced to reveal his true nature. And this revelation forces him to become more self-conscious, especially in recognizing that he has allowed his propensity to exhibit and project his power (omnipotence) to cloud his wisdom (omniscience). In contrast, because Job has been in the position of being God's victim, he has been able to see clearly from the beginning what was altogether unclear to God, that God had indeed mistreated him (1969, 10). From now on, God will begin to develop his capacity for wisdom against his exertion of power, and this development will reach its culmination in the incarnation portrayed in the New Testament, when God assumes human form.

But this development comes far too late to do Job any good. He remains God's victim, first, because he was the helpless victim of God's unthinking bargain with Satan in which God "had let himself be bamboozled" (1969, 17) and, second, because God's slowly dawning consciousness of what he allowed Satan to do led him to thunder at Job, as if Job, not Satan, were the one who had tricked God. In his thunderings, God accuses Job of harboring doubts about him, accusations that are actually self-projections: "Yahweh projects on to Job a sceptic's face which is hateful to him because it is his own, and which gazes at him with an uncanny and critical eye. He is afraid of it, for only in face of something frightening does one let off a cannonade of references to one's power, cleverness, courage, invincibility, etc." (1969, 18). As for Job, his submission to God in the wake of all this thundering is less than genuine. To be sure, his expression of fear and of self-loathing in the face of God sounds very much like Otto's abject creature standing before the "Holy":

> "Who is this that hides counsel without insight?"
> Therefore I have uttered what I did not understand,
> things too wonderful for me, which I did not know.
> "Hear, and I will speak:
> I will question you, and you declare to me."
> I had heard of thee by the hearing of the ear,
> but now my eye sees thee;
> therefore I abhor myself,
> and repent in dust and ashes [Job 42:3–6].

But in quoting God's own words back to him, Job is actually being quite disingenuous. Jung continues: "Shrewdly, Job takes up Yahweh's aggressive words and prostrates himself at his feet as if he were indeed the defeated antagonist. *Guileless as Job's speech sounds, it could just as well be equivocal.* He has learnt his lesson well and experienced 'wonderful things' which are none too easily grasped" (1969, 20, my emphasis).

In other words, Job is too smart to challenge God when God is in such bad humor. Better to say the things that God expects him to say, to "repent," even if he feels he has done nothing wrong. Thus, Jung disagrees with Otto's contention that Job repented because he was "inwardly convinced" of his depravity. He "repented" because he knew he was up against a more powerful and emotionally erratic opponent.

Like Otto, Jung fails to relate this scene in Job to the punishment scenario between a powerful adult and a terrified child, but surely the psychodynamics are similar. Confronted by the superior strength of the adult, and knowing that he is physically no match for the adult, the child "submits," "agreeing" with everything the adult says. The adult is "right" and the child is "wrong," for the child has nothing to gain by insisting that he may be in the right and that the adult, this time at least, is in the wrong. The child "submits" in order to get it over with, and sincerely hopes that the adult will perceive this "submission" to be genuine and heartfelt. One of the purposes of the child-rearing manuals that Miller cites is to assist the parent in discerning whether the child is "faking" or is genuinely repentant and remorseful.

Thus, unlike Otto, who takes a straightforward phenomenological view of the mysterium tremendum, Jung is more psychological. He fails to make the connection that I am proposing between the mysterium tremendum and childhood trauma, but he does demystify the mysterium tremendum, pointing out its inherent hollowness, its element of deceit and sham. Significantly, the moral delinquent in this case is Yahweh himself, for whom might makes right. By implication, the moral delinquent in the punishment scenario is the adult, whose violence toward the child is unwarranted, whatever the moral failing of the child may be. Not only do two wrongs *not* make a right, but also we expect a more fully developed morality in the adult than in the child.

We may wonder why Jung did not make this connection between the mysterium tremendum and childhood trauma and abuse. One possible clue is that, in his preface to *Answer to Job,* he makes a distinction between psychic and physical facts, and says that his book is purely about psychic facts. He is not concerned with the question of whether God is a reality in the physical world "out there" but is dealing only with the fact that God is a psychic reality, an "object" experienced within the psyche. Thus, his book is not concerned with the question of whether or not God exists independently of his existence within the psyche (1969, xii).

This distinction between psychic and physical facts serves the purpose of assuring his readers that he is only talking here about how God is psychologically experienced, that he is not making any statements as to what God is in fact. But this has the effect of so differentiating psychic and physical facts that the role of physical facts in the very creation of psychic facts is thereby minimized. If there *is* a physical fact behind the experience of God as mysterium tremendum—the fact of childhood trauma—Jung's distinction is likely to do more to obscure than to reveal it.

Still, if Otto inadvertently describes major aspects of the experience of childhood trauma in his portrayal of the mysterium tremendum, Jung indirectly identifies certain defenses that children employ to minimize the emotional pain or reduce the degree of violence perpetrated against them. He prefaces his quotation of Job's "repentence" speech with the observation that it was no doubt made "with downcast eyes and a low voice" (1969, 20). This is precisely the way a child is expected to repent: not defiantly but humbly and circumspectly. One of the child-rearing experts Miller cites puts it this way: " 'The eye discerns, the heart burns,' should be our preferred motto in punishing" (Miller 1984, 38). Yet, as Jung's suggestion that Job may have been equivocating indicates, the parent may not be able to discern from the child's humble demeanor whether he is repentent or not. As Jung says in the preface to *Answer to Job,* part of which I quoted earlier,

> It is far better to admit the affect and submit to its violence than to try to escape it by all sorts of intellectual tricks or by emotional value-judgments. Although, by giving way to the affect, one imitates all the bad qualities of the outrageous act that provoked it and thus makes oneself guilty of the same fault, that is precisely the point of the whole proceeding: the violence is meant to penetrate to a man's vitals, and to succumb to its action. He must be affected by it, otherwise its full effect will not reach him. But he should know, or learn to know, what has affected him, for in this way he transforms the blindness of the violence on the one hand and of the affect on the other into knowledge [1969, 4].

By pretending to be repentent, the child has at least gained in knowledge, especially knowledge of how to handle a situation in which one feels vulnerable and endangered. Also, Jung's view that God is experienced not as split asunder but as an antinomy—a totality of inner opposites—is precisely the child's experience of an adult who is abusive, for the child cannot separate the two faces or aspects of the adult (positive and negative, attractive and repelling), because these are experienced simultaneously. He experiences the adult's love in and through the violence, not apart from it, which, as I noted earlier, explains why some children continue to incur the adult's wrath, for only in this way does the child also experience the adult's love. Of course, the story of Job points also to the secondary gains that accrue to the child who is duly repentent. As the ending of the text reveals, God rewarded Job for "repenting" and, we assume, for keeping what he now knows about God under wraps. In other words, there is now a collusion of silence between them. The adult rewards the child for *not* revealing to others the fact that the child has been abused.

The Psychologist of Religion as Enlightened Witness

According to Miller, the lasting effects of child abuse may be countered by the "enlightened witness," an adult who confirms that abuse has indeed occurred and assures the child that he is right to feel victimized (Miller 1990a, 167–75). But Jung points out that Job's "comforters" side with his abuser, as they "do everything in their power to contribute to his moral torments, and instead of giving him, whom God has perfidiously abandoned, their warm-hearted support, they moralize in an all too human manner, that is, in the stupidest fashion imaginable, and 'fill him with wrinkles.' They thus deny him even the last comfort of sympathetic participation and human understanding, so that one cannot altogether suppress the suspicion of connivance in high places" (1969, 14).[5]

Job's comforters, then, actually collude with the abusive Yahweh, acting in a way opposite to that Miller ascribes to the enlightened witness, who would instead assure the victim that his perceptions of what is being inflicted on him are accurate and a basis for whatever resistance is possible. Enlightened witnesses not only take the side of the abused, unequivocally, but also affirm the aspect of the "self" of the abused that is determined not to collude with the abuser against himself. As the antithesis of Job's counselors who speak in support of the mysterium tremendum, the moral role of the psychologist of religion is to serve as a self-appointed enlightened witness to the physical fact that underlies the psychic fact, testifying to the painful truth about the childhood origins of the mysterium tremendum. Unlike Job, who confesses that he had "uttered what I did not understand, things too wonderful for me, which I did not know" (Job 42:3), the psychologist of religion should not be reluctant to say that there is nothing here that is beyond human understanding—no great mystery—other than the fact that an adult would act violently against a child, whatever the provocation may be. For however one may rationalize it (and the child-rearing manuals that Miller cites are replete with such rationalizations), an act of violence *is* an act of violence, and we should not be surprised if it engenders hate—either directly toward the perpetrator of the deed or, if this proves too threatening because it may provoke greater violence, then indirectly, in the internalization of the object, now ambivalently experienced as both loved and hated, simultaneously.

It seems clear, from biographical accounts, that the latter alternative was Otto's way of dealing with it, and that even his partial insight into the reasons for his suffering — the introspections disclosed in *The Idea of the Holy* — was insufficient to forestall his efforts to destroy the hated object. All that was left, it seems, was "the thrill of fear" and the "mighty shudder that excites" as — poised for suicide — he gazed, eyes downcast, on the empty space between himself and the ground below.

Jesus as Internalized Selfobject

As we have seen, Freud suggests that suicide — the killing of the internalized hated object — can be averted if there is also a strong enough ego-self to resist the act of self-inflicted violence. In other words, Freud creates a scenario much like Jung's description of God as an antinomy or "totality of inner opposites," only now it is the human individual who is so conflicted. The question this raises in Otto's case is whether he might have found in religion a resource that would have strengthened his ego-self, enabling him, in Troeltsch's words, to "pull [himself] together" by attending to "the peace of mind and the strength of the inner man." Otto's discussion of Jesus as a numinous figure in his chapter "Divination in Primitive Christianity" is relevant to this question.

Otto notes that the center of all religious movements is the "holy man," and that "what sustains the movement is always the peculiar power of his personality, the special impression he makes on the bystander" (*IH,* 157). What matters is not the holy man's self-claims but the fact that others experience him as uniquely holy. Otto suggests that Jesus was perceived as holy by other individuals, and that

> certain of the slighter touches in the Synoptic portrait of Jesus confirm the fact expressly in particular cases. We may instance here the narratives already referred to of Peter's haul of fishes (Luke 5:8), and of the centurion of Capernaum (Matt. 8:8; Luke 7:6), which point to spontaneous responses of feeling when the holy is directly encountered in experience. Especially apt in this connection is the passage in Mark 10:32 — "and Jesus went before them: and they were amazed; and as they followed, they were afraid." This passage renders with supreme simplicity and force the immediate impression of the numinous that issued from the man Jesus, and no artistry of characterization could do it so powerfully as these few masterly and pregnant words [*IH,* 158].

Otto explores how the gospels took this simple perception of Jesus as holy man and elaborated it into claims for his superiority over the demonic world, for his messiahship, and so on. He also notes how Jesus had his own teachings, based on his belief in the heavenly Father. In the following chapter, "Divination in Christianity Today," he explores the church's further elaboration of Jesus into Christ, focusing on the fact that the "Cross becomes in an absolute sense the 'mirror of the eternal Father' . . . and not of the 'Father' alone — the highest rational interpretation of the holy — but of Holiness as such" (*IH*, 172). As a Christian theologian, Otto writes passionately about these later "divinations" of Christ's true meaning, especially as they focus on the Cross, as these bring together "the most exalted love with the most awe-inspiring 'wrath' of the numen" (*IH*, 173). Against the backdrop of the punishment scenario in early childhood, where terror and love are intimately and confusedly intermingled, this scene of the Cross reenacts the earlier scenario without any significant dynamic change.

But let us suppose that Otto had taken Troeltsch's advice and had set theology aside for the sake of his own psychological well-being, in favor of "views which are for your own personal use." In that case, a perfectly usable idea would have been "the slighter touches in the Synoptic portrait of Jesus," those that portrayed Jesus as a man who evoked "spontaneous responses of feeling when the holy is directly encountered in experience." In this slighter portrait of Jesus — closer, one assumes, to the historical Jesus — the dynamic may have been very different. This "holy man" might have been internalized as the "inner man" Otto needed to "pull himself together," as Troeltsch put it, and find "peace of mind." To one for whom the holy was too much caught up in the melodrama of love and terror, the Cross could bring no peace, only more of the same. But the internalization of the "holy man," so as to feel that one is no longer so fragmented but more internally whole, may have made a profound difference. Whereas the "Holy" may destroy a man, a little holiness may bring genuine inner peace.

In this alternative scenario, Jesus becomes, in the language of Heinz Kohut, an "idealized selfobject" (Kohut 1971, 1977). Selfobjects are objects from the external world that are experienced as part of the self and play a vital role in the maintenance of self-cohesiveness and self-empowerment. By way of illustration, Kohut tells how German Chancellor Otto von Bismarck's severe and chronic insomnia was cured by Dr. Schweninger, a physician considered a quack by the German medical profession of his day: "Schweninger once came to Bismarck's house at bedtime one evening and sat next to the statesman's bed until he had fallen asleep. When Bismarck awakened the next morning, after a full night's sleep, Schweninger was still sitting at his bedside, welcoming him, as it were, into the new day. I believe it would be difficult to find a more striking clinical instance demonstrating how, via a transference enactment, the fulfillment of a patient's need for an empathically responsive selfobject can restore the patient's ability to fall asleep" (1984, 19–20). Kohut criticizes Schweninger for making himself an indispensable member of Bismarck's entourage, serving "as Bismarck's selfobject instead of bringing about that increase of the new or reinforced psychic structure that would have given Bismarck the ability to soothe himself into falling asleep with the aid of other selfobjects he would have to provide for himself" (1984, 20).

Our concern, though, is not with therapeutic technique but with religious ideas and the need to make discriminations between them. There are religious ideas, like that of the mysterium tremendum, which reflect and exacerbate fears for one's very survival, and there are religious ideas, like that of the "holy Jesus" who enables us to maintain self-cohesiveness and a sense of self-empowerment, which are restorative, enabling us to lay ourselves down to sleep at night, secure in the thought that our souls are in his keeping and that we shall live to see a new day. If we come down on the side of the latter, eschewing the crucified Christ of the church's elaboration, this may be because in matters of religious belief, and for personal reasons of our own, we find ourselves taking the child's point of view.

*"A Little Sun in His Own Heart": The
Melancholic Vision in* Answer to Job

When Carl Gustav Jung (born 1875, died 1961) was writing *Answer to
Job* in the months prior to its publication in 1952, he knew that it would be a
controversial book, even for him, an author accustomed to having his work
criticized and dismissed. Its actual reception substantiated his anticipatory
fears. The book was widely condemned. Viewed from our perspective several
decades later, its condemnation, while not altogether surprising, is odd in one
respect, namely, that many intellectuals without formal biblical training have
actually been praised for writing on Job, a text for which they lacked the
requisite scholarly background. What was there about Jung's interpretation of
the Book of Job that made it so negatively provocative? How had he given
offense? What was the nature of that offense?

For the reader who comes to it from considerable prior reading of other
works by Jung, *Answer to Job* is not a particularly startling book. As he
himself points out, he was building on themes previously explored in *Aion,*
"especially the problems of Christ as a symbolic figure and of the antagonism
Christ-Antichrist" (1969, ix; hereafter *AJ*). Yet, in comparison to James's
Varieties, Otto's *Idea of the Holy,* and Erikson's *Young Man Luther, Answer
to Job* does have a certain oddness or eccentricity about it. Gerhard Adler, one
of the editors of the Bollingen edition of Jung's works, suggests in his editorial
note that the book was "the most intimate and at the same time the most

controversial book [Jung] has ever written. Without claiming rigid scientific status it contains the most profound insights born out of an intense feeling of inner obligation" (*AJ*, v). Adler quotes Jung's own comments in letters to friends that "the motive for my book was an increasingly urgent feeling of responsibility which in the end I could no longer withstand," and that "if there is anything like the spirit seizing one by the scruff of the neck, it is the way this book came into being" (*AJ*, v). Adler suggests that Jung wrote the book as a reflection on the international calamity (World War II) just past, a war that claimed the lives of millions. At the same time, and relatedly, it was an attempt, from intense personal experience, to make his peace with the "ambivalent God" who could allow such destruction. In this sense, it was a book written by a man who had fought with God throughout his life and now, nearing the end of his days on earth — he was 76 when *Answer to Job* was published — wanted to "make his peace" with his lifelong adversary.

How Jung envisioned making his peace with God is suggested in a letter to a friend: "I had to wrench myself free of God, so to speak, in order to find that unity in myself which God seeks through man. It is rather like that vision of Symeon the Theologian, who sought God in vain everywhere in the world, until God rose like *a little sun in his own heart*" (*AJ*, v–vi, my emphasis). In other words, in *Answer to Job* he will follow the same procedure God used to find internal unity, only in reverse: If God found his unity through humans, Jung will find inner unity by wrenching himself free of God. Only then will he experience God as one who rises "like a little sun" in his heart.

He is surely aware that this places him in a most paradoxical situation. As he writes, he feels as though he has been seized "by the scruff of the neck." On the other hand, his writing is for the larger purpose of wrenching himself "free of God." If God's relationship to humanity is an ambivalent one, Jung's relationship to God is also ambivalent. In fact, his metaphors are reminiscent of the child who, having been grabbed forcefully by an adult, kicks and squirms until he breaks free. But there is also a reversal of the parent-child dynamic in his vision of God as being like "a little sun" rising in his own heart. There is a wordplay in this description of God as "a little sun" (German: *Sonne*), for it can also suggest "a little son" (German: *Sohn*), as if to imply that in breaking free of God as an external force, he will experience God as an inner presence. Moreover, God will no longer be a threatening parent but be his very own offspring, or the son he had experienced himself to be before this struggle between child and adult ensued. I shall return to this point later in discussing Jung's interpretation of the vision of John the Evangelist in the Book of Revelation, the concluding section of *Answer to Job*.

In his autobiography, *Memories, Dreams, Reflections* (1961), composed with the assistance of Aniela Jaffe several years after the publication of *Answer to Job,* Jung comments on his childhood reaction, or lack thereof, to the biblical story of Job. He tells of rummaging through his father's library when he was a boy, reading whatever he could on God, the Trinity, spirit, and consciousness. He devoured books, "but came away none the wiser" (1961, 42). His conclusion was precisely the same as when he listened to his father's sermons: "They don't know either." In retrospect, however, he wishes he had been able to read the Book of Job without the conventional interpretation: "I even searched about in my father's Luther Bible. Unfortunately, the conventional 'edifying' interpretation of Job prevented me from taking a deeper interest in this book. I would have found consolation in it, especially in chapter 9, verses 30ff.: 'Though I wash myself with snow water . . . yet shalt thou plunge me in the mire' " (1961, 42). That is, he would have realized that someone besides himself had experienced God as evil and sinister (1961, 41) and therefore would not have thought of himself as so utterly alone and inwardly depraved. Having recently dreamed of God befouling his own cathedral (1961, 39), he felt he had gained a deep insight into the nature of God that his father, a clergyman steeped in the pietistic tradition, lacked. Yet the dream "was a shaming experience," and it evoked in him "an overwhelming urge to speak, not about that, but only to hint that there were some curious things about me which no one knew of. I wanted to find out whether other people had undergone similar experiences. I never succeeded in discovering so much as a trace of them in others" (1961, 41).

As time went on, Jung grew increasingly skeptical of his father's sermons, and "those of other parsons became acutely embarrassing to me" (1961, 46). He alone seemed to understand that God could be "terrible." In consequence, "my doubts and uneasiness increased whenever I heard my father in his emotional sermons speak of the 'good' God, praising God's love for man and exhorting man to love God in return. 'Does he really know what he is talking about?' I wondered. 'Could he have me, his son, put to the knife as a human sacrifice, like Isaac, or deliver him to an unjust court which would have him crucified like Jesus? No, he could not do that. Therefore in some cases he could not do the will of God, which can be absolutely terrible, as the Bible itself shows' " (1961, 46–47). Jung concluded that when his father exhorted people to obey God rather than man, he was speaking sincerely but thoughtlessly:

> Obviously we do not know the will of God at all, for if we did we would treat this central problem with awe, if only out of sheer fear of the over-powering God who can work His terrifying will on helpless human beings, as He had done to me. . . . The Old Testament, *and especially the book of Job, might*

have opened my eyes in this respect, but at that time I was not familiar enough with it. Nor had I heard anything of the sort in the instruction for confirmation which I was then receiving. The fear of God, which was of course mentioned, was considered antiquated, "Jewish," and long since superseded by the Christian message of God's love and goodness (1961, 47, my emphasis).

At a later point in *Memories, Dreams, Reflections,* Jung relates how he came to write *Answer to Job.* He explains that the "inner root" of the book is to be found in *Aion,* a book that "had dealt with the psychology of Christianity": "Job is a kind of prefiguration of Christ. The link between them is the idea of suffering. Christ is the suffering servant of God, and so was Job. In the case of Christ the sins of the world are the cause of suffering, and the suffering of the Christian is the general answer. This leads inescapably to the question: Who is responsible for these sins? In the final analysis it is God who created the world and its sins, and who therefore became Christ in order to suffer the fate of humanity" (1961, 216).

In *Aion,* Jung had made reference to the bright and dark sides of the divine image and had discussed the "wrath of God," the commandment to fear God, and the petition in the Lord's Prayer "Lead us not into temptation," which implies that God is certainly capable of leading us into sin if he so chooses. In a similar way, "the ambivalent God-image plays a crucial part in the Book of Job. Job expects that God will, in a sense, stand by him against God; in this we have a picture of God's tragic contradictoriness. This was the main theme of *Answer to Job*" (1961, 216).

If the "inner root" of *Answer to Job* was to be found in *Aion,* Jung notes there were "outside forces, too, which impelled me to write this book" (1961, 216). Foremost among these were the many questions raised by the public and his own patients which made him feel that he must express himself more clearly "about the religious problems of modern man."

> For years I had hesitated to do so, because I was fully aware of the storm I would be unleashing. But at last I could not help being gripped by the problem, in all its urgency and difficulty, and I found myself compelled to give an answer. I did so in the form in which the problem had presented itself to me, that is, as an experience charged with emotion. I chose this form deliberately, in order to avoid giving the impression that I was bent on proclaiming some eternal truth. My *Answer To Job* was meant to be no more than the utterance of a single individual, who hopes and expects to arouse some thoughtfulness in his public. I was far from wanting to enunciate a metaphysical truth. Yet the theologians tax me with that very thing, because theological thinkers are so used to dealing with eternal truths that they know no other kinds [1961, 216–17].

If Jung's previous writings and desire to contribute to public religious discussion were major influences for writing the book, a more personal catalyst was that "the problem of Job in all its ramifications had likewise been foreshadowed in a dream" (1961, 217). In the dream, he was paying a visit to his long-deceased father, who was living in an inn at a spa in the country and was the custodian of a crypt containing the remains of many great personages who had died there. Besides his custodial position, his father was also "a distinguished scholar in his own right—which he had never been in his lifetime." Jung met him in his study, where a psychiatrist and the psychiatrist's son were also present:

> I do not know whether I had asked a question or whether my father wanted to explain something of his own accord, but in any case he fetched a big Bible down from a shelf, a heavy folio volume like the Merian Bible in my library. The Bible my father held was bound in shiny fishskin. He opened it at the Old Testament—I guessed that he turned to the Pentateuch—and began interpreting a certain passage. He did this so swiftly and so learnedly that I could not follow him. I noted only that what he said betrayed a vast amount of variegated knowledge, the significance of which I dimly apprehended but could not properly judge or grasp. I saw that Dr. Y. understood nothing at all, and his son began to laugh. They thought that my father was going off the deep end and what he said was simply senile prattle. But it was quite clear to me that it was not due to morbid excitement, and that there was nothing silly about what he was saying. On the contrary, his argument was so intelligent and so learned that we in our stupidity simply could not follow it. It dealt with something extremely important which fascinated him. That was why he was speaking with such intensity; his mind was flooded with profound ideas. I was annoyed and thought it was a pity that he had to talk in the presence of three such idiots as we [1961, 217–18].

The scene changed, and he and his father were in front of the house, which his father said was haunted. They entered the house and climbed a narrow staircase to the second floor. From there, Jung suddenly saw a steep flight of stairs ascending to a spot high up on the wall, at the top of which was a small door. His father said, "Now I will lead you into the highest presence." His father knelt down and touched his forehead to the floor. Jung imitated him, though for some reason he could not bring his forehead quite down to the floor: "But at least I had made the gesture with him." In the solitary room at the top of the ascending stairs was Uriah, the general whom King David had shamefully betrayed in order to take possession of Bathsheba, his wife. With this, the dream ended.

Jung suggests that this dream foreshadowed his *Answer to Job* in two important respects. First, there was the fact that Uriah lived above the room on the second floor, which appeared to be a throne room. Thus, "even higher than David stands his guiltless victim, his loyal general Uriah, whom he abandoned to the enemy. Uriah is a prefiguration of Christ, the god-man who was abandoned by God. 'My God, my God, why hast thou forsaken me?' On top of that, David had 'taken unto himself' Uriah's wife. Only later did I understand what this allusion to Uriah signified: not only was I forced to speak publicly, and very much to my detriment, about the ambivalence of the God-image in the Old Testament, but also, my wife would be taken from me by death" (1961, 219–20). He realized that "these were the things that awaited me, hidden in the unconscious. I had to submit to this fate," the fate revealed to him by his father.

The second foreshadowing of *Answer to Job* concerned Jung's inability to touch his forehead to the floor in imitation of his father's submission. What did this signify? It meant that "something in me was saying, 'All very well, but not entirely.' Something in me was defiant and determined not to be a dumb fish: and if there were not something of the sort in free men, no Book of Job would have been written several hundred years before the birth of Christ. Man has always had some mental reservation, even in the face of divine decrees. Otherwise, where would be his freedom? And what would be the use of that freedom if it could not threaten Him who threatens it?" (1961, 220). In short, "The dream discloses a thought and a premonition that have long been present in humanity: the idea of the creature that surpasses its creator by a small but decisive factor" (1961, 220).

Thus, the desire to continue explorations begun in a previous work, the questions of inquirers, and his dream of his father were all important factors in his decision to write *Answer to Job*. These factors, together with his advanced age, suggest that, for Jung personally, this was a book that would make or break him. In writing it, he would be placing himself in the position of Job. Like Job, he was determined to have it out with God, come what may. This would be his most personal book, a kind of confession, and anticonfession, of faith.

Taking the Step from Which Otto Recoiled

As we turn to the text itself, we may appropriately begin with the title: *Answer to Job*. Jung uses the phrase "answer to Job" in his discussion of Christ's despairing cry on the Cross, "My God, my God, why hast thou forsaken me?" In the crucifixion, Christ's "human nature attains divinity; at the moment God experiences what it means to be a mortal man and drinks to the dregs what he made his faithful servant Job suffer. *Here is given the answer to Job,* and, clearly, this supreme moment is as divine as it is human, as 'eschatological' as it is 'psychological.' And at this moment, too, where one can feel the human being so absolutely, the divine myth is present in full force. And both mean one and the same thing" (*AJ,* 46, my emphasis).

In other words, God's answer to Job's charges against God is that God will incarnate himself and take on human form, suffering as humans suffer. This means that the "answer" Job received from the whirlwind was not God's final response but only the beginning of a long process in which God, embarrassed by the truth of Job's accusations against him, determined to redeem himself in the eyes of his faithful servant. Through this long, self-remedial process, God's arrogant blustering against his human opponent would be replaced by genuine insight into his own inner character, including the evil within himself of which he had previously been oblivious. Christ's death on the Cross is a significant event in this process of divine self-recognition, but only a first step. As the last half of *Answer to Job* reveals, there are further developments in the process of God's self-recognition, especially as envisioned in the Book of Revelation, though also in the recent promulgation of the new dogma of the assumption of the Virgin Mary into heaven. Because the whole thread of Christian doctrine, with its ongoing development, may be viewed as an "answer to Job," the Book of Job is an early "landmark in the long historical development of a divine drama" (*AJ,* 3).

With regard to Jung's argument that the Book of Job is about God's ambivalent inner character, *Answer to Job* may usefully be read in relation to Otto's *Idea of the Holy.* Jung does not cite Otto's text; by this point in his career he is more influenced by his own earlier writings, such as *Aion,* than by the writings of others. So *Answer to Job* is not a direct response to Otto. On the other hand, as I pointed out in the previous chapter, Jung does take up the issue of the numinous, and he gives it a more radical interpretation than Otto does. Otto intended his own book to be phenomenological; he would not attempt to account for the holy on psychological, sociological, or historical grounds. As we have seen, he was especially wary of the dangers of psychologism, of accounting for the divine on the basis of human need. Of course, we would expect nothing less — and nothing more — from a Christian theologian who was concerned with asserting the objective reality of God as one who exists independently of human minds.

Jung takes precisely the opposite approach. As a psychologist, he cannot speak for the "nonpsychical" reality of God, but this does not matter, as the fact that something exists in the human psyche makes it real. After all, it is a psychic *fact.* Contrasting physical and psychic facts, and claiming that psychic facts, unlike physical facts, "cannot be contested and need no proof," he asserts that "religious statements are of this type. They refer *without exception* to things that cannot be established as physical facts. If they did not do this, they would inevitably fall into the category of the natural sciences. Taken as referring to anything physical, they make no sense whatever, and science would dismiss them as non-experienceable" (*AJ*, xii, my emphasis). Thus, "the psyche is an autonomous factor," and its "processes are not accessible to physical perception but demonstrate their existence through the confessions of the psyche" (*AJ*, xii).

Jung does not deny the existence of God independently of human minds, but he stresses that all we can know is the human psyche and what it perceives. However, like Otto, he insists on the inappropriateness of limiting ourselves to that which is rational only: "Although our whole world of religious ideas consists of anthropomorphic images that could never stand up to rational criticism, *we should never forget that they are based on numinous archetypes,* i.e., on an emotional foundation which is unassailable by reason. We are dealing with psychic facts which logic can overlook but not eliminate" (*AJ*, xiii, my emphasis).

What makes *Answer to Job* a more radical book than *The Idea of the Holy* is that Otto stops short of ascribing *evil* to God. Otto is interested in the holy as a *premoral* phenomenon. The holy terrifies, but this does not mean that the holy is evil. Although we bear the brunt of its terror, this has nothing to do with our moral guilt, only with the fact of our abject creaturehood. Conversely, Otto is critical of theologians, including Luther, who suggested in some of his writings that God might be above the law, as though God, when viewed from the human point of view, might be amoral.

Since Otto virtually abandoned his interest in the holy in later writings, is it possible that he had stared down into the abyss that Job—and Jung—had stared into, and backed away in horror? In ascribing to the holy the capacity to terrorize, had he come too dangerously close to saying that God has a capacity for evil? And if, unlike Jung's father, Otto would not dismiss the "wrath" of God as an Old Testament idea that was superseded in the New Testament, did he not nevertheless take refuge in the Christian theologian's recourse to "eternal truth" and conclude that, ontologically speaking, it simply cannot be said that God is an agent of evil? In other words, Otto was more courageous than Jung's father, but he was, after all, a Christian theologian, and this meant that he could not entertain the idea that, whatever else it may also be, the holy has an evil aspect.

Jung, who was surely aware of Otto's by then classic text, pursued the matter further. He wanted to offer an explanation for the holy as experienced by Job, and he did so by conjoining Otto's idea of the numinous and his own concept of the archetype, suggesting that our anthropomorphic images of God "are based on numinous archetypes, i.e., on an emotional foundation which is unassailable by reason" (*AJ*, xiii). Unlike Otto, Jung does not resist ascribing evil to God; he identifies Satan as a son of God and shows that, even as Adam and Eve succumbed to Satan's wily discourse, so did Yahweh himself. Furthermore, when confronted with his evil nature by Job, "a man who stands firm, who clings to his rights until he is compelled to give way to brute force" (*AJ*, 34), God set forth on a long and arduous task of redeeming himself by replacing his penchant for exercising brute force with a self-possessed wisdom: "The approach of Sophia betokens a new creation. But this time it is not the world that is to be changed; rather it is God who intends to change his own nature" (*AJ*, 35).

Otto laments the fact that later developments in the history of the holy were to take it in a *moral* direction, away from its emphasis on human creaturehood toward a focus on human sinfulness. Jung, however, believes that these developments are important, because they tell us about a certain progression in the evolution of God himself. The moral issue was always there, but the question is primarily, Is God capable of evil? and only secondarily, Is man a sinner? The story of Job tells us that God is indeed capable of evil — mistreating Job — and Job, with perfect justification, wants to know why God does evil to those who have placed their trust in him. As a psychologist and not a theologian, Jung challenges the holy as Otto understands it, arguing that there is something profoundly false about the holy as it was disclosed to Job, for the moral culpability in this case is on the side of God for allowing himself to be deceived by Satan and then to deny that he had wronged Job. Can the Book of Job be read in any way other than this? If this is *not* the point of the Book of Job, why, pray tell, was it ever written?

The Incarnation and the Suppression of Divine Evil

In Jung's reading of the history of the holy, by the time Christ appears on the scene, God has already gone through an important self-remedial process. Through the efforts of Sophia (or Wisdom), God has become a wiser, less power-invested deity. He is capable of greater self-reflection and exhibits genuine empathy with humans. The very fact that his second-born son (Satan being the firstborn) has assumed human form is itself testimony to God's empathy with humans for, through his second son, God will share in human joys and sorrows.

But the dilemma for Christ is that he doubts his father's total regeneration.

On the one hand, "as a result of the partial neutralization of Satan, Yahweh identifies with his light aspect and becomes the good God and loving father. He has not lost his wrath and can still mete out punishment, but he does it with justice. Cases like the Job tragedy are apparently no longer to be expected. He proves himself benevolent and gracious. He shows mercy to the sinful children of men and is defined as love itself" (*AJ*, 48). On the other hand, while affirming his complete confidence in his father and oneness with him, Christ "cannot help inserting the cautious petition—and warning—into the Lord's prayer: 'Lead us not into temptation, but deliver us from evil.' . . . The possibility that Yahweh . . . might yet revert to his former ways is not so remote that one need not keep one eye open for it" (*AJ*, 49). Christ himself "considers it appropriate to remind his father of his destructive inclinations towards mankind and to beg him to desist from them. Judged by any human standards it is after all unfair, indeed extremely immoral, to entice little children into doing things that might be dangerous for them, simply in order to test their moral stamina!" (*AJ*, 49).

Because this petition appears in the very prayer that Christ taught his disciples to pray, his confidence in his father's good character becomes somewhat questionable, and, in Jung's view, these doubts are well founded: "One must admit that it would be contrary to all reasonable expectations to suppose that a God who, for all his lavish generosity, had been subject to intermittent but devastating fits of rage ever since time began could suddenly become the epitome of everything good. Christ's unadmitted but none the less evident doubt in this respect is confirmed in the New Testament, and particularly in the Apocalypse. There Yahweh again delivers himself up to an unheard-of fury of destruction against the human race" (*AJ*, 49).

How are we to reconcile this new reaction of fury with "the behavior of a loving father, whom we would expect to glorify his creation with patience and love?" (*AJ*, 49). Jung guesses that when one attempts to secure an absolute and final victory for good, it leads to a dangerous accumulation of evil and hence to eventual catastrophe. If God is a personality, this means that he is a complex mix of positive and negative characteristics. The single-minded affirmation of his good traits and denial of his evil ones will eventually lead to an explosion. If God is unable to maintain control over his evil side, it will suddenly erupt with an incalculable destructive force. In Jung's view, the Book of Revelation envisions this destructive episode, God's reign of terror.

Thus, Jung suggests that the incarnation, while reflecting God's good intentions, also created a "dissociation" within God himself. The fact that he was acting as "the good father" made him oblivious to a very different truth: that he had got himself into a fearful dissociation through his incarnation. "Where, for instance, did his darkness go — that darkness by means of which Satan always manages to escape his well-earned punishment? Does he think he is completely changed and that his amorality has fallen from him? Even his 'light' son, Christ, did not quite trust him in this respect" (*AJ*, 70).

Most puzzling of all is that "this supremely good God" allows the purchase of his grace through an act of human sacrifice and, worse, through the killing of his own son: "This is an unsufferable incongruity which modern man can no longer swallow, for he must be blind if he does not see the glaring light it throws on the divine character, giving the lie to all talk about love and the Summum Bonum" (*AJ*, 68).

John's Self-Identification with the Divine Son

This reflection on the incarnation brings Jung to the Revelation of St. John, the next stage in the history of God's self-development. Assuming that the Book of Revelation was written by the author of the Epistles of John, Jung suggests that these revelations erupted out of the unconscious to compensate for the one-sidedness of John's "individual consciousness" as reflected in the Epistles' affirmation of a God who is light and in whom there is "no darkness at all" (I John 1:15). In the Epistles, John is overly certain that God is light and love, and he is therefore unusually susceptible to the irruption into consciousness of the counterposition, that God is capable of dark and fear-inspiring deeds. The letters that Christ commands John to write to the seven churches in Asia (Revelation 1:4, 3:22) are filled with terrible threats, including a massacre of the children of Thyatira that is all too reminiscent of the massacre of the children of Bethlehem from which the Christ child was miraculously saved. As Jung notes, "This apocalyptic 'Christ' behaves rather like a bad-tempered, power-conscious 'boss' who very much resembles the 'shadow' of a love-preaching bishop" (*AJ*, 74–75).

The Christ who reappears in Revelation does not behave at all like an innocent victim. On the contrary, in place of "the meek lamb who lets himself be led unresistingly to the slaughter" there is "the aggressive and irascible ram whose rage can at last be vented" (*AJ*, 75). Jung does not see any profound "metaphysical mystery" in this radically altered image of Christ. Rather, it is

the outburst of long pent-up negative feelings such as are frequently observed in people who strive for perfection. We can take it as certain that the author of the Epistles of John made every effort to practice what he preached to his fellow Christians. For this purpose he had to shut out all negative feelings, and, thanks to a helpful lack of self-reflection, he was able to forget them. But though they disappeared from the conscious level they continued to rankle beneath the surface, and in the course of time spun an elaborate web of resentments and vengeful thoughts which then burst upon consciousness in the form of a revelation [*AJ*, 76].

The terrible tragedy is that this outburst of emotions releases an act of divine terror contradicting "all ideas of Christian humility, tolerance, love of your neighbor and your enemies, and makes nonsense of a loving father in heaven and rescuer of mankind" (*AJ*, 76). All the good that had been done through the incarnation is undone in this "veritable orgy of hatred, wrath, vindictiveness, and blind destructive fury that revels in fantastic images of terror," overwhelming the world "which Christ had just endeavored to restore to the original state of innocence and loving communion with God" (*AJ*, 76).

Jung emphasizes that while John, whose personality betrays certain paranoid features, may have been unusually susceptible to a terrible vision of this nature, "it is not the conscious mind of John that thinks up these fantasies" (*AJ*, 87). Rather, "they come to him in a violent 'revelation,'" and "fall upon him involuntarily with an unexpected vehemence and with an intensity [that] far transcends anything we could expect as compensation of a somewhat one-sided attitude of consciousness" (*AJ*, 88). The "compensating dreams" of believing Christians whom Jung has met are quite weak in comparison to "the brutal impact with which the opposites collide in John's visions" (*AJ*, 88). Only mental psychoses rival these visions of John's in their emotional impact and power. But his visions are not psychotic delusions, for they "are not confused enough; they are too consistent, not subjective and scurrilous enough" (*AJ*, 88). These visions are not those of an unbalanced psychopath but those of a "passionately religious person with an otherwise well-ordered psyche," and they are therefore to be considered true revelations. It was precisely because John loved God that he, like Job, saw "the fierce and terrible side of Yahweh," and thus it was revealed to him that his gospel of love in his Epistles was one-sided and needed to be supplemented with the gospel of fear: "*God can be loved but must be feared*" (*AJ*, 88, his emphasis).

The Sun-woman and Her Divine Son

Jung, however, points out that even in the Book of Revelation there are mitigating visions that counter its dominant visions of a God whose terror knows no bounds. Especially noteworthy is the vision of the sun-woman in chapter 12. This vision is "altogether out of context" with what the Evangelist has seen so far. A woman clothed in the sun appears, with the moon under her feet and a crown of twelve stars on her head. She is experiencing the pangs of birth, and before her stands a great red dragon who threatens to devour her child. Jung notes that whereas the previous visions give the impression of having been revised, rearranged, and embellished, this one feels "original" and "not intended for any educational purpose" (*AJ, 76*). She is "a woman," not a goddess and not an eternal virgin immaculately conceived. Nor is the birth of her child "to be confused with the birth of the Christchild which had occurred long before under quite different circumstances" (*AJ, 77*).

While the story of Hagar and Ishmael may be a "prefiguration" of this vision, and John may have realized that his vision was also reminiscent of the myth of Leto and Apollo, Jung is persuaded that the vision arose out of John's unconscious, and that it reflects his own unconscious identification with the "divine child." Since Christ was already identified as the divine child, John would have had no difficulty in subsequently making a conscious association between the child in his vision and Christ. Nor would it have been difficult for him to identify the woman as a goddess (for example, the cosmic Sophia), because, as represented in the vision, she was obviously "a woman in heaven." But Jung contends that the vision as it first appeared in John's unconscious mind was an unconscious identification with the divine child. In a profound sense, John himself was the divine child. Thus, if the vision "were a modern dream one would not hesitate to interpret the birth of the divine child as the coming to consciousness of the self" (*AJ, 80*).

On the other hand, if John's Christ image "has turned into a savage avenger who no longer bears any real resemblance to a savior," then what his Christian consciousness does to this vision of the sun-woman and her child is to assimilate "the new-born man-child to the figure of the avenger, thereby blurring his mythological character as the lovely and lovable divine youth" who is so much a part of Greek mythology. "The enchanting springlike beauty of this divine youth is one of those pagan values which we miss so sorely in Christianity, and particularly in the somber world of the apocalypse—the indescribable morning glory of a day in spring, which after the deathly stillness of winter causes the earth to put forth and blossom, gladdens the heart of man and makes him believe in a kind and loving God" (*AJ, 81*).

Thus, in its original, unconscious form, the vision attests in its own way to the new birth of spring after the destruction of winter, and it evokes feelings and perceptions of a kind and loving God. In Jung's view, John's assimilation of this beautiful vision into the dark vision that pervades the Book of Revelation is unfortunate, but this later assimilation should not be allowed to cloud the fact that the vision itself signifies the birth of the divine child within John himself. Key to Jung's refusal to accept John's assimilation of the divine-child motif into his vision of Christ the avenger was his clinical observation that whenever a child appears in dreams, myths, and visions, it symbolizes new birth, not destruction and despair. He had made this point years earlier in his essay "The Psychology of the Child Archetype" (Jung and Kerenyi 1969, 70–100).[1]

In the concluding pages of *Answer to Job*, Jung focuses on the implications of "the dark side of the Apocalypse" for humanity today, which has "experienced things so unheard of and so staggering that the question of whether such things are in any way reconcilable with the idea of a good God has become burningly topical" (*AJ*, 91). He refers here to the devastations of World War II and new forms of destruction, such as the atom bomb and chemical warfare. In this situation, we are confronted with "a paradoxical idea of God" as one *who can be loved but must also be feared.* When so confronted, one finds oneself "in the situation of the author of Revelation, who we may suppose was a convinced Christian" (*AJ*, 91). How does this author endure the intolerable contradiction in the nature of the deity? While we may know nothing of his "conscious decision" about how he might continue to relate to a deity far more complex than the picture he gave of him in his Epistles, perhaps, suggests Jung, "we may find some clue in the vision of the sun-woman in travail" (*AJ*, 91).

For such a clue, Jung proposes that we consider the dreams of contemporary patients and draw on the experience of analysts who have recognized that "symbols of a reconciling and unitive nature do in fact turn up in dreams, the most frequent being the motif of the child-hero," who is precisely the figure we meet in the Apocalypse as the son of the sun-woman (*AJ*, 92). "This motif appears again in corresponding form and in corresponding situations in the dreams of modern man . . . [and therefore] the doctor, often very much against his will, is forced by the problems of psychoneurosis to look more closely at the religious problem" (*AJ*, 92).

The New Vision of the Divine Son

What, then, do contemporary patients' dreams of the "child-hero" tell us? What do they mean, religiously speaking? Noting that he is 76 years old and only now "catechizing" himself regarding the nature of those "ruling ideas" that decide our ethical behavior and have such a powerful influence on our practical life, Jung suggests that the vision of the sun-woman reveals the conflict into which Christianity inevitably leads, and under whose burden humanity has groaned, that "*God wanted to become man, and still wants to*" (*AJ*, 93, his emphasis).

But how, and in what form? If God, through Christ, has already incarnated himself as the unconscious child, Jung, citing Christ's own declaration "Except ye become as little children," suggests that the form God now wants to assume is of "the boy who is born from the maturity of the adult man" (*AJ*, 95). It was no mere coincidence that the vision of the sun-woman was that of an old man, one who could identify the divine child as himself. Henceforth, God will incarnate himself in the souls of mature men, though in the form of the boys whom they once were. These boys will restore the "indescribable morning glory of a day in spring, which after the deathly stillness of winter causes the earth to put forth and blossom, gladdens the heart of man and makes him believe in a kind and loving God" (*AJ*, 81).

Jung notes that a visible sign of this new dispensation, prefigured in the Book of Revelation, is that Roman Catholicism has recently promulgated the dogma of Mary's physical assumption into heaven. This suggests that she is now on a par with Christ, indeed, that she is the bride of Christ and hence the mistress of heaven even as he is mediator there. However, what this also implies is "the future birth of the divine child, who, in accord with the divine trend towards incarnation, will choose as his birthplace the empirical man" (*AJ*, 105). The new child symbolizes the wholeness of the self, its integration of the opposites that inhere in the human person, who after all is created in the image of God. This wholeness is very different from the self-abjection with which the Book of Job concludes, the portrayal of Job's acknowledgment of his insignificance before the overwhelming power of God. The self is no longer the quaking child before a threatening father but the mature man who is protective of the divine child inside him. Although this new self is no less conscious of his limitations, he is now aware of "his own limited ego *before the One who dwells within him,* whose form has no knowable boundaries, who encompasses him on all sides, fathomless as the abysms of the earth and vast as the sky" (*AJ*, 108, my emphasis). Thus, *Answer to Job,* like the Bible itself, ends on a visionary note. God's personal history is not concluded but continues its evolution into a new and uncharted future, and Jung looks within himself to discover its newest manifestation.

Childhood Traumas and Corresponding Visions

So far I have said nothing about how *Answer to Job* might fit the theme of melancholy. To address this, I want briefly to harken back to my chapter on Rudolf Otto, where I noted that Jung did not make any explicit connection between Job's encounter with God in the whirlwind and childhood trauma, in spite of the fact that his description of this encounter brings to mind episodes in which the child feigns remorse in order to placate an angry, emotionally volatile parent. I ascribed Jung's failure to make such a connection to his insistence on a clear differentiation between "physical" and "psychical" facts, a differentiation designed to mollify critics who might otherwise claim that he was attempting to "psychologize" the deity away.

Jung insists at the beginning and again at the very end of *Answer to Job* that his intention is not to reduce external realities to mental states. On the contrary, the very fact that *Answer to Job* is an exploration of the numinous *archetype* proves this is not his intention. While "there are no psychic conditions which could be observed *through introspection* outside the human being," and therefore "the behavior of the archetypes cannot be investigated at all without the interaction of the observing consciousness," we must nonetheless "concede to the archetype a definite measure of independence" of consciousness even as we accord "consciousness a degree of creative freedom proportionate to its scope" (*AJ*, 108, his emphasis). In other words, both archetype and consciousness are two "relatively autonomous factors" (*AJ*, 108). If, in turn, the archetypes persist in the collective unconscious of humanity, their contents are not reducible to the personal unconscious of individuals. Thus, John's vision is much more than a reflection of his own individual psyche, as its source exists outside himself.

However, while we cannot but admire Jung's effort to avoid psychologism, the risk he runs is that visions like that of the author of the Book of Revelation will be accorded a special epistemic status precisely because they are said to "transcend" or "exist independently of" the visionary's personal psychopathologies. What he sacrifices in this effort to avoid the charge of psychologism *in this particular case* is the opportunity to explore the dynamic relationship between the melancholic condition and the desire for visions of wholeness.

In a critically important passage for my argument here, Jung makes this observation: "The destruction of all beauty and of all life's joys, the unspeakable suffering of the whole creation that once sprung from the hand of a lavish Creator, would be, for a feeling heart, *an occasion for deepest melancholy* (*AJ*, 84). Yet, he goes on to note, John's vindictiveness and lust for destruction have gone to such lengths that he not only envisions but even cries out for such total destruction. This means that one side of John's psyche has gone beyond melancholy; it can no longer be touched by melancholy because his hatred is so great. However, this also explains why his vision of the sun-woman is so important and so inwardly powerful, as this vision suggests that there continues to beat in John a feeling heart, that somewhere deep in his personal unconscious persists a longing for beauty amid the destruction, and that his melancholia is precisely the source of his ability to envision "the indescribable morning glory of a day in spring, which after the deathly stillness of winter causes the earth to put forth and blossom" (*AJ*, 81). The vision arises from, not in spite of, his melancholy.

Of course, my primary interest here is not with the personal unconscious of the Evangelist but with that of Jung himself, and especially with the relationship between his own melancholia, which he does not personally acknowledge in *Answer to Job*, and his vision of God as "a little sun" arising in his own heart. The reader of *Answer to Job* can hardly ignore the fact that Jung and the Evangelist are old men, and that Jung is quite aware of their similarity in this respect. His statement about his own advanced age ("I myself have reached the age of seventy-six") precedes by only a page his observation that the Evangelist "had lived long and resolutely enough to be able to cast a glance into the distant future" (*AJ, 93*). Yet there is much more to Jung's personal identification with the Evangelist than their similarity in age, and the Evangelist's vision of the sun-mother is especially important in regard to this deeper, more profound identification.

As I have been arguing throughout this study, melancholy is rooted in the boy's loss of the perfect mother, the mother whose love for him is unconditional and whose ability to care for him is uncompromised. As Jung reveals in *Memories, Dreams, Reflections*, published posthumously in 1961 but begun in 1957 when he was 82, his emotional loss of his mother was unusually traumatic.

At the beginning of *Memories, Dreams, Reflections*, he portrays himself as an adventurous boy whose mother did all she could do to rein him in. For example, there is this early memory:

> Still another memory comes up: strangers, bustle, excitement. The maid comes running and exclaims, "The fishermen have found a corpse — came down the Falls — they want to put it in the washhouse!" My father says, "Yes, yes." I want to see the dead body at once. My mother holds me back and sternly forbids me to go into the garden. When all the men had left, I quickly stole into the garden to the washhouse. But the door was locked. I went around the house; at the back there was an open drain running down the slope, and I saw blood and water trickling out. I found this extraordinarily interesting. At that time I was not yet four years old [1961, 7–8].

This memory suggests that Jung was not inhibited by his mother's sternness but found ways to get around it. We saw something of the same evasion in his account of Job's seeming compliance with God. Jung did not disobey her openly but instead waited for his chance to disobey her when she was no longer present. But this episode involving his curiosity about a dead body is only the tip of the iceberg. Deeper and more pervasive were anxiety dreams that kept him awake at night and were connected to his emotional loss of his mother under very unfortunate circumstances.

The following memory dates back to when he was "not yet four": "Yet another image: I am restive, feverish, unable to sleep. My father carries me in his arms, paces up and down, singing his old student songs. I particularly remember one I was especially fond of and which always used to soothe me, '*Alles schweige, jeder neige. . . .*' The beginning went something like that. To this day I can remember my father's voice, singing over me in the stillness of the night" (1961, 8).

Why was it his father and not his mother who came in to soothe him? His further recollections of this episode provide the key: "I was suffering, so my mother told me afterward, from general eczema. Dim intimations of trouble in my parents' marriage hovered around me. My illness, in 1878, must have been connected with a temporary separation of my parents. My mother spent several months in a hospital in Basel, and presumably her illness had something to do with the difficulty in the marriage. An aunt of mine, who was a spinster and some twenty years older than my mother, took care of me" (1961, 8).

He recalls being "deeply troubled by my mother's being away" and remembers that from then on "I always felt mistrustful when the word 'love' was spoken. The feeling I associated with 'woman' was for a long time that of innate unreliability. 'Father,' on the other hand, meant reliability and—powerlessness. That is the handicap I started off with. Later, these early impressions were revised: I have trusted men friends and been disappointed by them, and I have mistrusted women and was not disappointed" (1961, 8). Clearly, his mistrust of women arose from the absence of his mother, and his suspicions of 'love' were associated with her unreliability.

Besides his aunt, the family maid also looked after him while his mother was away. He can still "remember her picking me up and laying my head against her shoulder. She had black hair and an olive complexion, and was quite different from my mother. I can see, even now, her hairline, her throat, with its darkly pigmented skin, and her ear. All this seemed to me very strange and yet strangely familiar. It was as though she belonged not to my family but only to me, as though she was connected in some way with other mysterious things I could not understand" (1961, 8).

He has another memory image from the period of his parents' separation. This is of a "young, very pretty and charming girl with blue eyes and fair hair leading me, on a blue autumn day, under golden maple and chestnut trees along the Rhine below the Falls, near Worth castle. The sun is shining through the foliage, and yellow leaves lie on the ground. This girl later became my mother-in-law. She admired my father. I did not see her again until I was twenty-one years old" (1961, 9).

His mother's absence was temporary, but the problems in his parents' marriage continued after her return. When he was seven or eight years old, he recalls,

> The nocturnal atmosphere had begun to thicken. All sorts of things were happening at night, things incomprehensible and alarming. My parents were sleeping apart. I slept in my father's room. From the door to my mother's room came frightening influences. At night Mother was strange and mysterious. One night I saw coming from her door a faintly luminous, indefinite figure whose head detached itself from the neck and floated along in front of it, in the air, like a little moon. Immediately another head was produced and again detached itself. This process was repeated six or seven times. I had anxiety dreams of things that were now small, now large. For instance, I saw a tiny ball at a great distance; gradually it approached, growing steadily into a monstrous and suffocating object. Or I saw telegraph wires with birds sitting on them, and the wires grew thicker and thicker and my fear greater until the terror awoke me [1961, 18].

The fact that his traumatic experiences began when he was three years old, or "not yet four," is most significant. It means that he had become accustomed to his mother's love prior to the separation caused by her hospitalization, and, indeed, the early pages of *Memories, Dreams, Reflections* make no mention of siblings who might have been rivals for her love and affection. In this regard, his earliest years were very different from those of both James and Otto but, as we shall see in the following chapter, similar to Erikson's early years. That he experienced prolonged separation from his mother at the age of three also has bearing on his response, as an old man, to the Evangelist's vision of the sun-woman and her child. When the sun-woman brought forth a male child, he was taken up to God and his throne, while she fled into the wilderness, "where she has a place prepared by God, in which to be nourished for one thousand two hundred and sixty days" (Revelation 12:5–6). This is roughly three-and-a-half years.

But there are other reflections of his parents' separation in the vision, as the vision indicates that the sun-woman's male child was threatened by a dragon that sought to devour him. This was why he was taken up to God and his throne, while his mother fled into the wilderness. As we have seen, it was his father who lifted Jung up and comforted him in his mother's absence, and the fact that his father was a clergyman would reinforce this connection between his father and God. Meanwhile, his mother's mental illness brought on by difficulties in his parents' marriage may be construed as both a physical and an emotional flight into the wilderness. Whether she actually was mentally ill is, of course, open to question. As Mary Elene Wood points out, it was very common in the nineteenth century for husbands to place their wives in mental asylums when marital problems arose (Wood 1994). Was Jung's mother hospitalized against her will? Jung does not say. But the vision of the Evangelist may, in any event, accurately capture the perceptions of the three-year-old boy, who would view her absence as taking flight for her own protection, leaving her son to fend for himself.

Yet, on another level, the vision of the sun-woman in Revelation is the very antithesis of Jung's experience of his mother, as his childhood images of her are overwhelmingly nocturnal. He identifies her with the terrors of the night. The person with whom he associates the sun is the girl who subsequently became his mother-in-law. In noting that the girl greatly admired his father, he implies that, as far as marital harmony was concerned, he would have been better off had *she* been his mother. This fantasy is more or less realized in his interpretation of the recent promulgation of the dogma of Mary's assumption into heaven, for Mary, in spite of the fact that she is Christ's mother, becomes his bride. She is the "sun-mother," while his own mother is associated with nocturnal terrors, including her own decapitation.

Thus, the promulgation of the doctrine of Mary's assumption into heaven, a Roman Catholic teaching that infuriated Protestants at the time, is viewed by Jung as a sign of something new. Perhaps his receptivity to this new doctrine as a further development in the reconciliation of God and humanity was due, at least in part, to its resonance with his childhood desire to be another woman's son. His associations of other women, never his mother, with acts of caring and love is revealing of this desire. He does not directly blame her for his nocturnal anxieties and terrors, but he does say that he "was deeply troubled by my mother's being away" and "from then on, I always felt mistrustful when the word 'love' was spoken."

The necessary ingredients for an especially severe melancholia are thus recorded in Jung's account of his early childhood years. His melancholia had a psychodynamic basis in the fact that, unlike a mother's physical death, which he could then have mourned, his experience of his mother's absence and subsequent return was fraught with ambiguity and mistrust. Although he does not say that she behaved as a crazed woman, he does associate her with nocturnal terrors, and it was not she but his father, and other women, who comforted him. He even slept in his father's bedroom. The Oedipal struggle so dear to Freud becomes, for three-year-old Carl, a moot issue. His fantasies are not those of a boy jealous that his father sleeps with his mother at night, for son and father share the same bedroom together, while mother sleeps apart from both of them. There is no competition in this respect between father and son, but, in consequence, father is viewed by son as reliable but powerless. Both males share a problem they seem powerless to do much about, the fact that wife and mother is estranged from both of them, though for different reasons. Helpless, the son may only fantasize an altogether different situation, one in which he and his father experience a shared happiness because the woman who can bring his father conjugal happiness is the same woman who can make the son feel that he is genuinely loved.

As this fantasy comes up against the hard reality of his mother's incapacity, for reasons that are surely beyond his, and perhaps her own, control, other fantasies take its place. One is the fantasy associated with the maid, the woman of dark complexion, who picked him up and laid his head on her shoulder. It was as though she belonged not to his family but to him alone. Of her, Jung writes: "This type of girl later became a component of my anima," and "the feeling of strangeness which she conveyed, and yet of having known her always, was a characteristic of that figure which later came to symbolize for me the whole essence of womanhood" (1961, 8–9). In other words, she evoked a sense of the uncanny in him, reminiscent perhaps of earlier times when his mother held him and laid his head on *her* shoulder. Yet the maid was not his mother, and this fact was especially brought home to him precisely when he was being held by her. Her acts of affection, while in one sense pleasurable, were reminders of his estrangement from his real mother.

The other fantasy is of the girl with blue eyes and fair hair who leads him under the golden maple and chestnut trees along the Rhine below the Falls. Unlike the girl of dark complexion, there is no mystery surrounding her, as she is associated not with the confusions of an unhappy, emotionally engulfing home but with the outdoors, with the shining sun and yellow leaves. But whereas he feels that the maid is his alone, belonging only to him, the same cannot be said of this girl, for she admires his father. And yet this seems not to threaten or disturb him. He seems to want for his father a woman's admiration, as this would enable his father to be less preoccupied with his own deficiencies as a man. Only later, in his dream of his visit to his long-deceased father, is he able to idealize his father and accord him the capacity to lead his son into the presence of Uriah. The dream contrasts dramatically with his account of his boyhood experience of his father, especially the embarrassment and disdain he felt toward him as he preached sermons that seemed so utterly hollow. Thus, of the two visions, the maid who held him in her arms and the girl who admired his father, the second is more holistic, more unitive, as it reflects the son's perception that his own happiness depends in large measure on the happiness of his father. His father's empowerment will empower him. Only in his late dream of his father do we detect such empowerment.

Should this reconstruction of his childhood fantasies seem tendentious and excessively speculative, what is incontrovertible is the fact that Jung's child-hood experiences set him up for a lifelong struggle with melancholia. The reader of his autobiography feels the sadness and despair in his account of his early years but senses the underlying rage as well. One finds oneself exclaim-ing, "No boy should have to suffer as this boy suffered." For the most part, the rage seems to be felt toward his mother. He is frustrated by his father's seeming powerlessness to do anything about the estrangement that exists between his parents, yet Jung seems to hold her primarily accountable, as she is the one toward whom fantasies of violence (decapitation) are directed. On the other hand, the fact that these *are* fantasies, of strange and terrifying things emanat-ing from her room at night, suggests that his rage is directed against some image of his mother, not necessarily the hapless woman who presumably sleeps more or less peacefully throughout the night.

Thus, he identifies with the Evangelist, who, having extolled the love of God in his letters, now invokes the avenger Christ, who will destroy everything in his wake, including the children of Thyratira. Yet he also identifies with the Evangelist who, having expended his rage, has a very different vision: a woman giving birth to another son, ushering in a new era in which God rises like "a little sun" in the hearts of aging men. This is a melancholiac's vision of renewal, of wholeness, after the rage has been expended. Knowing the nature of the traumas of Jung's own childhood, we are not surprised that he envisions a mother together with her son, or that this vision would arise out of the feeling heart of an old man looking back on his boyhood and finding within this feeling heart a deep and profoundly sympathetic love for the boy he had once been.

Yet there is more to the vision than an empathic reaching out to the child he once was. John's vision also entails something entirely new, a new develop-ment in the relation of God and humanity. As Jung puts it, "Christ's 'except ye become as little children' prefigures this change," for "what is meant is the boy who is born from the maturity of the adult man, and not the unconscious child we would like to remain" (*AJ,* 95). This new God-son would not have been possible had the man in whose heart he arises not already have experienced the bitterness of life, a bitterness so profound that he could welcome the destruc-tion of the world around him. This is a boy conceived out of the *maturity* of the adult man. After all, he is the mature man's vision. In this vision, a woman gives him birth, but she is not the author of the vision itself. In their latter days, the two old men have visions, and one of the two, although a "professed Christian," has dared to envision a new son of God coming to birth within him. This son is the man's own child, and he is divine, the little son who arises in a feeling man's heart. If other melancholiacs have had their hearts newly stirred by some external scene — a yellow jonquil, a drummer's tattoo — others feel the new life stirring up within, and these stirrings are no less identified with that which is divine.

Melancholy and the Mystery of Love

Given the falling out that occurred between Jung and Freud, I am mindful that followers of Jung often resent the use of psychoanalytic theories to explain matters in Jung's life and work for which there is already a Jungian explanation. In applying Freud's theory of melancholy to Jung's *Answer to Job,* however, I have not suggested or even implied that a Freudian interpretation is superior to a Jungian one. In fact, I have accepted Jung's own view that the "individuation process" is typically symbolized in dreams and myths by the divine child, and that the symbol of the divine child reveals "that there is in the unconscious an archetype of wholeness" (*AJ,* 106).

If I have preferred to focus on the relationship between Jung's presentation of the Evangelist's apocalyptic vision and his own childhood experiences, setting aside explorations of the divine-child archetype itself (as for example in Jung's "Psychology of the Child Archetype"), this is not because I have any particular brief against his claim that what we are witnessing in John's apocalyptic vision is the workings of the *collective* unconscious. Rather, in order to explore Jung's own religious answers to the problem of melancholia, it has been necessary to focus on his own *personal* unconscious, on experiences that he himself recounts in his autobiographical recollections of childhood. What I have argued, therefore, is that Jung's own melancholia, rooted in the emotional loss of his mother at the age of three, was integral to his mature vision of God as "a little sun" arising in his own heart. When the two texts of his late years, *Answer to Job* and *Memories, Dreams, Reflections,* are read in tandem, the reader senses that Jung himself makes this connection virtually explicit.

In the preface to *Answer to Job,* Jung notes that because he is dealing with "numinous factors," his feeling is challenged quite as much as his intellect: "I cannot, therefore, write in a coolly objective manner, but must allow my emotional subjectivity to speak if I want to describe what I feel when I read certain books of the Bible" (*AJ,* xv). In this chapter, I have focused on Jung's identification with John the Evangelist and on the fact that he feels within himself much the same emotions as the Evangelist, emotions that are the expression of a melancholy soul. There is the profound rage that envisions massive destruction, but there is also the healing vision of the rebirth of God in his own psyche, a rebirth that takes the form of a boy who is not an unconscious child—at best an observer of strange mysteries to which his parents' secrets hold the key—but a son like unto himself, as if the mature man were now father to himself. Thus, alongside his childhood desire to be another woman's son is the parallel desire to be his own father, as though he, an old man, is pregnant with new life.

If this vision reflects the human desire to be God, though in a qualified way, it also reflects God's desire to become human, in a correspondingly qualified way. Jung mistrusts the desire for identity with God, because this leads eventually to self-destruction. But he is open to the birth of God in his own heart, to what William James would call "the reality of the unseen world," though in this case *within* him. In the inner landscape of his heart there is a boy, spiritually alive, who dispels the deadly stillness of winter, gladdening the heart, and causing the old man to believe in a kind and loving God.

On the other hand, it is precisely this aspect of God—the lovingness of God—that is so difficult to talk about, to express in words. In the concluding sentence of *Answer to Job,* Jung acknowledges the difficulty of trying to encompass God in words when it is God who encompasses us, especially when God is felt inside us: "Even the enlightened person remains what he is, and is never more than his own limited ego before the One who dwells within him, whose form has no knowable boundaries, who encompasses him on all sides, fathomless as the abysms of the earth and vast as the sky" (*AJ,* 108).

The final chapter of *Memories, Dreams, Reflections,* which is followed by a brief "Retrospect," ends on a similar note of frustration as to how to speak of God. Jung confesses that he sometimes feels that St. Paul's words "Though I speak with the tongues of men and angels, and have not love" might well "be the first condition of all cognition and the quintessence of divinity itself" (1961, 353). He continues: "Whatever the learned interpretation may be of the sentence 'God is love,' the words affirm the *complexio oppositorum* of the Godhead. In my medical experience as well as in my own life I have again and again been faced with the mystery of love, and have never been able to explain what it is. Like Job, I had to 'lay my hand on my mouth. I have spoken once, and I will not answer'" (1961, 353).

Why is it so hard to speak of the mystery of divine love? The reason, he suggests, is that this mystery is the whole of which we are part. It is

> something superior to the individual, a unified and undivided whole. Being a part, man cannot grasp the whole. He is at its mercy. He may assent to it, or rebel against it; but he is always caught up by it and enclosed within it. He is dependent upon it and is sustained by it. Love is his light and his darkness, whose end he cannot see. . . . Man can try to name love, showering upon it all the names at his command, and still he will involve himself in endless self-

deceptions. If he possesses a grain of wisdom, he will lay down his arms and name the unknown by the more unknown . . . that is, by the name of God. That is a confession of his subjection, his imperfection, and his dependence; but at the same time a testimony to his freedom to choose between truth and error [1961, 354].

The melancholiac has a deep, natural mistrust of the word *love,* a mistrust deriving from early childhood experiences. At the same time, he knows that love is precisely that for which he yearns. Perhaps it was little Carl's experience of the maid caressing his head against her shoulder that afforded his first memory of the mystery, yes, the very uncanniness, of true human love, and perhaps this experience was somehow reminiscent of a more primordial experience of the mystery of his mother's love — mysterious because, in the final analysis, it cannot any longer be trusted, for he now knows it only as an alienated child. And yet over time Jung's predisposition to mistrust the women in his life proved again and again to have been misplaced.

So, too, perhaps, with one's predisposition to mistrust the love of God. The boy listening to his father preach is painfully aware that his father speaks superficially when he attests to the love of God: "Does he really know what he is talking about?" But the mature Jung, aided by the dream in which his father's mind "was flooded with profound ideas," comes in the end to his father's views concerning the love of God. In the concluding chapter of *Memories, Dreams, Reflections,* he dares once again to say what Job could not say, and what Paul only intimated: the mystery of love bespeaks another mystery — the mystery of God. If we refuse to ascribe the name of God to the mystery of love, we shall remain in the throes of endless self-deceptions. Which means that melancholia cannot but be deeply, inherently religious. It has its human players and counterplayers, yet, in the end, it always comes down to one's personal experience of the mystery, the uncanniness of love. And there is nothing more uncanny than a love that has no knowable boundaries.

Erikson

Melancholy and Motherhate: The Parabolic Fault Line in Young Man Luther

In his preface to *Young Man Luther,* Erikson leaves no doubt that what he believes is unique about his study of young Luther is its viewpoint of the clinician, especially a clinician who has spent the better part of his professional career treating individuals in their late teens and early twenties. In the opening sentence, he explains that his study of Luther as a young man "was planned as a chapter in a book on emotional crises in late adolescence and early adult- hood [1959]. But Luther proved too bulky a man to be merely a chapter" (1958, 7; hereafter *YML*). So "the clinical chapter became a historical book." Still, "clinical work is integral to its orientation" (*YML*, 7).[1]

Similarly, in chapter 1, entitled "Case and Event," Erikson begins by citing Kierkegaard's diary entry on Luther as "a patient of exceeding import for Christendom," and then comments: "In quoting this statement out of context, I do not mean to imply that Kierkegaard intended to call Luther a patient in the sense of a clinical 'case'; rather, he saw in him a religious attitude (patient- hood) exemplified in an archetypal and immensely influential way. In taking this statement as a kind of motto for this book, we do not narrow our perspec- tive to the clinical; we expand our clinical perspective to include a life style of patienthood as a sense of imposed suffering, or an intense need for cure, and (as Kierkegaard adds) a 'passion for expressing and describing one's suffer- ing'" (*YML*, 13).

Continuing, Erikson suggests that human nature can best be studied in the state of conflict, and that human conflict comes to the attention of interested recorders mainly under special circumstances. One of these is "the clinical encounter, in which the suffering, for the sake of securing help, have no other choice than to become case histories" (*YML,* 16). Another is where "extraordinary beings, by their own self-centered maneuvers and through the prodding of the charismatic hunger of mankind, become (auto) biographies. Clinical as well as historical scholars have much to learn by going back and forth between these two kinds of recorded history" (*YML,* 16).

Among such "extraordinary beings," Luther is "always instructive," because he "forces on the workers in both fields a special awareness. He indulged himself as he grew older in florid self-revelations of a kind which can make a clinical biographer feel that he is dealing with a client. If the clinician should indulge himself in this feeling, however, he will soon find out that the imaginary client has been dealing with him: for Luther is one of those autobiographers with a histrionic flair who can make enthusiastic use even of their neurotic suffering, matching selected memories with the clues given to them by their avid public to create their own official identities" (*YML,* 16). Thus, one needs all one's clinical skills to avoid being "taken in" by Luther "the autobiographer." *Young Man Luther* may be viewed as an attempt to find the real "young man Luther" precisely by maintaining a healthy skepticism toward the ways in which the "middle-aged Luther" reconstructed his earlier years.

In his initial chapter of *Childhood and Society* (1950; rev. ed. 1963), entitled "Relevance and Relativity in the Case History," Erikson set forth his manner of approaching any clinical case in which he was directly or indirectly involved (for example, the cases of a young boy who developed phobic reactions following his grandmother's death and of a combat marine who had been discharged from the armed forces as a "psychoneurotic casualty"). In discussing these cases, he suggests that there are essentially three processes that the clinician needs to consider: the *somatic process* (physiological processes inherent in the organism); the *ego process* (the individual's own "sense of coherent individuation and identity"); and the *social process* (family, class, community, and national factors that precipitate, sustain, and alleviate the illness). A human being "is at all times an organism, an ego, and a member of a society and is involved in all three processes of organization. His body is exposed to pain and tension; his ego, to anxiety; and as a member of a society, he is susceptible to the panic emanating from his group" (1963, 36). The clinician's task is to observe all three processes and be especially attentive to the ways they influence each other.

Guided by this model, Erikson explores in *Young Man Luther* the interrelationships among these three processes in Luther's case. Luther's *somatic processes* included his struggles with bodily diseases, his physical changes over the course of his life (especially the fact that his body weight increased considerably from young to middle adulthood, resulting in the "bulky" Luther of popular memory), his bouts with constipation and urine retention, and his unusual sensitivities to the organs of hearing and speaking. His *ego processes* were particularly noticeable in his struggle to find his true identity in terms both of his social role as monk turned reformer and, existentially, as a redeemed child of God. The *social processes* affecting Luther were especially reflected in the fundamental ideological changes widespread in sixteenth-century Europe as the medieval worldview was challenged and replaced by the new renaissance in political theory, the arts, the sciences, and views of human nature.

Of the latter, Erikson suggests that Luther "did the dirty work of the Renaissance, by applying some of the individualistic principles immanent in the Renaissance to the Church's still highly fortified home ground — the conscience of ordinary man," and that he "accepted for his life work the unconquered frontier of tragic conscience" (*YML*, 195). By conscience, Erikson means "that inner ground where we and God have to learn to live with each other as man and wife. Psychologically speaking, it is where the ego meets the superego; that is, where our self can either live in wedded harmony with a positive conscience or is estranged from a negative one. Luther comes nowhere closer to formulating the auditory threat, the voice of wrath, which is internalized in a negative conscience than when he speaks of the 'false Christ' as one whom we hear expostulate '*Hoc non fecisti*,' 'Again, you have not done what I told you' — a statement of the kind which identifies negatively, and burns itself into the soul as a black and hopeless mark" (*YML*, 195). As Luther saw it, this false Christ "becomes more formidable a tyrant and a judge than was Moses" (*YML*, 195).

Erikson's inclusion of ego processes in his clinical model was to become the hallmark of his own way of adapting psychoanalysis to the needs of his own era. From the very outset of his career as a psychoanalyst he identified with its egopsychology tradition, and by the time his first major book, *Childhood and Society*, was initially published (1950), he had already written several essays on ego psychology. In his clinical work with American veterans of World War II he began to describe their difficulties in readjusting to civilian life as "ego psychology" problems, mainly because the veterans perceived little continuity between their sense of self prior and subsequent to combat service. This led him to emphasize the need for a sense of continuity or coherence across the whole life span, and his theory of the human life cycle (with its eight psycho-

.social crises) sets forth the basic strengths that individuals require to counteract the disintegrative forces — both internal and external — that threaten to
undermine their sense of coherent individuation and identity. That the process
culminates in a crisis of "integrity vs. despair" is no accident. "Integrity"
implies that one has succeeded in maintaining a sense of continuity and sameness through the course of one's life, while "despair" signifies that one has
failed to do so, and that there is no longer time available to redirect one's life.
Erikson's life-cycle structure figures prominently in *Young Man Luther,* as he
uses it to inform his assessment of Luther's own struggle to realize a sense of
coherent individuation and identity (1963, 36).

Because it addresses the underlying reasons why this sense of continuity is so
problematic and difficult to realize, the chapter of *Childhood and Society* that
especially prefigures *Young Man Luther,* Erikson's second major book, is the
concluding one, entitled "Beyond Anxiety" (1963, 403–24). Erikson focuses
here on the major impediment to adults' inner sense of personal integration or
integrity: the fact that their childhood fears continue to manifest themselves in
adulthood, now in the form of inexplicable anxieties. If the child is justified in
having fears — after all, the child *is* vulnerable — the adult's anxieties are less
explicable, because they are typically experienced even when there is little or
no actual external threat. When there *is* such a threat, the adult reacts, as does
the child, with fear. Almost by definition, anxieties involve a sense of being
threatened that has no clear justification and thus no identifiable solution in
the external world.

The difference between fears and anxieties is that "fears are states of apprehension which focus on isolated and recognizable dangers so that they may
be judiciously appraised and realistically countered," whereas "anxieties are
diffuse states of tension (caused by a loss of mutual regulation and a conse-
quent upset in libidinal and aggressive controls) which magnify and even cause
the illusion of an outer danger, without pointing to appropriate avenues of
defense or mastery" (1963, 406–7). To be sure, "these two forms of apprehension obviously often occur together, and we can insist on a strict separation
only for the sake of the present argument" (1963, 407). Still, there *is* a difference between fear and anxiety, because it is not "the fear of a danger (which
we might be well able to meet with judicious action) but the fear of the associated state of aimless anxiety which drives us into irrational *action,* irrational *flight* — or, indeed, irrational *denial* of danger. When threatened with
such anxiety we either magnify a danger which we have no reason to fear
excessively — or we ignore a danger which we have every reason to fear"
(1963, 407).

Erikson argues that adult anxieties often have their origins in childhood fears that were never adequately resolved and therefore left the child with a lasting sense of being under threat. Such childhood fears fuel and exacerbate adult anxieties. As a result, everyone will carry into adulthood a deep sense of once having been small and vulnerable. "A sense of smallness forms a substratum in his mind, ineradicably. His triumphs will be measured against this smallness, his defeats will substantiate it" (1963, 404). Erikson identifies the most prominent fears that occur with regularity in childhood, such as the fear of sudden changes, of exposure, of being immobilized, but the fears that have greatest relevance to Luther are the fear of being attacked from the rear, which Erikson attributes to adult sadism, and the fear of being abandoned (1963, 410).

Like other childhood fears, the fear of being attacked from the rear involves a configuration of somatic, ego, and societal processes. The adult's attack on the child's buttocks (somatic) is a threat to the child's personal sense of wellbeing (ego) and reflects a particular understanding of how children are to become socialized to a particular worldview (social). Regarding the latter, Erikson notes that Native Americans expressed bewilderment when they saw Caucasian American parents beating their own children. They surmised that this was these parents' way of communicating to their children that earth is a living hell, and of inculcating in them a desire for the paradise that awaits them after death (*YML,* 69). He also notes that being struck from behind, the primary locus of Luther's fears, is forever associated with a guilty conscience, which was the focus of Luther's lifelong anxiety, as exhibited in his struggle with the "false Christ" who verbally condemned him: "You have not done what I told you." In this condemnation, the parental voice in the punishment scenario is unmistakable.

Thus, Erikson's clinical analysis of Luther is prefigured in the final chapter of *Childhood and Society,* where he argues that the neurotic anxieties of adults not only have their roots in childhood but are also the consequence of the fact that our child self survives into adulthood, forming an ineradicable substratum in our minds, permanently affecting our way of seeing and feeling things. This means that the child self cannot but form a significant part of the adult's ego, especially in its role as the source of anxieties that are otherwise inexplicable, because they have little or nothing to do with current threats to the adult's sense of personal wellbeing. Especially interesting to Erikson is the role played by a society's ideologies, often unexamined and taken for granted, in its attitudes toward and treatment of its children. Among psychoanalysts of his era, he was perhaps the most outspoken critic of the failure of psychoanalysis to explore the relationships between the psychological and the social. He was particularly interested in the ways that societies influence parents to rear their children so as to prepare them to assume a traditional "image" or "model" of adulthood that has not been subjected to careful examination, taking new social circumstances into account. He recognized that a society's religion is especially significant in this regard, because religion serves as an ideology that underwrites certain child-rearing practices which, in turn, result in the creation of childhood fears that are later manifested in adult anxieties. In circular fashion, religion produces fears that result in the anxieties that religion then seeks either to eliminate or to assuage.

The Boyhood Beatings of Martin Luther

What, in Erikson's view, was the actual basis for Luther's childhood fears? What was their primary source? In his chapter in *Young Man Luther* entitled "Obedience — To Whom?" Erikson explores the fact that Luther was severely and regularly beaten by his father and his teachers, and, at least on occasion, by his mother as well. In emphasizing that Luther was beaten as a child, he anticipates the objection that Luther's experiences could not have been unique in this regard; at the time, child beating was a very common, perhaps universal, practice. Against the views of one of Luther's biographers, he argues that the biographer's "statistical approach to a given effect — the assertion that the cause was too common to have an uncommon effect on one individual — is neither clinically nor biographically valid. We must try to ascertain the relationship of caner and caned, and see if a unique element may have given the common event a specific meaning" (*YML,* 64). What matters most, both clinically and biographically, is the effect of the beatings on the specific relationship involved. The decisive issue is that the beater was father, teacher, or mother, and that the beaten was "little Martin," not one of the other Luther children or schoolmates.

Erikson notes that the clinician needs a "framework" within which to evaluate the beatings that were inflicted on "little Martin." This framework includes, among other things, a very careful listening to what the individual sufferer has to say about the beatings that he endured as a child. "Many authorities on Luther, making no attempt at psychological thinking, judge this matter of punishment either to be of no importance, or on the contrary, to have made an emotional cripple of Martin. It seems best, however, to outline a framework within which we may try to evaluate these data. In my profession one learns to listen to exactly what people are saying; and Luther's utterances, even when they are reported secondhand, are often surprises in naive clarification" (*YML,* 64).

Erikson first takes up the fact that Luther's father beat him. What especially attracts his clinical ear is Luther's later observation that on one occasion when his father beat him, "I fled him and I became sadly resentful toward him, until he gradually got me accustomed (or habituated) to him again" (*YML*, 64). In Erikson's clinical judgment, the "meaning" the beating had for Luther was that when he was mortally afraid of his father he hated him, but not absolutely, for he also felt a deep sense of sadness. Conversely, while his father would not allow the boy to come close and was murderously angry at times, he could not let "little Martin" go for long. "They had a mutual and deep investment in each other which neither of them could or would abandon, although neither of them was able to bring it to any kind of fruition" (*YML*, 65). Erikson views Martin as the child who had been selected from among his many siblings to justify his father. Thus, a great premium was placed on what Martin was — or was not — accomplishing, on what he had — or had not — recently done for his father.

There were also the beatings inflicted by his school teachers. At the age of seven, Luther was sent to Latin school, where the teachers "were apt to express their impatience with life in their treatment of the children, which was very similar to the treatment that the town miller's men gave their donkeys." They "drummed" facts into the children's minds by relentless mechanical repetition, and "they also drummed the children . . . on the behind, other body parts being exempt" (*YML*, 78). Erikson notes that Luther's biographers differ radically on the long-term effects of his teachers' beatings, depending on whether or not they consider the adult Luther to have been seriously neurotic. One suggests that a "lusty caning" did not harm Martin any more than it did the other children. Others, however, have made "the most of Luther's statement, made in middle age, that the hell of school years can make a child fearful for life" (*YML*, 78). Erikson believes that an adult's assertion that "I was beaten, but it didn't do any permanent damage" expresses the speaker's capacity to make the best of what cannot be undone, but whether or not it actually did them harm "is another question, to answer which may call for more information about the role they have come to play in adult human affairs" (*YML*, 68–69).

In Luther's case, what Erikson finds significant about his teachers' beatings is that Luther would have been beaten for speaking German, for swearing, and for speaking impulsively out of turn. Beatings were therefore associated with an injunction against "verbal freedom" (*YML*, 79). In light of this injunction, the episode that Erikson chooses to introduce Luther to his readers (in his chapter "The Fit in the Choir") is especially significant. This episode was reported to have occurred when Luther was training to become a monk. The scripture text read in the monastery chapel that day was Mark 9:17–29, the story of the man who brought his son to Jesus because he had a "dumb spirit." When Luther heard the story, he reportedly roared like a bull, "It isn't me!" In denying identification with the son who could not speak by verbally disrupting the Mass, Luther unwittingly confirmed that he identified with this troubled individual. To Erikson, verbal freedom is precisely the issue here. Would Luther ever find a way truly to speak his mind, and if he ever did, how might he be assured that his words were divinely sanctioned?

There were also the beatings inflicted by Luther's mother. Erikson centers on Luther's account of the time she beat him "until the blood flowed" for his theft of a single nut, and his claim that this beating drove him into the monastery. Luther had told this story to illustrate the importance in parent-child relations of ensuring that the punishment truly fits the offense (*YML*, 67). While Erikson believes that the father was the predominant parent in Luther's life, guarding the father-son relationship so jealously "that the mother was eclipsed far more than can be accounted for by the mere pattern of German housewifeliness" (*YML*, 65), the fact that Luther's mother also severely beat him must not be ignored. Erikson wonders: Does this mean that she failed to stand between the father and the son to whom she had given birth? Was she acting as his father's agent when she beat him, or was she acting on her own initiative? To explore the meaning of her own beatings of young Martin, Erikson relates them to the fact that several of Luther's siblings died in infancy, raising the issue of the possible relationship between his fear of being attacked from the rear and his fear of being abandoned. Erikson asks: "And what did she feel when she bore and lost so many children that their number and their names are forgotten? Luther does mention that some of her children 'cried themselves to death,' which may have been one of his after-dinner exaggerations; and at any rate, what he was talking about then was only that his mother had considered these children to have been bewitched by a neighbor woman" (*YML*, 72). This startling information about Luther's dead siblings is followed by a paragraph in which Erikson comments on the personality of Luther's mother:

> The father seems to have been standoffish and suspicious toward the universe; the mother, it is said, was more interested in the imaginative aspects of superstition. It may well be, then, that from his mother Luther received a more pleasurable and more sensual attitude toward nature, and a more simply integrated kind of mysticism, such as he later found described by certain mystics. It has been surmised that the mother suffered under the father's personality, and gradually became embittered; and there is also a suggestion

that a certain sad isolation which characterized young Luther was to be found also in his mother, who is said to have sung him a ditty: "For me and you nobody cares. That is our common fault" [*YML,* 72].

What is to be made of this, clinically speaking? Erikson sets aside the historian's natural caution and makes a claim based entirely on his clinical expertise: "A big gap exists here, which only conjecture could fill. But instead of conjecturing half-heartedly, I will state, as a clinician's judgment, that nobody could speak and sing as Luther later did if his mother's voice had not sung to him of some heaven; that nobody could be as torn between his masculine and his feminine sides, nor have such a range of both, who did not at one time feel that he was like his mother; but also, that nobody would discuss women and marriage in the way he often did who had not been deeply disappointed by his mother — and had become loath to succumb the way she did to the father, to fate" (*YML,* 73).

As a clinician, Erikson is willing to go out on a limb, to make assertions that he cannot in fact support with historical facts. I find it significant, however, that Luther's relationship to his mother is the occasion for Erikson's assertion of his clinical qualifications. Is this because he has worked therapeutically with young men of whom Luther is reminiscent? This is surely part of it. But another, more significant explanation is that Erikson is deeply aware that Luther's early relationship with his mother is a prefigurement of his own "prehistoric" relations with *his* mother, whom he was both very much alike and deeply disappointed by. I shall return to this point later in the chapter.

Luther's Pathology: Melancholy with "Teeth in It"

For now, I want simply to note that the passage about Luther's prehistoric relation to his mother is especially relevant to the theme of this study, as it concerns Erikson's "expanded" clinical interpretations of Luther's sufferings from melancholy. By exploring the melancholy issue in *Young Man Luther* we may see how Erikson uses this theme to establish a position for himself between psychiatry and religion. This in-between position proved risky, as it failed to satisfy either the psychiatric or the religious community. The reception that *Young Man Luther* got from both professional groups bears this out. The psychiatric community felt that Erikson had written a book that was too favorable toward Luther in light of his religiously based pathologies, while the religious community questioned a psychoanalyst's right to explore Luther's theology from a clinical perspective. Historians also joined the controversy, contending that Erikson had exceeded his own competence by presuming to write a historical book. After all, Erikson was not a trained biographer.

A useful way of approaching *Young Man Luther* is to focus on Erikson's effort to find a workable position between psychiatry and religion. This effort carries great risks of failure, and it is reminiscent of John Dominic Crossan's comparison of myth and parable, myth being the affirmation that psychiatry and religion are somehow reconcilable, and parable being the counterargument that no such reconciliation is possible. Crossan states:

> Myth has a double function: the reconciliation of an individual contradiction and, more important, the creation of belief in the permanent possibility of reconciliation. Parable also has a double function which opposes that double function of myth. The surface function of parable is to create contradiction within a given situation of complacent security but, even more unnervingly, to challenge the fundamental principle of reconciliation by making us aware of the fact that *we made up* the reconciliation. Reconciliation is no more fundamental a principle than irreconciliation. You have built a lovely home, myth assures us; but, whispers parable, you are right above an earthquake fault [1975, 56–57].

I suggest that ostensibly Erikson's case study of Luther is mythic, in that it reflects his confidence that disciplines and professions can be reconciled to one another. His metaphor for such reconciliation is the boundary, or borderline. He speaks of the borderline between history and psychology, and of his interest in working as a psychohistorian (*YML*, 15–16). And there is also the borderline between psychiatry and religion. Writing about Luther's "fit in the choir," he notes that "the paroxysm occurred in a holy spot and was suggested by a biblical story, which places the whole matter at least on the borderline between psychiatry and religion" (*YML*, 38).

As a practitioner and scholar who wants to situate himself in the boundary between disciplines, Erikson believes—or at least wants to believe—in "the permanent possibility of reconciliation." His will to believe may be warranted. But surely anyone who claims to be clinically aware will be placed on guard by his use of the word *borderline* to depict the relationship between psychiatry and religion, as the "borderline personality disorder" is defined in *DSM* as "a pervasive pattern of instability of interpersonal relationships, self-image, and affects," which may entail "an identity disturbance characterized by markedly and persistently unstable self-image or sense of self" (1994, 650–51). The irony here is that Erikson's own contribution to the psychiatric diagnostic lexicon—"identity disturbance," or, as he preferred to call it, "identity diffusion" — is a telling argument against the very reconciliation between disciplines that he envisions. To put it another way, he is presenting the symptom as the cure or, as Crossan more poetically puts it, he is attempting to build a lovely home right above an earthquake fault. By centering on Erikson's discussion of Luther's melancholy, we may see just how risky is the effort to reconcile psychiatry and religion, but also how fruitful it can be.

As I noted earlier, Erikson introduces the reader to Luther by citing the claim by three of Luther's contemporaries that in his early or middle twenties Luther suddenly fell to the ground in the choir of Erfurt monastery, "raved" like one possessed, and roared with the voice of a bull, "It isn't me!" All three reporters agree that Luther was responding to the reading of Jesus's cure of a man possessed by a dumb spirit. Erikson says this can only refer to Mark 9:17ff., where Jesus asked about the cause of a disturbance in the crowd nearby and "one of the crowd answered him, 'Teacher, I brought my son to you, for he has a dumb spirit.' " As the son in the biblical story had a habit of falling on the ground, writhing and foaming at the mouth, the chroniclers of Luther's "fit in the choir" considered young Luther to be demon-possessed (*YML*, 23).

Erikson uses this story of the choir fit both to introduce Luther and to build his case that historians and biographers of Luther have created portraits of him to which Luther would justifiably object, "It isn't me!" Erikson wonders, "Am I likely to fare any better?"

I shall not discuss all of Erikson's agreements and disagreements with the four biographers he presents as representative (a German Protestant theologian, a Dominican priest and Vatican archivist, a Danish psychiatrist, and an American historian who applied some psychoanalytic ideas to Luther in 1915). What I do wish to focus on is the fact that two of these authors, the German Protestant theologian and the Danish psychiatrist, refer to Luther's melancholia, though they differ in their views concerning its origins or etiology. The theologian, Otto Scheel, claims that Luther's fits of overwhelming anxiety and states of brooding despair were "catastrophes" that came directly from God and therefore had nothing whatever to do with Luther's mental condition. The Danish psychiatrist, Paul J. Reiter, considered these attacks "endogenous," or biological, and therefore believed it futile "to try to find any 'message,' either from a divine or an inner source, in Luther's abnormalities other than indications of erratic upsets in his nervous system" (*YML*, 27).

Erikson seems especially interested in Reiter's work, in part because we might have expected something much like it from Erikson himself. In Erikson's own estimation, Reiter provides "as complete an account of Luther's 'environment, character, and psychosis' as I have come across. His study ranges from the macrocosm of Luther's times to the microcosm of his home and home town, and includes a thorough discussion of his biological make-up and of his lifelong physical and emotional symptoms" (*YML, 33*). On the other hand, Erikson thinks that Reiter, who accuses psychoanalysis of being too dogmatic, is himself too rigid and doctrinaire: "He shows much insight in his asides; but in his role of bedside psychiatrist, he grimly sticks to his central view by asserting that a certain trait or act of Luther's is 'absolutely typical for a state of severe melancholia' and 'is to be found in every psychiatric textbook'" (*YML, 33*).

Erikson agrees that the older Luther may have approached "textbook states," but

> when it comes to the younger Luther and the psychiatrist's assertion that his *tentationes tristitiae* — that sadness which is a traditional temptation of the *homo religiosus* — is among the "classical traits in the picture of most states of depression, especially the endogenous ones," we must be decidedly more doubtful. For throughout, this psychiatric textbook version of Luther does not compare him with other examples of sincere religious preoccupation and corresponding genuine giftedness, but with some form of *Ausgeglichenheit* — an inner balance, a simple enjoyment of life, and an ordinary decency and decided direction of effort such as normal people are said to display. Though the psychiatrist makes repeated allowances for Luther's genius, he neverthe-less demands of him a state of inner repose which, as far as I know, men of creative intensity and of an increasing historical commitment cannot be ex-pected to be able to maintain [*YML, 34*].

Thus, Erikson does not challenge the psychiatrist's diagnosis of Luther as suffering from melancholia, perhaps a severe form of it, but he rejects his insistence on treating Luther as a "textbook case," especially with respect to how the disease originated in the first place and to why Luther proved incur-able. For Erikson, Luther's melancholic episodes did not, as the theologian Scheel suggests, come "straight down from heaven," but nor were they, as the psychiatrist Reiter suggests, mere "indications of erratic upsets in his nervous system." Against Scheel, Erikson argues that Luther's melancholia, whether "fits of overwhelming anxiety" or "states of brooding despair," had psycho-dynamic roots. Against Reiter, he contends that Luther's melancholic epi-sodes, especially those that did approach the most severe "textbook cases," were religious experiences. While there is little reason to believe that Scheel's religious position and Reiter's psychiatric position are reconcilable, we may, as Erikson sees it, be able to find some mediating position born not of a spirit of irenicism but of a desire to make a better, more clinically astute assessment of Luther's real condition.

Thus, against Scheel, Erikson claims that Luther's melancholia is psychodynamically rooted in his pre-historic relation to his mother. This is implied in his observation "that a certain sad isolation which characterized young Luther was to be found also in his mother" (*YML*, 73). If his sadness may be traced to her, his despair might also, for he was "deeply disappointed" by her inability to stand up to his father. However, what Erikson does *not* attribute to Luther's pre-historic relation to his mother is as significant as what he *does* attribute to it. While Freud, in "Mourning and Melancholia," ascribes to the melancholiac deep feelings of rage, even hatred, toward the one who has been the cause of such deep disappointment, Erikson characterizes Luther's feelings toward his mother quite differently: Toward his mother, Luther felt only love.

Erikson agrees with the American historian Preserved Smith that Luther undoubtedly had an "Oedipus complex which was aroused by a forceful and libidinal attachment to the vivacious and, as far as we know, gifted and imaginative mother, and accentuated by the sinister harshness of the father toward him, toward the siblings and maybe also to the mother" (Smith, quoted in *YML*, 73). Building on Smith's contrast between the vivacious mother and the harsh father, Erikson adds: "We would not wish to see any boy — much less an imaginative and forceful one — face the struggles of his youth and manhood without having experienced as a child the love and the hate which are encompassed in this complex: love for the maternal person who awakens his senses and his sensuality with her ministrations, and deep and angry rivalry with the male possessor of this maternal person" (*YML*, 73). Hence, so far as Luther's Oedipus complex is concerned, love and hate are divided — all too neatly, in my judgment — between mother and father. It appears that, in Erikson's rendering, young Martin feels only love for his mother; his rage at what his mother had done, or permitted to happen, is magically erased.

In his later chapter "Allness or Nothingness," however, Erikson returns to the matter of Luther's melancholia and comes much closer to Freud's view that, in melancholia, love and hate are experienced toward the selfsame person, the lost object. In what appears to be a digression, Erikson introduces a long passage from James's *Varieties,* a text that seems to have been much on Erikson's mind while writing *Young Man Luther.* He has just been talking about how the sadness of Luther's youth stemmed from his awareness of having lost his childhood and, even more than that, of having sustained a profound loss in infancy itself. What Luther lost back then, in those pre-historic times, was the infant's sense of "original unity" with his basic provider, the maternal person herself. And what destroyed this basic unity? "All religions and most philosophers agree that it is *will* — the mere will to live, thoughtless and cruel self-will" (*YML*, 120). Then comes the long quotation

from *The Varieties,* one of the concluding paragraphs of James's chapter "The
Sick Soul," which I referred to in chapter 2 as "the parable of the prehistoric
reptiles" (*VRE,* 163–64, quoted in *YML,* 120).

Erikson follows the quotation from *The Varieties* with this comment on the
mood that it ascribes to the melancholiac:

> The tenor of this mood is immediately convincing. It is the mood of severe
> melancholy, intensified tristitia, one would almost say tristitia with teeth in
> it. . . . James is clinically and genetically correct, when he connects the horror
> of the *devouring* will to live with the content and the disposition of melan-
> cholia. For in melancholia, it is the human being's horror of his own ava-
> ricious and sadistic orality which he tires of, withdraws from, wishes often to
> end even by putting an end to himself. This is not the orality of the first, the
> toothless and dependent stage; it is the orality of the tooth-stage and all that
> develops within it, especially the prestages of what later becomes "biting"
> human conscience [*YML,* 120–21].

Then he alludes to Luther's own depiction of God "as a devourer, as if the
wilful sinner could expect to find in God's demeanor a mirror of his own
avarice, just as the uplifted face of the believer finds a countenance inclined
and full of grace. . . . Thus, in the set of god-images in which the countenance
of the godhead mirrors the human face, God's face takes on the toothy and
fiery expression of the devil, or the expressions of countless ceremonial masks.
All these wrathful countenances mirror man's own rapacious orality which
destroys the innocent trust of that first symbiotic orality when mouth and
breast, glance and face, are one" (*YML,* 121–22).

Erikson does not say that the mother may have done something to invite this
attack. Nor does he indicate that the attack, because motivated by the will to
live, may have been born of the perception that the giver of life is withholding
it instead. Still, his description of melancholy with "teeth in it" expresses the
tone of the melancholy from which young Luther suffered, for he was more
than a sad and pensive young man. He was struggling for life, and his writhing, as though some vicious animal had pinned him to the ground, was all part
of fighting back. The "fit in the choir," in which he roared like a bull, was an
instance of melancholy with teeth in it, a refusal to allow others to define who
he was and, on this basis, leave him as if for dead.

Yet this was all prefigured in Luther's early infancy, in the fact that he lived
to survive his infancy when several of his siblings did not. We recall his own
recollection that they "cried themselves to death" and his mother's attempt to
place the blame for their deaths on a woman neighbor who had presumably
bewitched them. If, as Erikson notes, "the most deadly of all possible sins is the

mutilation of a child's spirit" (*YML*, 70) and Luther, as the son of a vicious father, was threatened with such mutilation almost every day of his life, we should not be surprised if little Martin's loss of "unity" with his mother was due not only to her own "succumbing" to father and fate but also to his insistence on having life on whatever terms he could get it, even if this meant attacking her, *forcing* her to give him the emotional nurturing that any child needs in order to live. Better to have it by force than to cry himself to death.

Erikson does not disagree with the Protestant theologian and the Danish psychiatrist that Luther was melancholic. But he wants to insist that Luther's sadness had "bite" to it, that underlying his monumental sadness was a deep, potentially towering rage, so that the sadness and rage were related dynamically. What Erikson does not say, but what needs to be said, is that the sadness and rage were both evoked by the selfsame person, his mother, as her own self-pity allowed her to absolve herself of responsibility for what had become of her children. Blaming a neighbor for bewitching them is symptomatic of her failure, and her own participation in the abuse that the father inflicted on his children suggests that she was all too willing to collude with the father so as to ensure her own survival. Erikson notes that, in contrast to Luther's comments on the physical abuse his father inflicted upon him, his "statement of the maltreatment received at the hands of his mother is more specific; however, whatever resentment he felt against her was never expressed as dramatically as was his fatherhate, which took the form of a burning doubt of divine righteousness" (*YML*, 67). This does not mean, however, that he did not have motherhate or that he did not express it just as indirectly as he expressed his fatherhate against God. As Freud's "Mourning and Melancholia" suggests, the expression of this hate was *self*-directed, which is, of course, how melancholiacs find a way to hate without acknowledging that their hate has an identifiable object. What Luther rages against is the internalized mother, the mother, no longer an object in the objective world, who has become internalized as one with the ego. Because she was identified with "real injury or disappointment" (Freud 1963, 170), causing her son to doubt her love and withdraw his own, he will continue to attack her, though the attack is now inflicted on himself.

Thus, Luther's object loss began early in his life, when he lost the infant's natural confidence in his mother's will to sustain his life and perceived that his survival depended upon his capacity to save his own life by taking matters into his own hands. If this happened in his pre-history, we should not be at all surprised that as a young man he was quite unconscious of what had occurred between them. But middle-aged Luther, the Luther of "Table Talk," is perhaps more open to the idea that it happened, and happened like this. He is at least able to recall the other children in the Luther household who cried themselves to death, and he seems not quite willing to accept his mother's explanation that a woman neighbor bewitched them. Middle-aged Luther is on to something. Is he beginning to ask himself the very question that Erikson asks himself: "And what did she feel when she bore and lost so many children that their number and their names are forgotten?" (*YML,* 72). And what *could* she feel for the surviving ones?

One is reminded here of Alice Miller's essay on the artist Käthe Kollwitz (1990b), in which Miller focuses on the fact that Kollwitz's mother's first two children and her last born died when they were very young. Miller sees the surviving children growing up in the shadow of their mother's cult of the dead, "raised in a way to rid them of their bad behavior and make them acceptable in the future. To be too affectionate would be dangerous, for too much love could ruin them. The parents seem to think that affection and tenderness should be carefully measured out in the child's best interest. And so the poor well-raised mother feels a duty toward her living children to train them well and to suppress their true feelings" (1990b, 28). Her "relationship" to her dead child is very different from this, and the surviving children feel it:

> But it's a different matter in the case of her dead child, for that child needs nothing from her and does not awaken any feelings of inferiority or hatred, does not cause her any conflict, does not offend her. Since she need not be afraid of spoiling the child with her love, when she goes to the cemetery she feels genuine inner freedom in her grief. Compared with that feeling, being with her other children can make her suffer because they clearly do not measure up to the dead child and its fantasized goodness and wisdom. Their vitality, their demands and claims on her can make a mother in love with her dead child feel distinctly insecure [1990b, 28–29].

Here we have the problem of mourning and melancholia on the mother's side. She mourns the dead child but has melancholic reactions to her living child, which in turn feeds the living child's own melancholia: Mother and child are a disappointment to each other.

Miller's suggestion that the bereaved mother does not dare to be affectionate toward her surviving children, carefully measuring out warmth and tenderness and emphasizing that they must be purged of bad behavior, fits what Erikson tells us about Luther's mother. The Luther of "Table Talk" complained that she beat him bloody for stealing a nut, adding, "Such strict discipline drove me to a monastery although she meant it well" (*YML,* 64). Also relevant to Luther are Miller's reference to the mother's insecurity when she is with her living children and her suggestion that she is drawn, emotionally, to her dead child and is unable to respond to the living child who claims her love and attention. If, as Freud says, the shadow of the lost love object falls upon the melancholiac, it is because in this instance the love object lived her life in the shadow of her own lost object.

Father-Son Theology Versus Mother-Child Mysticism

Thus far I have addressed Erikson's response to the theologian Scheel's view that melancholia is a heaven-sent catastrophe and have presented the alternative argument that melancholia has its origins in the mother-son relationship. But what of Erikson's response to the psychiatrist Reiter's contention that Luther's melancholia may be adequately explained as being endogenous, the manifestation of an erratic, unbalanced nervous system? In response to him, Erikson takes the side, at least provisionally, of the theologian — not Scheel, however, but Luther himself, whom Erikson considers the far more astute theologian, especially where his own struggles and conflicts are concerned.

In his chapter entitled "The Meaning of 'Meaning It,'" Erikson indicates that he is essentially persuaded by Luther's own attempt to make religious sense of his lifelong struggles with melancholia. Especially important in this regard are key passages in Erikson's text that focus on the role Luther assigned to Christ in coming to terms with his own internalized self-hatred. Erikson notes that Luther "made a virtue out of what his superiors had considered a vice in him (and we, a symptom), namely, the determined search for the rock bottom of his sinfulness: *conformis deo est et verax et justus.* One could consider such conformity utter passivity in the face of God's judgment; but note that it really is an active self-observation, which scans the frontier of conscience for the *genuine* sense of guilt. Instead of accepting some impersonal and mechanical absolution, it insists on dealing with sincere guilt, perceiving as 'God's judgment' what in fact is the individual's own truly meant self-judgment" (*YML,* 212, my emphasis).

What Luther seems determined to differentiate is the real guilt for which he is accountable from the false guilt that derives from a false conscience, attributable to his internalization of and hostility toward the lost object. For Luther, Christ becomes a new internalized object — what Heinz Kohut would call a selfobject (Kohut 1971, 1977, and as in my discussion at the end of chapter 3). This selfobject replaces the debilitating self-image with a self-empowering one. As Erikson puts it, "Yet now, in finding Christ in himself, he establishes an inner position which goes beyond that of a neurotic compromise identification. He finds the core of a praying man's identity, and advances Christian theology by an important step" (*YML,* 212).

This discovery of "Christ in himself" meant that Luther found himself rejecting or abandoning other theories of Christ's role in the life of the believer: "It is clear that Luther abandoned the appreciation of Christ as a substitute who has died 'for' — in the sense of 'instead of' — us; he also abandoned the concept of Christ as an ideal figure to be imitated, or abjectly venerated, or ceremonially remembered as an event in the past. Christ now becomes the core of the Christian's identity. . . . Christ is today here, in me. . . . God, instead of lurking on the periphery of space and time, became for Luther 'what works in us'" (*YML,* 212–13). This is the theological "answer" to the psychological "problem." It may be stated in Luther's simple aphoristic form as "Not I, but Christ lives in me." The self-hatred that was so integral to Luther's melancholy is profoundly relativized. So long as the son of God lives within him, he has no grounds for hating himself, for that would be to hate the son of God, who has done nothing to merit his wrath. Through him, Luther receives God's very recognition. Having "sought to dispel the angry cloud that darkened the face of the fathers and of the Father," Luther "now said that Christ's life *is* God's face" (*YML,* 213).

Erikson affirms this resolution of Luther's melancholia, or, more precisely, of that aspect of Luther's melancholia which centered on his internalized self-hatred (the other aspect being his terrible sadness). In doing so, he takes the side of the theologian against the psychiatrist for whom the resolution involves achieving some sort of "psychic balance." Erikson agrees with the theologian — Luther, in this case — even at the risk of seeming to endorse Lutheran theology, because Luther's position offers a far more radical solution to the problem, one befitting the severity of the pathology. The need is not for psychic balance but for a new core to one's own identity: Christ in me, Christ the agency of every new beginning. In an odd sense, the biblical story of the young man who is demon-possessed gets it right, or at least half-right, as it goes on to tell of how Jesus commanded the dumb spirit to come out "and never enter him again" (Mark 9:25). So the hated self, the self that has been causing such inner suffering and anguish, gets expelled from the body. What Luther perceives is that an "object" must take its place — which is the other half of the story. And what better object than the exorcist, Christ himself?

Yet, if Erikson endorses Luther's resolution, he nonetheless wants to have the clinician's last word. He begins the paragraph that immediately follows his account of Luther's internalization of Christ with this proposal: "Let us rephrase somewhat more psychologically what we have just put in theological terms" (*YML,* 214). This "rephrasing" returns to the issue he had raised in his earlier comments on Luther's having been "deeply disappointed in his mother" and, more specifically, to his rather allusive observation that "if the soul is man's most bisexual part, then we will be prepared to find in Luther both some horror of mystic succumbing and some spiritual search for it, and to recognize in this alternative some emotional and spiritual derivatives of little Martin's 'pre-historic' relation to his mother" (*YML*, 73).

Having accepted Luther's own theological explanation for how one breaks the deadly grip of melancholia, Erikson returns to the matter of Luther's mother's legacy, the fact that from her he "received a more pleasurable and more sensual attitude toward nature, and a more simply integrated kind of mysticism, such as he later found described by certain mystics" (*YML*, 72). In light of his disappointment in his mother for her willingness to "succumb" to the father and fate, this was a legacy that Luther viewed ambivalently, having both "some horror of mystic succumbing and some spiritual search for it."

It occurs to Erikson that much of what Luther describes in theological terms could also be said in more mystical terms. He wonders whether the natural climate might have a lot to do with it, citing William James's remark that "the Latin races seem to be able more easily to split up the pressure of evil into, 'ills and sins in the plural, removable in detail,' while the Germanic races tend to erect one 'Sin in the singular, and with a capital S . . . ineradicably ingrained in our natural subjectivity, and never to be removed by any piecemeal operation'" (*YML,* 215). Erikson observes: "Just because Luther's periodic states of melancholy repeatedly forced him to accept despair and disease as final, and death as imminent, he may have expressed in his most pessimistic and philosophically most untenable concepts (such as the total predestination of individual fate, independent of personal effort) exactly that cold rock bottom of mood, that utter background of blackness, which to Northern people is the condition of spring" (*YML,* 215). He then quotes a German lyric which says that "winter is gone and summer is at the door, and that the flowers are coming up; and that Whoever has begun such a process will surely complete it" (*YML,* 215–16).

By offering a more mystical, non-Christocentric explanation for Luther's release from melancholic despair, Erikson gives a psychological "rephrasing" of what has been put in theological terms. But there is more to it than the word *rephrasing* implies. This is the suggestion, nay, the clinician's considered judgment, that the theological vision of rebirth will always find itself up against the superior power of nature — Mother Nature, we should say — which has its own established patterns of dying and rising, of birth and rebirth. The theological vision is certainly authentic, and certainly points to something real, yet it also seems a bit melodramatic. It has a certain logic — it *is,* after all, theo-*logical.* But is it not, ultimately, a game that is played by fathers and sons, who have become adept at whistling as the dark deepens around them? In other words, if Luther's melancholy had its origins in the mother-son relationship, we are likely to view theological visions of rebirth — where sons and fathers are reconciled to one another — with considerable caution, for the fact is that these visions fail to take sufficient account of the power of the mother to cast her deathly shadow over her son's entire earthly life.

Just prior to his discussion of melancholy with "teeth in it," Erikson points out that Luther "always objected to the Madonna's mediation in the then popular scheme of religion. He wanted *God's* recognition. A long way stretched ahead of him before he was able to experience, through Christ rather than through Mary, the relevance of the theme of mother and child in addition to that of father and son" (*YML,* 119). One *can* attempt to banish one's self-hatred by replacing one's self-image with the image of Christ and, in doing so, gain the heavenly Father's recognition. But this does not address and bring adequately to consciousness the fact that the self-hatred had its origins in the son's motherhate. Thus, the theological resolution that Luther himself proposes — "Not I, but Christ lives in me" — addresses the symptomatology of the problem but fails to penetrate to its roots. It fails to take the absolutely essential further step, the step back into "little Martin's 'pre-historic' relation to his mother" (*YML,* 73). By itself, Luther's theological resolution contributes to the continued repression of "little Martin's" rage toward his mother for failing, in his view, to provide a secure defense against his father's frequent abuses.

Where Melancholia Is, Let Mourning Be

I suggest that the "clinical" solution to the problem of melancholia is to mourn the loss of the mother and of the self who believed that she would do all in a mother's power to save her son from the evil one. In saying that mourning is the key, I am mindful of Paul Watzlawick's ironic observation that "any reality testing is bound to lead to disappointing anticlimaxes" (1983, 51). But if we wish to go beyond what Freud calls "the attitude of revolt" that characterizes the melancholic view of life and of death, mourning is the answer. Here is Freud on what mourning involves:

> Now in what consists the work which mourning performs? I do not think there is anything far-fetched in the following representation of it. The testing of reality, having shown that the loved object no longer exists, requires forthwith that all the libido shall be withdrawn from its attachments to this object. Against this demand a struggle of course arises — it may be universally observed that man never willingly abandons a libido-position, not even when a substitute is already beckoning to him. This struggle can be so intense that a turning away from reality ensues, the object being clung to through the

medium of a hallucinatory wish-psychosis. *The normal outcome is that deference for reality gains the day.* Nevertheless its behest cannot be at once obeyed. The task is now carried through bit by bit, under great expense of time and cathectic energy, while all the time the existence of the lost object is continued in the mind. Each single one of the memories and hopes which bound the libido to the object is brought up and hyper-cathected, and the detachment of the libido from it accomplished. Why this process of carrying out the behest of reality bit by bit, which is in the nature of a compromise, should be so extraordinarily painful is not at all easy to explain in terms of mental economics. It is worth noting that this pain seems natural to us. *The fact is, however, that when the work of mourning is completed the ego becomes free and unhibited again* [1963, 165–66, my emphases].

What remains ambiguous in Erikson's case study of Luther is whether Luther ever clearly understood that his real grievance was not with his father but with his mother. While *Erikson* is certainly aware that Luther had a deep and lasting grievance with his mother, Luther's disappointment in his mother is essentially a subtext in a case study concerned with the father-son relationship, on both the human and the divine level. Why Erikson focused so much on the father-son relationship has itself been a matter of considerable conjecture (see Johnson 1977), some of it centering on his own autobiography (to which I shall return). However, the fact that I have been able to make a case for the importance of the mother-son relationship using only Erikson's own case study for supporting evidence testifies to his clinical perceptiveness, since he included in his case study "facts" that were peripheral to his own interpretive schema. Indeed, he seems to feel that his approach to Luther was dictated in part by the historical context, for Western religion itself so emphasizes "the divine Father-Son," a schema within which "the mother remains a counterplayer however shadowy" (*YML*, 263).

In any event, following Freud's suggestion that melancholia reflects a failure in the mourning process, we need to affirm the necessity of mourning. In the case of the melancholiac, this means mourning not only the lost object (the beloved mother) but also the child ("little Martin") whose implicit belief in his mother's will to save him from whatever evil might befall him was undermined, never to be restored. An aphoristic rendering of this mourning process, this acceptance of the child's disillusionment, would be something like "Where hatred was, let pure sadness be." This, however, raises a very serious problem for the religionist, as it seems less than self-evident that the mourning process the melancholiac needs to undergo is inherently "religious." On the contrary, as we saw in our discussion of Luther's "theological breakthrough," there is the danger that in finding a role for religion, we shall abort a natural grieving process before it has been completed. Why allow a theo-logic to intervene in a process which, if left to itself, may complete itself?

In his discussion of the weaning process that a young adult undergoes, Bert Kaplan notes that many young adults "report that the sense of being weaned from family care develops slowly over a period of years and that it is experienced partly as a function of their own desire for independence and freedom. Nevertheless, the full force of the fact of being alone in an indifferent world is a good deal more than they have bargained for. The crisis of this period of life may be regarded as a re-experiencing of the anxieties of the earlier period of weaning, but this time without the support of the family" (1977, 392). He suggests that the young adult's first reaction is to search and hunt for the lost object. When this fails, we experience the suffering that comes with deprivation, and the suffering itself may come to replace the lost object. However, this suffering may lead in time to a qualified recovery, one involving "a certain limited optimism that lost objects will sometimes return" as well as the discovery that we may create our own "new objects of value" from a world literally teeming with objects. Hence, there is "a loosening of ties to particular loved objects and the emergence of a relationship to the world taken as a whole" (1977, 400).

But another, more painful act in this mourning process is also requisite: the relinquishing of the self who believed in the lost object. As Freud puts it, in mourning, a part of oneself must be "suppressed" or smothered. In Luther's case, this would have meant putting "little Martin" — the self who had wanted so much to believe in his mother — to death. In so doing, Luther would have been united with those other siblings who had "cried themselves to death." The "weaning process" is not finished until "little Martin" has been put to death, but the "mourning process" is not complete until "little Martin" has been grieved over — and this, I believe, was what the middle-aged Luther's after-dinner reminiscences were designed, in part, to accomplish. What remains unclear, but is well worth asking, is, When Luther thought of Christ reborn in him, did he think of little Martin? One wishes he did.

In any case, Erikson began his study of Luther with a quotation from Kierkegaard about Luther's passion for expressing and describing his suffering. I conclude my discussion of the necessity of mourning lost objects with reference to Kierkegaard's *Fear and Trembling,* which focuses on Abraham's aborted sacrifice of his son, Isaac. Kierkegaard imagines several different scenarios for how this "test" of Abraham's faith might have gone differently and then, in the concluding paragraph to each scenario, comments on the mother, Sarah, who was left behind. These paragraphs all begin with the phrase, "When the child is to be weaned, the mother . . . ," and Kierkegaard then describes actions the mother takes to effect a separation between herself and her child. This is followed in each instance with a sort of beatitude, "How fortunate the one who did not need more terrible means to wean the child" or "How fortunate the child who has not lost his mother in some other way" (Kierkegaard 1983, 9–11; see also Capps 1995, 78–95).

If "religion" is what was going on atop Mount Moriah, where fathers and sons have it out, appealing to each other for justification and deliverance, then I suggest that we would do well to set religion aside, at least provisionally, so that we may attend to the seemingly mundane experience of a mother and son who know in their hearts that they are losing each other through the natural process of weaning, when the "good objects are at least partially withdrawn and provided only on a conditional basis" (Kaplan 1977, 392). This natural process was exacerbated in Luther's case by the fact that his dead siblings were like magnets pulling his mother's love into the dead earth. How fortunate, then, the son who is able to mourn the loss of his mother and put an end to the terrible ordeal of misplaced self-hatred. And how fortunate the son who finds in this immense world of objects one whom he can love and, in loving, can regain his capacity to believe.

This brings us back to the methodological issue with which we began, specifically the matter of Erikson's own apparent belief in the permanent possibility of reconciliation, including the reconciliation of psychiatry and religion. If we find such myths a bit hard to swallow, it is due in no small measure to Erikson's insertion of a parable (James's "Parable of the Carnivorous Reptiles of Geologic Times") into the very middle of his own text, in a chapter appropriately entitled "Allness or Nothingness" (*YML,* 120). This parable about the desperate fight for life among all living species, a parable which prompted James himself to observe that "it may indeed be that no religious reconciliation with the absolute totality of things is possible" (*VRE,* 164), alerts us to the fault line beneath the myths that we ourselves construct, especially the one that banishes the language of hate from the stories we tell about mothers and sons. If we want to speak truly about what occurs between mothers and sons, we must speak in parables.

The Bible as Maternal Matrix

Thus far, I have argued that Luther's "deep disappointment" in his mother at an early age was the source not only of his sadness but also of his deep sense of self-hatred. I have suggested too that a religious view which gives primacy to the Father-Son relationship can only imperfectly and indirectly address this disappointment. For it to be adequately addressed, there needs to be a natural process of mourning, one entirely separate from religious symbols and images, as these have a way of inhibiting the mourning process. Certainly Luther's recourse to the idea of the divine Father-Son contributed only tangentially to this mourning process, for its object was first, foremost, and always the mother whose love was unconditional.

On the other hand, there is a feature of Erikson's account of Luther's religious breakthrough in his chapter "The Meaning of 'Meaning It'" that we have not yet considered, one that I believe suggests a way in which a religious object may both aid the mourning process and take the place of the lost object. This is Erikson's representation of the Bible as being, for Luther, the "maternal matrix" (*YML*, 208). Although in his "Epilogue" Erikson says that "Father religions have mother churches" (*YML*, 263), in his account of Luther's theological breakthrough he focuses not on Mother Church but on the Bible as maternal voice. In his discussion of Luther's emphasis on prayer as key to a religious man's identity, he notes that for Luther rebirth by prayer is passive: "It means surrender to God the Father, but it also means to be reborn *ex matrice scripturae nati,* out of the matrix of the scriptures" (*YML*, 208). Observing that "matrix" is as close as Luther will come to saying "mater," Erikson also suggests that Luther "cannot remember and will not acknowledge that long before he had developed those wilful modes which were specifically suppressed and paradoxically aggravated by a challenging father, a mother had taught him to touch the world with his searching mouth and his probing senses" (*YML*, 208).

In other words, Luther remains unconscious of the connection between the "matrix" of the scriptures and his mother's ways of teaching him how to experience the world around him. He therefore does not realize that the passivity which seemed so hard to acquire "is only a regained ability to be active with his oldest and most neglected modes" (*YML*, 208). Erikson asks:

> Is it coincidence that Luther, now that he was explicitly teaching passivity, should come to the conclusion that a lecturer should feed his audience as a mother suckles her child? Intrinsic to the kind of passivity we speak of is not only the memory of having been given, but also the identification with the maternal giver: "the glory of a good thing is that it flows out to others." *I think that in the Bible Luther at last found a mother whom he could acknowledge: he could attribute to the Bible a generosity to which he could open himself, and which he could pass on to others, at last a mother's son* [*YML,* 208, my emphases].

Continuing, Erikson suggests that the word *passivity* is too flat to capture the "total attitude of living receptively and through the senses," a receptivity that

Luther experienced in and through those experiences with his mother in which he had felt, in all of his senses, her glorious love (*YML,* 208). Because it goes to the very heart of melancholy — its sadness, its rages — the Book of Psalms was the scripture text that first evoked in Luther this new receptivity, this renewed ability to hear his mother's voice that had "sung to him of some heaven" (*YML,* 72). In a very real and tangible sense, the scriptures *are* the lost object. Unlike the mother who was cause of disappointment, anger, and despair, they are the perfect mother, the son's ideal mother. No wonder, then, that Luther insisted on their adequacy for a saving faith — *sola scriptura.*

In noting the psychodynamic importance of the scriptures to Luther, their capacity to dispel his deep melancholic anxieties and despair, Erikson puts forward an argument that he had only recently made with respect to Freud's discovery of the importance of dreams. In "The Dream Specimen of Psychoanalysis," published in 1954 (see Erikson 1987, 237–79), Erikson quotes Freud's observation that "every dream has at least one point at which it is unfathomable; *a central point,* as it were, connecting it with the unknown." Noting that the English "central point" is *Nabel* (a navel) in the original German text, Erikson suggests that for Freud the dream in question was not only about woman but was itself "a mother image." She, the dream itself, "is the one, as the Bible would say, to be 'known' " (1987, 270). Thus, if for Freud it was the dream that promised restoration to the lost object, for Luther it was the scriptures. For Luther, the key to keeping his melancholy from overwhelming him throughout his life was the availability of the scriptures, to which he could always repair for solace and reassurance. The scriptures became even more important to him as his melancholia assumed dangerous depths in his middle years and continued to do so until his death at the age of 63.

The Return of Little Martin

Although Luther's symptoms were not unique in his own times, and his gift of language enabled him to give them a melodramatic flair, Erikson is concerned in his final chapter, "Faith and Wrath," to discern what meaning they had for Luther. He is especially impressed in this regard by two features of Luther's symptomatology. One is that Luther talked frequently about matters best described as "anal." He spoke often of his buttocks, his constipation and problems of urine retention, his diets (which included gorging himself so that he might force the elimination process to work), his farts and feces, and so forth. He once described himself as a "ripe turd" about to cut itself loose from the world, that "gigantic asshole" (*YML,* 245ff.). The other feature is that Luther was much given to explosively uncouth invectives hurled at his enemies and at the devil himself — whose "face" was Luther's "ass" (*YML*, 246). While these verbal expletives might be explained as the "manic" side of Luther's manic-depressive state, Erikson believes that the very form they took is significant. It was as though the only way he *could* continue to pray was by allowing himself to give voice to all the invective and cursing of which he was capable.

Also significant to Erikson is that Luther suffered in later life with a chronic middle-ear infection, which caused a constant buzzing in his ears. Erikson suggests that this buzzing "became the mediator between his physical and his mental torments, the weapon of his inner voice" (*YML*, 244).

In Erikson's judgment, Luther's obsessive preoccupation with his backside, and the endless vocal competition between divine supplication and demonic invective, reveal "the active remnants of his childhood repressions" (*YML*, 245). There are obvious somatic symptoms here, as well as social circumstances connected to Luther's controversial public position (after all, he *did* have various mortal enemies). But what Erikson sees here is a man's desperate struggle to hold himself together, to maintain a sense of continuity and sameness in spite of enormous internal pressures threatening the loss of the sense of identity he had achieved as a young, articulate reformer. Childhood fears that were held at bay throughout his career as a revolutionary force for change had returned with a vengeance, fueling severely neurotic anxieties and threatening his ego identity to its core (*YML*, 247ff.).

This middle-aged Luther interests Erikson as much as, if not more than, young man Luther, enabling him to view Luther as a tragic figure who, for reasons that were in part beyond his control, discovered that the personal solutions rooted in a self-understanding which was religiously grounded, and had worked so well in his young adulthood, were failing him now. Erikson observes that Luther was losing confidence that Christ was indeed "today, here, in me," that Christ was indeed "working in him," that Christ was indeed "the core of his identity." As his childhood fears returned, so also did his original — false — view of Christ as tyrant and judge, as provocateur of a guilty conscience, accusing him, "Again, you have not done what I told you." Coincident with his guilty conscience was a deep and pervasive sense of self-pity, itself reflecting an anxiety that Erikson traces back to childhood fears of being left empty or, more simply, of being left, of being abandoned (Erikson 1963, 410–11).

To lose his Christ was to lose his sense of having an identity, for he had staked everything that he was or hoped to become on the assurance that Christ was and ever would be the guarantor of his identity, without whom he was absolutely, abjectly nothing. In the "Epilogue," however, Erikson implies that Luther turned the tables on his anxieties and doubts by the same method of introspection, based on self-observation, that had secured his ego identity back in the days of his young adulthood. Only this time the insight his self-observation yielded was that for a man of heightened religious sensibilities the issue of ego identity, of the ability to experience one's sense of self as something that has continuity and sameness, is an inevitably chronic problem that will never be resolved in some once-and-for-all fashion. As Erikson puts it, "the integrity crisis" that comes last in the lives of ordinary persons is "a life-long and chronic crisis in a *homo religiosus*" (*YML,* 261).

Thus, on the one hand, the *homo religiosus* is one "who can permit himself to face as permanent the trust problem which drives others in whom it remains or becomes dominant into denial, despair, and psychosis" (*YML,* 262). On the other hand, the homo religiosus "is always older, or in early years suddenly becomes older, than his playmates or even his parents and teachers, and focuses in a precocious way on what it takes others a lifetime to gain a mere inkling of: the questions of how to escape corruption in living and how in death to give meaning to life" (*YML,* 261).

What Erikson seems to be saying here is that the religiously sensitive man experiences *discontinuity* as the deepest reality of all, both because he is an "adult" in his childhood years and because he is very much a "child" in his adult years.

As homo religiosus, Luther must have realized that he could not but be a seriously endangered self, that he could never take for granted his claim on his ego identity, his desire to have an intact, invulnerable, inviolable sense of self. Yet, as Erikson also suggests, it was precisely his acceptance in his later years of his profound vulnerability to discontinuity, dissociation, and fragmentation that became, as it were, his real meaning to himself and others. To make this point more clinically, we would say that the one anxiety to which Luther was chronically subject was the anxiety of losing himself. Yet in this regard his childhood fears — of being abandoned to evil forces — were, paradoxically, supportive. For even in his most desperately melancholic moments their survival in the unconscious substratum of his mind were living proof that he was continuous with the infant whose mother sang to him of some heaven.

This does not mean that the abuses he suffered as a child may be excused or pardoned; as Erikson notes, "the most deadly of all possible sins is the mutilation of a child's spirit, for such mutilation undercuts the life principle of trust" (*YML,* 70). It does mean, however, that through the very *survival* of our childhood fears we recover whatever "continuity and sameness" we may confidently affirm as our own. The felt "smallness" that is an ineradicable substratum of our adult mind may be the only assurance we have (or need?) that we will not lose our fundamental identity. Strangely enough, the fearful child becomes the ineradicable core of this very identity.

In an allusion to the biblical story in which Jesus invites a child to stand in the midst of his disciples (Matthew 18:1–4), Erikson concludes that what Luther and Freud did, each in his own way, was to place the child at the very center of adult life. Thus, "in this book, I have described how Luther, once a sorely frightened child, recovered through the study of Christ's Passion the central meaning of the Nativity; and I have indicated in what way Freud's method of introspection brought human conflict under a potentially more secure control *by revealing the boundness of man in the loves and rages of his childhood.* Thus both Luther and Freud came to acknowledge that 'the child is in the midst.' Both men perfected introspective techniques permitting isolated man to recognize his individual patienthood" (*YML,* 253, my emphasis).

While Erikson celebrates the "healthy" young man Luther, he also has great sympathy for middle-aged Luther, the Luther who understood himself too well ever to imagine that he might shake off his patienthood, no matter how long he lived or how hard he tried. For how could he eradicate the *fearful child* who was deeply imprinted in the recesses of his mind? Nor, Erikson seems to say, should he want to. Thus, the logic of Erikson's psychoanalysis of old man Luther points beyond Christ, Luther's savior in his young adulthood, to Luther's own child self as savior, as that which "works inside" him and becomes the core of his identity. The similarities here between Erikson and Jung on this matter of the child self are striking.

Thus, in the reemergence of profound melancholia in Luther's later years, a melancholia now expressed in biting and explosive invective, there was nonetheless one bright spot in an otherwise grim and dismal picture: the return of "little Martin." What this meant, clinically speaking, has already been noted — that Luther could not succumb to the total fragmentation of his obviously threatened and deeply troubled self because his melancholia reenacted the sufferings of little Martin. *Theologically* speaking, the logic of Erikson's psychoanalysis of middle-aged Luther points beyond Christ, Luther's savior in his young adulthood, to Luther's own child self — little Martin — as savior, as that which "works inside" him, as the essential core of his identity.

Of course, to suggest this is to admit to the limits of Luther's own self-observations, for it appears he never consciously made this transfer to — or association between — the saving Christ and the saving child who is Luther himself in the form of little Martin. But the biblical story in which Jesus places the child in the midst of his disciples is clear on this point: It is not to himself that Jesus bids his disciples attend but to the child — the child who is their very own self. If we agree with William James that our beliefs are reflected in what we choose to attend to (James 1950, 2:295), then it follows that what Jesus is encouraging his disciples to believe in is the child self who is the sole guarantor of their sense of continuity as they undergo the inevitable disintegrative effects of aging.[2]

Erikson indirectly supports this conclusion when he describes, in the "Epilogue," the "three objects [that] awaken dim nostalgias" in the adult self. One is the simple and fervent wish for a hallucinatory sense of unity with the maternal matrix. Another centers on the paternal voice of guiding conscience. The third, the most primordial of all, concerns "the pure self itself, the unborn core of creation, the—as it were, preparental—center where God is pure nothing: *ein lauter Nichts,* in the words of Angelus Silesius" (*YML,* 264). If the "pure self" is the core of one's identity, access to this pure self occurs when we admit our childhood fears into our adult consciousness. When these fears are not raised to consciousness, they continue to manifest themselves in adult anxieties, which in turn jeopardize the pure self itself.

The Portrait: The Recognition of the Self in the Other

Thus far, I have focused exclusively on Erikson's exploration of Luther's lifelong struggle with melancholia and have had nothing directly to say about Erikson's own experience of melancholia. I realize that there is considerable conjecture in my view that Erikson, too, suffered from melancholia. But I am bold enough to put this argument forward because, if true, it affords a new way of looking not only at *Young Man Luther* but also at the whole corpus of his work.

We may begin to get at the issue of Erikson's own melancholia by asking why it was that he wrote a book in the mid-1950s on Martin Luther. Of course, we have his wry comment that he did not intend to write a *book* about Luther but Luther proved too "bulky" a subject for a mere chapter. This does not, however, explain why Erikson wanted to write about Luther in the first place. In his preface to *Young Man Luther,* he suggests that he wrote it out of a desire to "take account of recent thinking about the ego's adaptive as well as its defensive functions," and he adds that his study of Luther will enable him to "concentrate on the powers of recovery inherent in the young ego" (*YML,* 8). If a deeply troubled youth like Luther could be salvaged, so, he believes, may equally troubled contemporary youths. But having said this, he goes on to acknowledge personal doubts as to whether "the impetus for writing anything but a textbook can ever be rationalized," and he notes that his choice of subject forced him to deal with problems of faith and problems of Germany, "two enigmas which I could have avoided by writing about some other young great man. But it seems that I did not wish to avoid them" (*YML,* 9). This implies that he had personal reasons for writing *Young Man Luther.* I suggest that the most critical personal reason was that he recognized something of himself in Luther, and that this self-recognition did not exclude Luther's melancholia.

The catalyst for this self-recognition was his resignation in 1951 of his professorship at the University of California over his refusal to sign a special oath of loyalty to the United States government (Erikson 1987, 618–20). The reader who is aware of this experience in Erikson's life cannot but sense resonances of it in his chapter "The Meaning of 'Meaning It,'" in which he portrays the period in Luther's life that culminated in his famous refusal to recant his writings at the Diet of Worms. The same tragic sense that one must take a stand, and can do no other, is poignantly expressed in Erikson's explanation for why he could not, in good conscience, sign the special oath of loyalty.

There was also a deeper, long-standing vocational interest in his decision to write on Luther. This related to Erikson's desire as a young man to become an artist. We have already noted his observation that Luther "proved too bulky a man to be merely a chapter" in a book (*YML*, 7). Since his preferred medium as a young artist in Munich was woodcuts of enormous size (Coles 1970, 15), we might say that his own artistic ambitions were a factor in his discovery that young man Luther was "too bulky" for a single chapter, especially in light of his observation that "the early Luther was by no means the typical pyknic, obese and round-faced, that he became in his later years. He was bony, with furrows in his cheeks, and a stubborn, protruding chin" (*YML*, 196). His artist's rendering of Luther's portrait continues:

> His eyes were brown and small, and must have been utterly fascinating, judging by the variety of impressions they left on others. They could appear large and prominent or small and hidden; deep and unfathomable at one time, twinkling like stars at another, sharp as a hawk's, terrible as lightning, or possessed as though he were insane. There was an intensity of conflict about his face, which might well impress a clinician as revealing the obsessive character of a very gifted, cunning, and harsh man who possibly might be subject to states of uncontrolled fear or rage. Just because of this conflicted countenance, Luther's warmth, wit, and childlike candor must have been utterly disarming; and there was a total discipline about his personality which broke down only on rare occasions. It was said about Luther that he did not like to be looked in the eye, because he was aware of the revealing play of his expression while he was trying to think [*YML*, 196].

This visual portrait of Luther reflects Erikson's discovery as a student at the Psychoanalytic Institute in Vienna that he could become a clinician and still "keep contact with the artist in me" (Erikson 1975, 29), a judgment confirmed several decades later when, in writing his first book, *Childhood and Society,* he found that "clinical writing lent itself to artistic as well as theoretical expression" (1975, 29–30).[3]

On the artistic level, Erikson provides in *Young Man Luther* a portrait of Luther, one composed of several critical scenes in Luther's life: the "fit in the choir"; the banquet scene where Luther was publicly humiliated by his father; the altar scene where he experienced an anxiety attack when performing his first mass; and the "revelation in the tower" scene. The banquet scene recalls Breughel's *Wedding Banquet,* while the altar scene — by way of contrast — recalls the Budapest Master's *Mass of Pope Gregory the Great,* a depiction of the pope's vision of Christ as he lifted the Host. But the artist who is closest to Luther's own way of looking at things is, in Erikson's view, Albrecht Dürer. In the crucial passages in which Erikson discusses Luther's theological breakthrough via the internalized Christ, he suggests that "the artist closest to Luther in spirit was Dürer, who etched his own face into Christ's countenance" (*YML,* 213).

Erikson also addresses the common complaint by portrait artists' subjects (and their relatives) that the painter has failed to capture the subject's essential character. In his chapter "The Fit in the Choir," in which he reviews and critiques as inadequate the portraits of Luther offered by other biographers, contending (as we have seen) that they have either spiritualized him, demonized him, or reduced him to a clinical diagnosis, he quotes with favor Jacob Burkhardt's contention that Luther "should be taken for what he was."

> But how does one take a *great* man "for what he was"? The very adjective seems to imply that something about him is too big, too awe-ful, too shiny to be encompassed. Those who nonetheless set out to describe the whole man seem to have only three choices. They can step so far back that the great man's contours appear complete but hazy; or they can step closer and closer, gradually concentrating on a few aspects of the great man's life, seeing one part of it as big as the whole, or the whole as small as one part. If neither of these works, there is always polemics; one takes the great man in the sense of appropriating him and of excluding others who might dare to do the same [*YML,* 36].

The implication here is that those who cannot find an appropriate artistic way of "focusing" and "focusing on" the great man resort to polemics instead. While Erikson knows that his clinical orientation will enable him to avoid partisan polemics, the artist in him nonetheless worries that Luther, as a ghost from the grave and the subject of the portrait, will condemn his efforts with the very same words that he allegedly roared forth in the monastery chapel: "*It isn't me!*" The portrait painter's nightmare. All that Erikson can say to his unwilling subject is that he — the artist/clinician — knows from personal and professional experience how powerful is the "need to negate" ("it isn't me") before one can affirm anything at all. This feature of Luther's personality Erikson understands, as he has witnessed it time and time again in his work with other gifted youths suffering from "identity diffusion."

Many other examples of Erikson's artistic perspective in *Young Man Luther* could be cited (such as his discussion of the Florentine schools, which reflects his own years of residence in Florence as an aspiring artist [*YML*, 191–92]), but the example most relevant to my argument that Erikson himself suffered from melancholy is to be found in the "Epilogue." Here, as I have already noted, he is concerned with images of God and self and describes the experience of looking "through a glass darkly," where one finds oneself "in an inner cosmos in which the outlines of three objects awaken dim nostalgias." The first is the image of the mother, "symbolized by the affirmative face of charity, graciously inclined." The second, chronologically later, is the voice of the father that puts an end to the simple paradise as he sanctions — or, more likely, demands — energetic action. Third, but chronologically prior to the others, "the glass shows the pure self itself, the unborn core of creation, the — as it were, preparental — center where God is pure nothing: *ein lauter Nichts,* in the words of Angelus Silesius." These three images, he concludes, "are the main religious objects" (*YML*, 264). Note that he sees the "objects" of religious devotion, fear, and purity as internalized images, as pictures in the mind, and that the luminosity of the maternal image is in marked contrast to the utter darkness of the original image of the pure self. The image of the father is, as we have come to expect from Erikson's earlier analyses of the father-son relationship, a far more threatening image than that of the mother.

However, if we focus on the images of the pure self and the self who experiences the mother's affirmative face, we gain the distinct impression that for Erikson the work of one's lifetime is to clarify the image of the self, to bring it to light, and this is possible only if the self is recognized by another self, and thereby confirms its very existence. If William James emphasized introspection as the primary means of self-discovery and discernment, and therefore the primary method of psychology itself (James 1950, 1:185), Erikson emphasizes the mediated nature of self-recognition. One knows oneself by being known by another. The search for identity is not the incessant asking of the question, Who am I? Rather, it is the searching of other faces to discover oneself through others: Who do *you* say I am?

What makes this a religious searching is that its ontogenetic source is in the self-recognitions which occur in the infant-mother relationship. In a section of *Toys and Reasons* entitled "Infancy and the Numinous: The Light, the Face, and the Name," Erikson notes that the infant "develops a benevolent self-image (a certified narcissism, we may say) grounded in the recognition of an all-powerful and mostly benevolent (if sometimes strangely malevolent) Other" (1977, 87). This "first and dimmest affirmation, this sense of a hallowed presence, contributes to mankind's ritual-making a pervasive element which is best called the *numinous*" (1977, 89). While he acknowledges that "of all institutions that of organized religion has the strongest claim to being in charge of the numinous," the visual arts best capture the transcendent power of the numinous: "The human being which at the beginning wants . . . to be gazed upon and to respond to the gaze, to look up to the parental countenance and to be responded to, continues to look up, and to look for somebody to look up to, and that is somebody who will, in the very act of returning his glance, lift him up. . . . In the Visconti Hours, where Barbello depicts Maria's death, God in heaven is shown holding in his arms her spirit in the form of a swaddled baby, and 'returning the gaze of Mary's soul' " (1977, 91). Maria, the one who was looked up to by the infant Jesus, is now the one who is looking upward as God returns her hopeful gaze. Yet the form of the encounter is the same.

In his study of the art of portraiture (1991), Richard Brilliant lends considerable support to Erikson's view that the original experience of "hallowed presence" is the event of mother and infant recognizing each other. But he goes farther, claiming that all portraiture has its ontogenetic source in this infantile experience. Erikson could not agree more with Brilliant's view that "the dynamic nature of portraits and the 'occasionality' that anchors their imagery in life seems ultimately to depend on the primary experience of the infant in arms. That child, gazing up at its mother, imprints her vitally important image so firmly on its mind that soon enough she can be recognized almost instantaneously and without conscious thought; spontaneous face recognition remains an important instrument of survival, separating friend from foe, that persists into adult life" (1991, 9).

Brilliant uses Erikson's own term — "identity" — to characterize the life-long process begun in this original recognition scene. The essential constituents of a person's identity are "a recognized or recognizable appearance; a given name that refers to no one else; a social, interactive function that can be defined; in context, a pertinent characterization; and a consciousness of the distinction between one's own person and another's, and of the possible relationship between them" (1991, 9).

Most difficult to realize on canvas is the "pertinent characterization," because it is related to but separate from physical appearance, which is unstable over time, and social effect, which too is passing. Whether or not this "persistent inner character or 'soul' can be empirically demonstrated," the portrait artist believes that it exists, and he depends on "his insight as an analyst of character and on the accumulation of his own memories of the subject" to render it visually (1991, 12–13).

An especially important feature of portraiture is the role of the artist's own self-identity in the artistic rendering of his or her subject. Brilliant notes that

Francis Bacon's portraits of popes, friends, patrons, and himself "all seem to look alike, as if he were seeking to express himself through their contorted images" (1991, 156). If Bacon's portraits "implicate the artist in each image as if he mirrored his own anxious appearance in their faces," this is an extreme case of a more general phenomenon of the artist's "presence" in the painting even as he maintains an objective distance from his subject. In an early essay on children's narratives, Erikson makes this comment: "We could say about the artist that he withdraws behind his art while offering an image of himself in his work" (1987, 46).

Assuming that this is also true of Erikson's portrait of Luther, in what ways is *Young Man Luther* a self-portrait? In what sense does it, like Dürer's portrait of Christ, reflect the artist's own self-image? Following Brilliant's suggestion that the ontogenetic source of all portraiture is the mother-infant relationship, I suggest that the most important reflection of Erikson's own self-image in *Young Man Luther* is precisely the mother-son theme that lies, shadowlike, behind the melodramatic story of father and son. While Erikson claims to base his "conjectures" about the maternal sources of Luther's higher aspirations as well as his inner torments on his "clinician's judgment," there are grounds for these conjectures that are much closer to home: his relationship with his own mother.

In his essay "'Identity Crisis' in Autobiographic Perspective" (1975, 17–47), Erikson responds to the request that he write autobiographically about his "discovery" of the problem of identity.[4] He accepts the fact that this will require him to say something about his own origins, as the question of origins "often looms large in individuals who are driven to be original" (1975, 26–27). He says of his origins,

> I grew up in Karlsruhe in southern Germany as the son of a pediatrician, Dr. Theodor Homburger, and his wife Karla, née Abrahamsen, a native of Copenhagen, Denmark. All through my earlier childhood, *they kept secret from me the fact that my mother had been married previously; and that I was the son of a Dane who had abandoned her before my birth.* They apparently thought that such secretiveness was not only workable (because children then were not held to know what they had not been told) but also advisable, so that I would feel thoroughly at home in their home. As children will do, I played in with this *and more or less forgot the period before the age of three, when mother and I had lived alone* [1975, 27, my emphases].

He makes this "forgetting" seem natural, almost benign, yet under the circumstances the psychoanalytic term *repression* certainly applies to such "forgettings" as this.

Continuing, Erikson contrasts the earliest years of his life during which he and his mother lived alone with the years that ensued from the time his step-father entered the picture:

> Then her friends had been artists working in the folk style of Hans Thoma of the Black Forest. They, I believe, provided my first male imprinting before *I had to come to terms with that intruder, the bearded doctor, with his healing love and mysterious instruments.* Later, I enjoyed going back and forth between the painters' studios and our house, the first floor of which, in the afternoons, was filled with tense and trusting mothers and children. *My sense of being "different" took refuge (as it is apt to do even in children without such acute life problems) in fantasies of how I, the son of much better parents, had been altogether a foundling.* In the meantime, however, my adoptive father was anything but the proverbial stepfather. He had given me his last name (which I have retained as a middle name) and expected me to become a doctor like himself [1975, 27, my emphases].

Later, Erikson comments further on his "stepson identity" and its role in his tendency to work on the boundaries between disciplines: "That a stepson's negative identity is that of a bastard need only be acknowledged here in passing — and by myself. But a habitual stepson might also use his talents to avoid belonging anywhere quite irreversibly; working between the established fields can mean avoiding the disciplines necessary for any one field; and, being enamored with the aesthetic order of things, one may well come to avoid their ethical and political as well as their methodological implications" (1975, 31).

In this attempt to explain the early origins of his discovery of the problem of identity, Erikson gives primacy to the stepson theme, to the fact that he was the adoptive son of Dr. Theodor Homburger, whose name he retained as his middle name after adopting the rather enigmatic last name of "Erikson," which *could* refer to the mythical father that a foundling imagines — "I am Erik, *son of Erik*" — or *might* instead suggest that he had to become his own father as he had no trust or confidence in his stepfather. Either way, the later name change, which occurred after his immigration to America in 1933, suggests that young Erik never fully accepted his mother's marriage to the man to whom she brought him for medical attention.

On the other hand, by focusing on the stepson theme, Erikson deftly minimizes the fact that he was "a bastard," which "need only be acknowledged here in passing." The very wording of the fact of his illegitimacy minimizes the scandal involved: "They kept secret from me the fact that my mother had been married previously; and that I was the son of a Dane who had abandoned her before my birth." The reader is likely to take this to mean that he was the son of the man to whom his mother was married, who then abandoned her before Erik's birth. In point of fact, however, he was the child of a man — a Gentile — with whom his Jewish mother had had an affair (see "Obituary," *New York*

Times, May 13, 1994). If this man subsequently "abandoned" her, it was also true that she had "abandoned" her own husband to have an affair with a man on whom she had little claim, a man who apparently abandoned her; faced with the scandal of having conceived out of wedlock, she went by herself to Germany to bear her child.

Erikson acknowledges that these "acute life problems" made him feel different, and he mentions that his sense of differentness was accentuated by the fact that, while ostensibly the son of Dr. Homburger, he was nonetheless "blond and blue-eyed, and grew flagrantly tall" (1975, 27). He is notably uncritical of his mother for her role in all this. He not only writes protectively of the circumstances of his conception but also excuses the fact that she and her new husband created additional difficulties for him by keeping him in the dark as to the real circumstances surrounding his parentage. Whatever overt criticism he allows himself is directed toward his stepfather, the man who "intruded" into his life with his mother, and in whose home he never felt fully at home. Years later, he calls it *"their* home."

This positive account of his mother continues throughout his autobiographical essay. Noting that "the malignancy of the identity crisis is determined both by defects in a person's early relationship to his mother and by the incompatibility or irrelevance of the values available in adolescence," he writes:

> I must say that I was fortunate in both respects. Even as I remember the mother of my early years as pervasively sad, I also visualize her as deeply involved in reading what I later found to have been such authors as Brandes, Kierkegaard, and Emerson, and I could never doubt that her ambitions for me transcended the conventions which she, nevertheless, faithfully served. On the other hand, she and my stepfather had the fortitude to let me find my way unhurriedly in a world which, for all the years of war and revolution, still seemed oriented toward traditional alternatives, and in which threatening cataclysms could still be ascribed to the episodic transgressions of criminal men and evil nations or classes [1975, 32–33].

The reason he considers himself "fortunate" is that he had a mother who, while faithful to the conventions she upheld as the wife of Dr. Homburger, encouraged her son to aspire to something higher or greater. She did this by reading books in his presence. If her husband's medical instruments were cold and harsh reminders of the real world of pain and suffering, her books were just the opposite, conveying her higher ambitions for her son. Integral to the whole "maternal matrix," they represented the unspoken relationship that continued to exist between them, a relationship Dr. Homburger could not intrude upon.

But have we not heard all this before? Surely it is reminiscent of these words he wrote about Luther's mother: "It has been surmised that the mother suffered under the father's personality, and gradually became embittered; and there is also a suggestion that a certain sad isolation which characterized young Luther was to be found also in his mother" (*YML,* 72). And these: "I will state, as a clinician's judgment, that nobody could speak and sing as Luther did if his mother's voice had not sung to him of some heaven; that nobody could be as torn between his masculine and feminine sides, nor have such a range of both, who did not at one time feel that he was like his mother" (*YML,* 72–73). Here we have two sad women, one of whom sang, the other of whom read, but both of whom inspired their sons to transcend the conventions of a patriarchal society that they themselves faithfully served.

Like Luther's, Erikson's melancholy was early and forever linked to his relationship to his mother. What especially impresses Erikson about Luther, and is the crux of his own self-recognition in his portrait of Luther, is Luther's capacity to conquer his melancholia by depending on the reassuring words of the Bible (*YML,* 208). In them, he has perennial access to the "numinous" quality of his mother's reassuring face. The mother, then, is identified with books, and books, especially inspirational books, compensate for the loss of the original maternal image, as they are the boy's link to the era in his life when he had his mother all to himself, before the advent of "the intruder." To read them, or even simply to watch his mother read them, is to reawaken that dim nostalgia when mother and son were as one.

If Erikson also "dis-identifies" with Luther, this is in the fact that he never discusses autobiographically the internalized rage, even hate, underlying the more visibly apparent sadness of melancholia, which in Luther's case he explores through Luther's very ambivalent commentary on Mary, the mother of Jesus (*YML,* 119–22). Erikson makes no corresponding acknowledgment of rage or hatred toward his own mother. Instead, there is a strong desire to be protective of her, to use his own very skillful facility with words to veil the truth of his own conception, placing the blame squarely on the shoulders of the man who abandoned her. In a sense, the adult Erikson has chosen to protect his mother not only from an inquisitive public, which does not have an inherent right to know about these matters, but also from the child Erik, who *did* feel that he had a right to know, a right to be told the truth. He excuses his mother's failure to be truthful to her child on the grounds that parents in those days assumed that children would not know "what they had not been told," as if children would not hear it from some other, less sympathetic source. But the fact remains that she and her husband placed him in the awkward position of having to pretend that he did not know that what they had told him was untrue.

Whatever rage he may have felt then at their having deceived him is now obliterated by his effort to understand the matter from his mother's perspective. She did this, he believes, because she and her husband wanted him to "feel thoroughly at home in their home." Also obliterated, however, are the first three years of his life, as he represses "the period before the age of three, when mother and I had lived alone." Thus, he attempts to deal with the rage he felt toward his mother with an empathic understanding of her own plight, her own "pervasive sadness," and with a psychohistorical explanation that in those days parents had ideas to which we ourselves no longer subscribe.

So far as portraiture is concerned, then, there is considerable self-recognition in *Young Man Luther,* but there is also an attempt to distance himself from his subject where rage is concerned. Is this distancing a reflection of Erikson's own failure to be relentlessly introspective, or might it be due to his belief that he has worked these issues through in the course of being psychoanalyzed, that his earlier emotions of rage have been replaced by insight? Has mourning displaced melancholia? As I am suspicious of adults' efforts to explain parental malfeasance on the grounds that it was done with good intentions (see Miller 1984), I am reluctant to take such a sanguine view of Erikson's adult disposition to defend his mother's deceptions, no matter how understandable they were. I believe that a lingering rage is discernable in his writings on womanhood and the "inner space," essays to which I now wish to turn.

The Still Life: Womanhood and the "Inner Space"

In his "Epilogue" to *Young Man Luther,* Erikson offers a defense of his portrait of Luther and, in this context, makes his first reference to the "inner space": "I have implied that the original faith which Luther tried to restore goes back to the basic trust of early infancy. In doing so I have not, I believe, diminished the wonder of what Luther calls God's disguise. If I assume that it is the smiling face and the guiding voice of infantile parent images which religion projects onto the benevolent sky, I have no apologies to render to an age which thinks of painting the moon red. *Peace comes from the inner space"* (YML, 265–66, my emphasis). Exactly ten years later he published an essay entitled "Womanhood and the Inner Space" (1968, 261–94). Because this essay engendered considerable controversy and criticism, he wrote a second essay, "Once More the Inner Space" (1975, 225–47), which concluded with a similar refusal to apologize for the religious views expressed in the earlier essay.

If Erikson was ill-prepared for the controversy that followed the publication of *Young Man Luther,* he seemed even more startled by the negative response to his first essay on womanhood. Women had been among his most enthusiastic readers and most stalwart supporters, in part because his writings and personal demeanor reflected an identification with women that was patently missing in the writings of other male psychoanalysts. The negative response, led by Kate Millett's devastating critique (1969), had a kind of domino effect, leading to feminist critiques of his life-cycle theory as male biased (Gilligan 1982; but see Capps 1993, 134–36) and to objections to his portrayal of the American "Mom" in his essay "Reflections on the American Identity" (1963, 285–325). His efforts to dissociate himself from Freud's views on women, as in his critique of Freud's treatment of "Dora" (Erikson 1964, 166–74; see also Decker 1991, 113), were overwhelmed by this wave of negative response. Even today there is a prevailing reluctance to reconsider his essays on womanhood in light of changes in feminist ideology. In contemporary literature on women's issues, his first essay is usually summarized (and rejected) with a brief cryptic sentence, and the second essay is completely overlooked.

In the original essay, he indicates that he is very much aware that he is embarking on a subject that "always retains an intense actuality" both for himself and for the reader (1968, 265). Invoking the comment made by the Vermont farmer to a driver who asked him for directions — "Well, now, if I wanted to go where you want to go, I wouldn't start from here" — he acknowledges that his professional identity as a psychoanalyst is a liability, as he decidedly does *not* want to begin his analysis of womanhood with Freud's own theories about penis envy and the like. On the other hand, he believes this may be a strength as well, because psychoanalysis always alerts us to the danger that new insights into matters of identity may produce new repressions.

The major section of this essay centers on Erikson's contribution in the 1940s to a research study involving children aged ten to twelve. Over a two-year span, he saw 150 boys and 150 girls three times each, presenting them with the task of using toys to construct "an exciting scene" from an imaginary movie and then verbally relate its "plot." He soon discovered that the children were more involved in the "spatial" than the "narrative" feature of the assignment. Gender differences were not the initial focus of interest, but as the study progressed he found that girls and boys used space differently, that girls tended to emphasize inner space while boys emphasized outer space (1968, 270). A typical girl's scene

is a house *interior,* represented either as a configuration of furniture without any surrounding walls or by a simple *enclosure* built with blocks. In the girl's scene, people and animals are mostly *within* such an interior or enclosure, and they are primarily people or animals in a *static* (sitting or standing) position. Girls' enclosures consist of low walls, i.e., only one block high, except for an occasional *elaborate doorway.* These interiors of houses with or without walls were, for the most part, expressly *peaceful.* Often, a little girl was playing the piano. In a number of cases, however, the interior was *intruded* by animals or dangerous men. Yet the idea of an intruding creature did not necessarily lead to the defensive erection of walls or the closing of doors. Rather the majority of these intrusions have an element of humor and pleasurable excitement [1968, 270–71].

In contrast, boys' typical scenes involved high towers that collapse, people and animals outside enclosures, elaborate automotive accidents, and so on.

Erikson notes that various interpretations have been offered for these differences in play constructions, some based on psychoanalytic psychosocial theory, others on social-role theory. He argues, however, for "an altogether more inclusive interpretation, according to which a profound difference exists between the sexes in *the experience of the ground plan of the human body*" (1968, 273, my emphasis). Unlike men, women have "a productive interior" that not only affords "a sense of vital inner potential" but also "exposes women early to a specific sense of loneliness, to a fear of being left empty or deprived of treasure, of remaining unfulfilled and of drying up" (1968, 277). This theme of "emptiness," particularly reminiscent of the "Beyond Anxiety" chapter of *Childhood and Society* (1963, 410–11), is especially associated with women, because "emptiness is the female form of perdition — known at times to men of the inner life" but "standard experience for all women" (1968, 278).

He finds support for his view of women being identified with inner space and men with exterior, or outer, space in a motion picture taken in Africa — "visual data" — showing how in a wandering troop of baboons the males protectively surround the females. He observes that the body structure, posture, and behavior of the males and females fit into "an ecology of divided function," both sexes adapted "to their respective tasks of harboring and defending the concentric circles, from the procreative womb to the limits of the defensible territory" (1968, 280). Obviously, *human* society and technology have transcended this early evolutionary arrangement, making room for "cultural triumphs of adaptation." Yet "when we speak of biologically given strengths and weaknesses in the human female, we may yet have to accept as one measure of all difference the biological rock-bottom of sexual differentiation. In this, the woman's productive inner space may well remain an inescapable criterion, whether conditions permit her to build her life partially or wholly around it or not" (1968, 281).

However, he also comments on the tendency of the *young* woman to become "free from the tyranny of the inner space" as she ventures "into 'outer space' with a bearing and a curiosity which often appears hermaphroditic if not downright 'masculine.' A special ambulatory dimension is thus added to the inventory of her spatial behavior, which many societies counteract with special rules of virginal restraint" (1968, 282).

Erikson concludes that "only a total configurational approach—somatic, historical, individual—can help us to see the differences of functioning and experiencing in context, rather than in isolated and senseless comparison" (1968, 289). If the somatic has a vital role to play, so does history, and so does the individuality of each woman (and man). He notes that psychoanalytic ego psychology has emphasized the importance of the ego as mediator among the somatic, the historical, and the uniquely personal, "for the ego is the guardian of the indivisibility of the person" (1968, 289). But he insists that his emphasis in this particular essay on the "somatic" is not a "renewed male attempt" to argue that woman's procreative endowment "dooms" every woman to perpetual motherhood and provides a warrant for denying her the "full equivalence of individuality" and "full equality of citizenship." On the other hand, he worries about a "militant individualism and equalitarianism" that has "inflated this core of individuality to the point where it seems altogether free of somatic and social differences" (1968, 290). The real question, "is how these three areas of life reach into each other—certainly never without conflict and tension and yet with some continuity of purpose" (1968, 291).[5]

Toward the end of the essay he refers to his last conversation with Paul Tillich, who worried that the psychoanalytic emphasis on the ego and its adaptation to the world might have the unintended effect of making individuals ill-equipped to face "ultimate concerns." Erikson believes Tillich agreed with his response that, on the contrary, only when ego adaptation is achieved is one free to face and recognize these ultimate concerns. He ends the essay on a decidedly religious note: "One may add that man's Ultimate has too often been visualized as an infinity which begins where the male conquest of outer spaces ends, and a domain where an 'even more' omnipotent and omniscient Being must be submissively acknowledged. The Ultimate, however, may well be found also to reside in the Immediate, which has so largely been the domain of woman and of the inward mind" (1968, 293–94).

In "Once More the Inner Space," published seven years later, Erikson begins with an artistic allusion that recalls his comment at the close of *Young Man Luther* that "if I assume that it is the smiling face and the guiding voice of infantile parent images which religion projects onto the benevolent sky, I have no apologies to render to an age which thinks of painting the moon red"

(*YML*, 266). He asks his reader to turn with him to his earlier paper so that he may show "how some sentences, when used for political rhetoric, lost their theoretical half tones and, instead, took on one (inflammable) color" (1975, 228). The critic who made Erikson "see red" was Kate Millett, author of *Sexual Politics* (1969). Her primary criticism of Erikson was that in viewing anatomy as one of the three "defining" features of sexual differentiation, he merely repeated and reinforced "psychoanalysis' persistent error of mistaking learned behavior for biology. . . . Anatomy is only destiny insofar as it determines cultural conditioning" (Millett 1969, 215; quoted in Erikson 1975, 228).

He responds that if his critics are saying that anatomy does in fact to some extent "determine cultural conditioning," there is really no argument between them. But he believes that this "agreement" between his critics and himself, if such it is, obscures his basic point that the somatic, the historical, and the individual—"the three aspects of human fate"—are *relative* to one another, for each *codetermines* the others: "Such 'systematic going around in circles' (as I have called it, so as not to overdo the word 'relativity') takes some thought which is indispensable to the study of human facts" (1975, 228). So a significant difference between Erikson and his critics is that he tends to think "configurationally" (in circular fashion), while they impute to him a way of thinking that is basically linear (or simple cause-effect reasoning).

He also reminds his readers that if Freud, the physician, made his famous "biology is destiny" statement to challenge the hubris of the politician Napoleon's assertion that "history is destiny," Erikson, "an heir of ego psychology," has dared to ask "rather modestly whether we ourselves are not also part of our destiny. I find myself in a body that exists in a particular social place and historical period, and I must attempt to make the most and the best of that. . . . A freer choice nobody can claim or grant to anybody" (1975, 229).

As for his emphasis on the inner space, he notes that one publication (approvingly) took him to mean that men are "penetrators," women are "enclosers," that men are "outer-directed," women "inner-directed." Another author (disapprovingly) understood him to be saying that men are active, women intuitive, that men are interested in things and ideas, women in people and feelings. Another critic (Millett) took him to be saying that a woman who has not experienced childbirth will forever feel unfulfilled, and that with each menses a woman cries to heaven over a child not conceived, when in fact he was referring to a mother's loss of her child by miscarriage or in childbirth. He acknowledges that his writing style is partially to blame for such misreadings, for in addition to some vagueness of language, the essay included "a few imprudent words and phrases as well as some ambivalently poetic ones" that he would want to change. But such misreadings are also due, he feels, to the fact that in America the dominant discourse is the social one, so that whatever a psychologist might write about "womanhood" (or "manhood") is quickly recontextualized in terms of its "social role" implications. While not adverse to having his views so recontextualized, he thinks it important then to differentiate between "the role concepts which emerge in a given country" and "the role ideology dominant in it" (1975, 236). Noting that in America "the emphasis on *choice* in all social roles has become an ideological faith," he sees a danger that this ideology may obscure what "no true role *concept* would ignore," namely, "the fact that functioning roles . . . are tied to certain conditions: a role can only provide leeway within the limits of what bodily constitution can sustain, social structure can make workable, and personality formation can integrate" (1975, 236).

Concerned that women may be taken in by the same ideology that had men believing they could be whatever they chose ("self-made men"), he nonetheless discusses in the last half of the essay ways in which the sociocultural meanings traditionally ascribed to the somatic dimension of the overall configuration of human life may be reconfigured. He argues that the traditionally negative view of the inner space as a metaphor of confinement and passivity (and, in more extreme cases, of masochistic suffering, with its "secondary gains of devious dominance") may be replaced with a more positive view of the inner space as self-empowering. Here he supports those who argue for the right of a woman to exercise personal autonomy over and within the inner space, defining "autonomy" in this instance not as "separateness" (as Gilligan does in *In a Different Voice*) but as "self-governance."

Yet, equally important is the need to challenge the fact that in the past young women were forced to restrain their "ambulatory" modes of somatic being in favor of a certain "inner-directedness." Their "self-centered strength and peace" was bought at the price of abandonment of "much of the early locomotor vigor and the social and intellectual initiative and intrusiveness which, potentially, girls share with boys" (1975, 242). He sees the need for women (and men) to develop those potentials which in the past were not developed because "each sex overdeveloped what was given" and then "compensated for what it had to deny." In effect, each received "special approbation for a divided self-image" (1975, 242).

This essay concludes, then, much as the original did, noting that men have traditionally sought the Ultimate in the far reaches of "outer space," whereas women have traditionally experienced it in the innermost core of their being. Instead, we need a new "guiding vision," in which men withdraw their "commitment from a variety of overextended fighting fronts" and engage in "a new search for anchor in that inner space which we all share," while women bring their "special modes of experience" to "the overall planning and governing so far monopolized by men" (*YML,* 247). It is clear from this concluding statement that the inner space has a religious — *numinous* — quality for Erikson. Precisely for this reason he "still believes" and will not "apologize for" what he said in the earlier essay "in somewhat creedal terms about the Ultimate residing in the Immediate" (1975, 247). This statement, in turn, recalls his religio-poetic reflections on the "inner cosmos" in the concluding paragraphs of *Young Man Luther.*

I believe that Erikson was basically correct in his complaint that he had been misread by his critics, especially in their tendency to read social-role implications into what he was describing as an unconscious, or at best a preconscious, fear characteristic of women — that is, of being "left empty" or, more simply, of being left, being abandoned. Similar misreadings of his life-cycle theory (e.g., Gilligan 1982) have made it difficult for a new generation of readers to engage Erikson's texts on their own terms. Like Freud, Erikson is now numbered among those unfortunate authors to whom readers are most likely to be introduced by their critics, and rare is the critic who does not to some degree misrepresent the views of the author being criticized.

On the other hand, I believe that Erikson's essays on womanhood and the inner space reflect a deep ambivalence regarding motherhood, an ambivalence that is in turn revealing of melancholia. To make this case, I want to introduce another artistic genre, still life, because it gives us a unique angle from which to understand how the inner space has traditionally been gendered and how men, especially those with artistic — and religious — sensibilities identify the inner space with their own unrealized potential.

In *Looking at the Overlooked: Four Essays on Still Life Painting* (1990), Norman Bryson notes that for still life "no theoretical body of work exists at a level of sophistication comparable to that found in contemporary discussions of history painting or landscape; it is to the higher genres, regarded as intrinsically more interesting, that modern art gravitates" (1990, 136). Why this ambivalent response to still life? And what connections exist between the terms of this ambivalence and the cultural construction of gender? Since the "basic routines of self-maintenance" (such as cooking and eating, shopping, seeing to domestic chores, keeping our creatural habitat in viably good repair) are necessary for our welfare and respond to the inescapable conditions of human life, the *value* that is placed on the life of creaturely routine is very much a matter of culture and of history: "Whether these activities are respected or dismissed, valued or despised, depends on the work of ideology" (Bryson 1990, 137). Presumably, the need to devalue the life of creaturely routine arises from the threat it poses for those who think that some other level of culture affords access to superior or exalted modes of experience.

Bryson suggests that one possible dimension of threat is the fact that the *forms* represented in still life are virtually indestructible. While bowls, vases, and dinner plates reflect the cultural values of their creators and manufacturers, their forms change very little over long periods of time because they are meant for purposes that do not vary. Although their names seem demeaned — jug, jar, bowl, pitcher — the

> forms of still life have enormous *force*. As human time flows around the forms, smoothing them and tending them through countless acts of attention across countless centuries, time secretes a priceless product: familiarity. It creates an abiding world where the subject of culture is naturally at ease and at home. . . . The forms of still life are strong enough to make the difference between brutal existence and human life: without them there is no continuity of generations, no human legacy, only an intermittent and flickering chaos; with them, there is cultural memory and family; an authentically civilized world. . . . While complicated tools and technologies are subject to rapid change, simple utensils obey a slow, almost geological rhythm [Bryson 1990, 138–39].

Thus, what still life threatens are the ideological assumptions that ascribe high cultural significance to historical events and low cultural significance to the routines of self- and household maintenance: "This is not simply a formal choice between genres, but a genuine crisis in which painting is forced to contemplate two utterly different conceptions of human life: one that describes what is important in existence as the unique event, the drama of great individuals, the disruptions of creaturely repetition that precipitate as narrative; and one which protests that the drama of greatness is an epiphenomenon, a movement only on the surface of earthly life, where greater mass is made up of things entirely unexceptional and creatural, born of need on a poor planet" (1990, 154).

To Bryson, this opposition does not exist in a vacuum: "*It is overdetermined by another polarity, that of gender*" (1990, 157, his emphasis). With the exception of monks, the "delegates" of still life are far more likely to be women than men. In the case of seventeenth-century Dutch still life, "the interior of the house is regarded as intrinsically female space. It is women rather than men whose job it is to guard the moral and physical purity of households" (1990, 158). Furthermore, when men occupy this inner space, as in Vermeer's *Soldier and Young Girl Smiling,* they seem awkward and ill-at-ease.[6] And when their cherished objects (helmets, swords, pistols, trumpets) are depicted in a still life, they seem out of place, invasive, intrusive, as though the "man of the house" is bent on asserting a power that in this setting is not rightfully his. "When still life of the table sounds the theme of disorder, asymmetry of the sexes is an important factor in the emotional nuancing of the scene. . . . In this littering of the table with masculine paraphernalia, there is signalled the male's inability or refusal to harmonize with the domestic space" (1990, 160).

Bryson also turns his attention to the artist, specifically to the tendency of the male artist to paint still life as an outside observer. Chardin's work reflects the desire "to enter the feminine space of domesticity gently and invisibly . . . to capitulate, to make himself and his canvas *porous* to the female space" (1990, 167, his emphasis). Yet even Chardin "encounters an obstacle which is without equivalent in the other genres, and which must be negotiated. The asymmetry of the sexes with regard to domestic life constantly works to place the male painter of still life in a position of exteriority to his subject. Inevitably, still life's particular mode of vision bears the traces of this exclusion" (1990, 169). The male painter of still life is highly focused, almost glaringly so, "as if the world of the table and domestic space must be patrolled by an eye whose vigilance misses nothing." The result "is often the production of *the uncanny: although everything looks familiar, the scene conveys a certain estrangement and alienation*" (1990, 170, my emphasis).

To explain this phenomenon of male estrangement, Bryson turns to Freud's essay "The 'Uncanny,'" noting Freud's point that the uncanny is something that is secretly familiar but has undergone repression, and then returned from it. He also notes Freud's claim that the locus of greatest uncanniness is the mother's body. The boy, says Bryson, is made aware that "the persistence of his desire to remain within the maternal orbit represents a menace to the very center of his being, a possibility of engulfment and immersion that threatens his entire development and viability as a subject" (1990, 172). He must escape, and "he can do so by no other means than by claiming as his another kind of space," a space "that is definitely and assuredly *outside*," a space "where the process of identification with the masculine can begin and can succeed" (1990, 172). Thus, "still life bears all the marks of this double-edged exclusion and nostalgia, this irresolvable ambivalence which gives to feminine space a power of attraction intense enough to motor the entire development of still life as a genre, yet at the same time apprehends feminine space as alien, as a space which also menaces the masculine subject to the core of his identity as male" (1990, 172–73).

On the other hand, Bryson's analysis suggests that the male who has been most willing to place his "male identity" at risk is precisely the still-life painter. He cites the eighteenth-century English art critics (Reynolds, Shaftesbury, and Burke) who claimed that men who painted still life were "effeminate," lacking in the "manly virtues," and suggested that there are two distinct modes of vision, divided between the sexes at birth: "To the male, vision under abstraction, rising above mere detail and sensuous engagement to attain the general over-view; to the female, vision attuned to the sensuous detail and surfaces of the world, color and texture, rich stuffs and silks. For the male to be drawn away from abstraction towards the mode of female vision is for him to desert his sex: even to *look* at still life, which entails a descent into the sensuous particularity of things, is to put manhood at risk" (1990, 177).

Bryson's discussion of still life offers us a new way of looking at Erikson's essays on womanhood and the inner space. We may view these essays as a man's effort to "apprehend" feminine space, to make himself and his verbal canvas "porous" to female space. But, if so, his "ambivalently poetic" phrases reveal just how "alien" and "exclusive" this space appears to men. In contrast to *Young Man Luther,* where Erikson writes with a certain surefootedness (after all, he is writing "a study in psychoanalysis *and history*"), his essays on womanhood and the inner space are written with some degree of awkwardness, as though he is writing about a subject that "bears all the marks of a double-edged exclusion and nostalgia." His confession in the second essay that he had included "a few imprudent words" in the first essay indicates that he was aware of writing about something "alien," while his observation that he would now want to withdraw certain "ambivalently poetic" words and phrases suggests that he had written out of deep nostalgia for what was once familiar but had since been de-familiarized.

Erikson takes particular offense (suppressed rage?) at Millett's rather jeering reaction, noted above, to the following passage:

> For, as pointed out, clinical observation suggests that in female experience an "inner space" is at the center of despair even as it is the very center of potential fulfillment. Emptiness is the female form of perdition—known at times to men of the inner life . . . but standard experience for all women. To be left, for her, means to be left empty, to be drained of the blood of the body, the warmth of the heart, the sap of life. How a woman thus can be hurt in depth is a wonder to many a man, and it can arouse both his empathic horror and his refusal to understand. Such hurt can be re-experienced in each menstruation; it is a crying to heaven in the mourning over a child; and it becomes a permanent scar in the menopause [1968, 278].

Millett read the word *it* in the phrase "it is a crying to heaven in the mourning over a child" to mean "mourning over each menstrual loss, wherefore she undertook to count how many periods women average in a lifetime and how often, therefore, Erikson thinks, they are crying to heaven over a child not conceived" (1975, 234). Erikson partly blames himself for this misunder-standing, for if he had italicized the word *it* one would surely know that he was referring to the "hurt" that registers so deeply when a woman weeps over her dead child: "To older people like myself, the loss of a child by death was once a more expectable experience in family life, whereas in past generations all living children represented a triumph of survival" (1975, 234). One hears overtones in this passage of Luther's dead siblings and of Erikson's own pre-carious infancy, as his mother fled to Germany and reared him all by herself.

In spite of all his efforts to clarify his original, intended meanings, the impression that I have of these essays is similar to Bryson's impression of the still-life paintings of Chardin: Although everything looks familiar, the scene conveys a certain estrangement and alienation. Indeed, Erikson confesses as much, for, as we have seen, both essays end with the lament that men, with a divided self-image, view the inner space as outsiders.

Kate Millett, too, observes the "awkwardness" reflected in Erikson's origi-nal essay, though she attributes "the uneasy, even contradictory, tone of the essay . . . to the fact that Erikson vacillates between two versions of woman, Freud's chauvinism and a chivalry of his own" (Millett 1969, 212). I attribute this "contradiction," if you will, to something much deeper: Erikson's sense of being an outside observer of what he experienced earlier as a certified insider. Hence, he is ambivalently alienated and nostalgic. At issue is not "women in general" but Erikson's personal experience of his mother and the space she embodied as things long since de-familiarized. Millet notes that "maternity is something of a preoccupation with him" (1969, 211). Here again I agree, but this too has a highly personalized connotation for him, because he identifies his own mother with the woman for whom childbirth and a deep sense of being bereft and abandoned go together. His references to the woman's fear of "being left" (abandoned), like his suggestion that men are essentially "in-truders" into the inner space (an indirect allusion to his stepfather), are thus deeply autobiographical. And the "chivalry" that Millett detects in the tone of his essay is born ultimately of the son's effort to understand and, if necessary, to forgive his mother for the "acute life problems" he experienced as an illegiti-mate son. If the essay betrays his "awkwardness," as Millett suggests, it is the awkwardness of an unacknowledged melancholia.

Jesus: Disturbing the Peace of the "Inner Space"

To conclude our exploration of Erikson's own melancholy, I now want to link together the self-recognition theme of portraiture and the inner-space theme of still life. Our point of convergence is Erikson's essay on Jesus, "The

Galilean Sayings and the Sense of 'I,'" published in 1981 when he was 79 years old (Erikson 1981).

In his description of girls' play themes, Erikson noted that the walls around the enclosure were low, and that "the idea of an intruding creature did not necessarily lead to the defensive erection of walls or the closing of doors." Rather, "the majority of these intrusions have an element of humor and pleasurable excitement" (1968, 271). This description is a valuable preface to his "Galilean Sayings and the Sense of 'I.'" A few months after its publication, I had a long conversation with Erikson at his home in Tiburon, California, during which we discussed his essay on Jesus. He said that he, raised a Jew, felt he was in rather familiar territory as he wrote the essay, because it centers on the early Jesus in his role of itinerant rabbi in Galilee. He added that he wanted to write about the Jesus who went down to Jerusalem and made history there but was not sure if he was personally qualified to do so.

In the essay he *did* write, he sounds a theme which was central to his *Toys and Reasons* (1977), that between the individual life cycle and the arena of historical events lies the mediating phenomenon of "the ritualization of everyday life" (1977, 85ff.). In *Toys and Reasons* he repeats a story he told in *Childhood and Society* (1963, 176–77) of Fanny, the Yurok shaman, who described the right way to conduct an ordinary meal. A native tribe in Northern California, the Yurok were dependent on the salmon and its elusive ways of propagating and migrating. The child who was old enough to "have sense" was taught to eat in prescribed ways, putting only a little food on the spoon, taking the spoon up to his mouth slowly, and putting it down again while chewing the food, all the while concentrating on the idea of becoming wealthy by thinking of shell money and salmon. Erikson suggests that "such ritualization . . . is anything but neurotic symptomatology where it supports the formation of a set of behavior patterns combining human propensities in a cultural system within a circumscribed section of nature and technology. Thus daily ritualization can serve as adaptive interplay deemed central to both the natural and the social universe" (1977, 81–82).

In his essay on Jesus, Erikson suggests that the great yearly holidays celebrated at the temple in Jerusalem "were no doubt occasions of ritual self-transcendence and of national renewal," whereas "the services in the synagogues had turned more to textual preoccupation with the wording of scriptures, even as the daily and weekly prayers were (as Jesus was to point out) occasions demonstrating one's righteousness" (1981, 340). He views this hardening of ritual negatively, noting that "all of these concerns with strictness in ritual life are, of course, a potential found in all institutions that have outlived the ideological conditions of their origins" (1981, 340). A third form of ritual especially interests him, however: the "ritualization of everyday life which must have played a great role in the survival of Judaism" (1981, 340). Here, in the rituals of family life, the holy was not profaned but brought down to earth, while the secular life was transformed into the sacredness of religious duty. Key to this ritualization of everyday life was the Jewish mother, who played "the role of a most down-to-earth goddess of the hearth" (1981, 340).

Erikson suggests that the Galilean Jesus made this feature of Judaism's ritual forms the focus of his reforming activity. This meant introducing a "new disposition" regarding the cultural meanings associated with the inner space. For one thing, Jesus was remarkably intrusive, as though he simply assumed that the woman, or women, of the house would respond to his entry with humor and pleasurable excitement. As for Jesus's tendency to upset the tranquil ecology of the home itself, Erikson cites the story of the men who, unable to enter the house where Jesus was staying because it was already too crowded, lowered through a hole in the roof the paralyzed man they had tied to a bed. More focally, however, there was Jesus's habit of breaking traditional rules of the table. Erikson writes:

> When challenged by some Pharisees who saw his disciples sit down to a meal without washing their hands properly and without seeming concerned about "the washing of pots and cups and vessels of bronze," Jesus says tough things, as Mark reports it, about their "teaching as doctrines the precepts of men," thus "making void the word of God through your tradition." Mark continues: "And he called the people to him again, and said to them, 'Hear me, all of you, and understand: there is nothing outside a man which by going into him can defile him; but the things which come out of a man are what defile him'" (Mark 7:14–16) [1981, 345].

Later, in conversation with his disciples, Jesus explained that a man cannot be defiled by things that enter the body, because they enter not his heart but his stomach and then pass on, taking "their natural course." What *does* defile a person is that which emanates from the heart: evil thoughts and deeds.

Judged by Norman Perrin to be "the most radical statement in the whole Jesus tradition" (cf. Erikson 1981, 346), Jesus's insistence that what one ingests does not defile him "seems to do away with many deeply ingrained distinctions between clean and unclean which serve the phobic avoidances and the compulsive purifications by daily and weekly ritualisms — at the time probably reinforced by Pharisaic circles by their disdain for the intrusion into Jewish life of Hellenic mores. By then, of course, Jesus had publicly demonstrated not only his unorthodox daily habits but also the liberality of his choice of table fellows" (1981, 346).

In effect, Jesus introduced a new sense of interiority (of "I-ness") even as he challenged traditional boundaries of human association (of "we-ness" versus "they-ness"). Although he proclaims the right of John, his mentor and baptismal initiator, to "emphasize radical asceticism in *his* part of the story," Jesus "insists on the legitimacy of his own ritual use of a joyous table-fellowship in which he — so shockingly for his times — includes tax collectors and sinners of all kinds who are not welcome at anybody else's table or, for that matter, inside anybody else's house" (1981, 351). We might add that what makes all this the more shocking, and disruptive, is that neither the table nor the house belongs to him. He is a guest in someone else's home. Could he have got away with this had he not been able to count on the complicity of that shadowy figure who rarely speaks, the goddess of the hearth? (See Goodwin 1993.)

Erikson is suggesting that the ritualism of the synagogue revealed a Jewish community which had become defensive and exclusive, so that Jesus saw his greatest opportunity for communal rebirth in the traditional restrictions placed on table fellowship. By taking control of the table — upsetting it, even as he made history by upsetting the money changers' tables in the temple in Jerusalem — he also created new vistas of personal inwardness. He was a man who did not hesitate to intrude upon the "interior space" where the mother — "a most down-to-earth goddess of the hearth" — presided. Readers of the gospels sense that his troop of wandering disciples and hangers-on disturbed whatever peace and tranquility the family had enjoyed prior to his coming, a disturbance undoubtedly welcomed by the daughters, for whom such intrusions had an element of humor and pleasurable excitement. At the same time, like the painter Chardin, Jesus made himself porous to the female space and seemed willing and able to risk his male identity. He understood that "his desire to remain within the maternal orbit" was not "a menace to the very center of his being" but rather, more truly, a reflection of his desire to be whole, to overcome the split self-image to which men, alienated from the inner space, are especially susceptible.

But perhaps for Erikson himself there is even more. In his analysis of Jesus's story of the prodigal son who longs to return home, Erikson notes that the father, in his steadfast love *of both sons,* was "almost like a mother to them," and that the audience, in listening, "becomes tuned to the story-teller's peculiar *caring* about the [generational] dimensions" of the story, in which "the father and the sons can find themselves and one another only by gaining their own identity in the very fulfillment of their intergenerational tasks within their cultural and economic matrix" (1981, 356). If Erikson then asks — explicitly — whether we might view this "matrix" as "the missing mother" in the story, he also suggests — implicitly — with his statement of the storyteller's own "peculiar caring" that there is something altogether motherly in the *way* the story is told, almost as though Jesus himself is the goddess of the hearth.

With Erikson's discussion of the Parable of the Prodigal Son, we return to the issue of myth and parable, though with a new aspect, because what he has done here is made the parable itself mythic. It becomes a story in which the theme of reconciliation receives such focal attention that the irreconciliation — between father and *elder* son — which is at the heart of the parable becomes shadowy at best. Erikson makes his case for the father's being "almost like a mother" to his two sons on the grounds that he was steadfast in his love for both. From the perspective of generative adults, the father's evenhandedness is surely commendable, even loving. Yet from the perspective of the son who has been steadfast in his love for his father, this evenhandedness is decidedly unfair, and he is justifiably enraged by the fact that his father has acted so "lovingly" toward the brother who treated the father's legacy with such disdain.

Of what experience in Erikson's own life is this parable reminiscent? I suggest that it calls to mind events that occurred when he was only three, events that caused his whole world to tremble and shake. For three years Erik and his mother lived together as one. Then, out of the blue, an intruder came into their lives, and his mother's welcome of this intruder made little Erik feel as though *he* were the real intruder. No doubt his mother felt that she could love them both with equal fervor, and conceivably she did. From the perspective of the three-year-old boy, however, he had been shunted aside, losing his place of privilege; and from the perspective of the old man looking back on these scenes many decades later, it was clear that she was pervasively sad, having relinquished her own freedom — for the sake of her child? — for a conventional life as the wife of the bearded doctor. Her son had to perceive that in her reading of books she was encouraging him to a higher ambition.

As Erikson indicates, his reaction to being shunted aside as a child was to create a personal myth, one in which he was "the son of much better parents," "altogether a foundling" who belonged neither to his mother nor his adoptive father (1975, 27). Of such myths is a propensity to religion born in a small child, reflecting as it does the desire for a mythical Father and Mother. So far as his mythical *father* was concerned, there was considerable reality in this, as he could appropriately imagine himself the son of a much better father than his stepfather. It is reported that Erikson later tried — unsuccessfully — to find his birth father. But why the mythical mother when his real mother was still present? I believe this was because she was no longer the mother whose exclusive company he had enjoyed in the first three years of his life. Herein lay the fault line in their relationship together, and out of this melancholy situation the young boy created a personal myth.

Yet if the child in this case entertained fantasies of being the child of mythical parents in order to explain and rationalize his feelings of alienation in the inner space he shared with his mother and adoptive father, these fantasies seem to have served emotional needs only in the short term. What he found more helpful in the long run were his return visits to the forest, where he discovered an accepting inner space in the painters' studios. It was not the synagogue but the studio that offered compensations for the loss of his mother's undivided love.

I suggest that Erikson's tendency to mythicize the parabolic fault lines of his own early childhood may be traced back to the days when little Erik perceived that his mother was very sad, which made him determined not to be the occasion for any further grief. However, in terms of Freud's theory of how melancholia works, this meant that whatever rage he felt toward her was internalized in the form of a certain self-hatred. That it did not become a debilitating self-hatred was due in large measure to the fact that he had the imagination of an artist and was able to paint for himself a reasonably comfortable position out on the boundary, in the free space between the doctor's office and the artist's studio, where a boy can be alone with his thoughts.

Conclusion

In this exploration of four key texts in the psychology of religion, my concern has been to account for the origins of a boy's disposition to be religious. I have proposed that the origins of such a disposition are in the loss of the mother whom he had perceived as loving him unconditionally but now doubts that she really does. The religious disposition emerges from the sense that something has been lost, perhaps irrevocably and irretrievably. It has, however, two discernible features, each reflecting in its own way the child's uncertainty as to the irreversibility of the loss.

One is the formation of a moral, perhaps even hypermoral, consciousness, whose purpose is to win his mother back through the moral determination to be "a good boy." The other is to redress the loss in other venues, in "worlds" that are reminiscent of the mother who is no longer accessible, who, as originally experienced, no longer "exists." Both are related to melancholy, but the second more centrally, as melancholy is not based primarily on a genuine sense of guilt for having behaved in such a way that mother was forced to respond punitively. Instead, it is based principally on the perception that she has unaccountably turned against him, revealing a "side" of herself which he had never seen before and which frightened and terrified him or, alternatively, impressed upon him her incapacity to protect him from those things that he already feared. Thus, melancholy has its origins more in the perception that the loss is irrevocable, and less in the sense that he might do something to restore what has been lost. Melancholy centers less on the boy's moral resolve — though this may be one way in which he becomes religious — and more on the resulting nexus of sadness (with overtones of self-pity) and rage (or the blaming of the mother).

I have therefore focused less on the boy's efforts to win his mother back through moral behavior, and more on his efforts to find consolations for his loss and means of avenging it, consolations and avengings that invariably assume a religious form, because they cannot be realized in what James would call "the seen world." Even the "real" mother, as distinguished from the boy's original image of the "perfect" mother, is unable to provide consolation, for she after all is only human, and this is *not* good enough. Moreover, she is too negligible a target for the deep rage he feels against the perfect mother.

However, precisely because the boy becomes aware of this deep rage within him, he knows there is some "fault" that underlies his life which is deeper than his moral determination to be "good" can ever penetrate. While the rage itself is misdirected, for he has internalized the original object of his love and turned against "her" by turning against himself, the sense of sin that ensues from awareness of the rage that he experiences within himself is, as Otto suggests, deeper than a moral self-judgment and goes instead to the very core of his sense of creaturehood. To a significant degree, melancholia provides an explanation for why theologians like Luther and Otto insisted that "sin" is not essentially moral but ontological.

In this study, I have explored the ways in which the four authors I have focused on sought compensations for their loss in and through religion, as well as how they sought in religious ways to mitigate their suffering. James turned his attention to nature, discerning in the natural world the consolations that are often hidden and masked behind its overwhelming power to threaten and injure. For him, the world is animistically alive and testifies, in its way, to the reality of the "world" he had lost in losing his mother. For Otto, experiences of the "numinous" also brought back memories of the loss he had sustained as a child, though these experiences were self-punishing as well, because they repeated in a new venue the very scenarios that were instrumental in the loss itself. Jung found his consolations in a biblical text, entering into its visions of a restorative spiritual world that exists inside the world of human forms. In a similar way, Erikson also turned to the biblical text, recognizing it as a consoling "maternal matrix" and, more specifically, the source of myths of reconciliation between mother and child.

On the other hand, all four authors seem to have had a degree of mistrust or suspicion of such consolations. All four experienced them as sources of hope, but not as any once-and-for-all compensation for their original loss. One is struck by the fact that in all four cases their experiences of wholeness were occasional, short-lived, and subject to future erosion. Each found himself clinging to a tenuous image or fleeting vision, aware that it could be extinguished, like a candle, in a moment. Of course, this awareness led them to seize on these experiences and to mine them as fully as possible, with the introspective method itself frequently serving this very purpose.

If religious consolations are occasional and fleeting, this raises the question of whether religion is the appropriate locus in which to address one's melancholic condition. I have suggested, especially in the chapter on Erikson, that there is in fact another way. This is to mourn the loss of the mother and, having mourned, to seek in the world of flesh and blood — the *seen,* not the *unseen,* world — the means and sources of consolation and compensation. As I put it, "How fortunate the son who finds in this immense world of objects one whom he can love, and, in loving, can regain his capacity to believe." Undoubtedly, this *was* the experience of the four authors, but to varying degrees.

James, though he married relatively late, experienced the lifelong devotion of his wife (though he left *her* for both brief and extended periods of time). Also, he had genuine affection for his wife's mother, to whom he dedicated *The Varieties* "in filial gratitude and love." Erikson, too, was blessed with a very devoted wife, who shared almost every facet of his work. In a testimony to his old friend Peter Blos, he notes that they both "solemnly approved of each other's [marital] choices and, what is more, we still do, knowing full well that our wives have saved us from our wandering selves and from *too much Geistigkeit*" (1987, 711). Jung's marital infidelities are well known. In his only reference to his wife in his autobiography, he notes that he would have made the legend of the Holy Grail a study of his own had "it not been for my unwillingness to intrude upon my wife's field" (1961, 215). Still, as we have seen, he writes in *Memories, Dreams, Reflections* of having been pleasantly surprised throughout his life that women had proven far more trustworthy than his early childhood experiences might have led him to imagine. Otto, though he never married, experienced the loving support of older sisters and aunts.

And yet there are indications in the case of all four men that the mother image is projected onto these other women. Erikson is no doubt joking when he says in his tribute to Peter Blos that their wives saved them from their wandering selves and from too much *Geistigkeit,* but there is certainly an element of projection of the ambivalence originally felt toward his mother in this joking comment. Moreover, the fact that for all four the religious search persisted throughout their lives indicates that, in the words of James, there was something "More" (*VRE*, 508; also Otto, *IH*, 32, 46) for which they longed, something not even a loving woman could fulfill. Each in his own way was irrevocably religious, in spite of protests (for example, James's responses to Pratt's questionnaire) and actions (such as Otto's suicide attempts) that might suggest otherwise. In all four there seems to have been an aspect of themselves that was inaccessible even to those who were most devoted to them—an uncanniness, as it were. And it was this inaccessibility, ultimately traceable to a deep disappointment in their mothers, that marked them as religious melancholiacs.

Perhaps, then, the idea of turning from the unseen world and making a full and exclusive commitment to the real world around him is to expect too much "reality testing" from the melancholiac, even though it may well be the "healthiest" solution available to him. On the other hand, if he is "destined," as it were, to be incurably religious, some ways of being religious are better than others. I have suggested, especially in the chapters on Otto and Erikson, that the better forms of religion for the melancholiac are those that encourage him to replace self-hatred with a sense of self-cohesion and empowerment. I proposed that Otto's image of Jesus as the holy one might serve as an internalized selfobject who consoles him and empowers him to face the new day. I also suggested in my chapter on Erikson that the image of Christ may point beyond itself to the child self as the guarantor of one's sense of continuity and inner integrity as one undergoes the inevitable disintegrative effects of aging. These suggestions find support in Jung's view of "the little sun" arising in his own heart and in James's view of the importance of having a self that we genuinely want to care for.

In other words, if there is a need for the melancholiac to be "religious," his religion should be such that it contests what Erikson calls "that unbearable prejudice against the self [which] is at the bottom of much of the human proclivity for compulsive, obsessive, and depressive disorders" (1977, 95). The image of Jesus as the holy one or as the one who draws attention to that inner or primordial self evocative of our own love and affection may not have the power to restore the lost mother, but it may have the power to confront and exorcise our self-hatred, which, as Freud argues, is a consequence of the internalization of the original lost object. If religion has a constructive role to play in the mitigation of the pain and distortions of melancholia, it needs to be as "internal" as the roots of melancholia itself. The image of Jesus may well be an answer, especially if, as Erikson suggests, Jesus is, in his bearing and voice, uncannily reminiscent of the missing mother. But even more vital is the recovery of the child self to which Jesus, in the episode recounted in my discussion of Erikson—"the child is in the midst"—directs our attention. The point is less to make Jesus the object of one's gaze — and veneration — and more to look where he looks, to follow *his* eyes.

Finally, because this study reverses Erikson's priorities in *Young Man Luther* by focusing on the mother-son relationship and relegating the father, even the Father God, to "shadowy" status, I want to say something by way of conclusion about fathers and their potential role in the mitigation of the pain and distortive effects of melancholia.[1]

Jung's dream of his father as suddenly speaking with such wisdom and erudition that his own son was annoyed that his father "had to talk in the presence of three such idiots as we" suggests a deep desire to be able now, as an old man, to idealize a father whom he could not idealize earlier in real life. Jung does not suggest that the need for such idealization of his father has any direct bearing on his melancholia, but the self theorist Heinz Kohut has written extensively about the child's need to idealize the parent so as to secure his own sense of self. Parents who resist such idealization on the grounds that it is false or inappropriate fail to appreciate how much the child's own sense of self depends on this idealization of parents being mirrored back to the child. In their essay on the disorders of the self, Kohut and Ernest Wolf offer the following illustration: "A little boy is eager to idealize his father, he wants his father to tell him about his life, the battles he engaged in and won. But instead of joyfully acting in accordance with his son's need, the father is embarrassed by the request. He feels tired and bored and, leaving the house, finds a temporary source of vitality for his enfeebled self in the tavern, through drink and mutually supportive talk with friends" (1986, 184).

While such idealization of one of the parents raises the danger of image splitting, in which one parent is idealized as the other becomes demonized, I do not sense that this was the case for the four boys discussed in this study. There is little evidence that James, Otto, Jung, and Erikson idealized their fathers as young boys. James and Jung, whose fathers were much into religion themselves, were at best objects of amusement. For the title page of his father's latest book young James drew a picture of a man beating a dead horse. Carol Holly notes that the James children, subtly encouraged by their mother, teased their father in his presence about his "ideas" (1995, 30–31). Jung, as we have seen, confesses to having felt great discomfort in listening to his father preach. Otto's father, who died when Rudolf was twelve, was, according to Philip Almond, too busy building up his business to pay any attention to his children. (To be sure, this saved the family from economic ruin after his early death.) Erikson speaks of having "a strong identification with my stepfather, the pediatrician," but this was "mixed with a search for my own mythical father." If he had a desire to idealize someone, one guesses that his natural father was a better candidate than his stepfather. As noted earlier, it has been reported that in mid-life Erikson engaged in a search, apparently unsuccessful, to find his birth father.

Thus, not one of the four gives the impression of having been able to hold his father in the sort of high esteem or regard that would bolster his own self and make it more secure. If they could have revealed their true feelings about their fathers (in Erikson's case, his stepfather), they would probably have confessed to the desire to be another man's son (cf. my discussion of this phenomenon in Capps 1995, 112–115).

On the other hand, the very absence of idealizations of their fathers left these boys more vulnerable to the sadnesses and rages they felt toward their mothers. They lacked the protection that an idealization of their fathers might have provided from the deeper emotions, especially the self-hatred, to which their melancholy already disposed them. One also senses that, on the whole, their efforts as young adults to find a "father surrogate" whom they could idealize did not bear lasting fruit. Erikson can make much of Dr. Staupitz as "the best father figure Luther ever encountered" (*YML*, 37) because his own efforts to find such a figure in older men, including Freud, were far more ambiguous. He writes very positively of his "adoption" by the Freudian circle but describes it as "a kind of positive stepson identity" (1975, 29). He was not, to Freud, a real surrogate son.

A common characteristic of the four men is that they come across as essentially "self-made men" (the term used by Erikson in his original essay on womanhood and the inner space). To be sure, they have intellectual and professional debts and occasionally speak of such debts, but each seems to be a lonely pioneer, not someone who was "mentored" into an intellectual and professional tradition, at least not by an older and trusted male. As we have seen, Erikson's "spiritual mentor," the term he uses for Dr. Staupitz (*YML*, 17), was *Anna* Freud. In this sense, all four seem to fit quite nicely Erikson's description of the homo religiosus as being, as it were, his own father (*YML*, 261ff.). Jesus's attestations to his experiences of his Father in heaven are convincing precisely because we imagine him as being virtually fatherless, humanly speaking. And for the four men we have represented in this study Jesus is the paradigmatic homo religiosus.

While good father surrogates (like Dr. Staupitz) are in no position to cure their adoptive sons of melancholia, they may in fact be the closest thing that these sons will experience to a lasting remedy, especially if the father surrogates have personal knowledge of melancholy and its self-destructive potential. In support of this conclusion, I bring this book to a close with a brief account of one of the most celebrated and poignant friendships in English letters, that of Samuel Johnson and his chronicler, James Boswell (Boswell 1980).

"I Could Not Be So Easy with My Father"

When Boswell and Johnson first met, Johnson, a widower in his early fifties, was one of London's literary giants. In contrast, Boswell was only 25 and had come to London to escape the influence of his father, a jurist in Scotland, who wanted him to study law. More interested in literature than in law, he hoped to become part of the London literary scene. After several abortive attempts, he succeeded in meeting Johnson and eventually persuaded him to go to dinner with him.

They ate alone together at the Mitre Tavern, Boswell sitting awed at the realization that he was actually conversing one-on-one with a famous literary figure. They discussed poetry at some length, and then Boswell acknowledged that he had been struggling with his religious beliefs, at which point Johnson reached out his hand and said warmly, "I have taken a liking to you." Johnson spoke of a period in his own life when he had neglected religion, and this prompted a discussion of belief in ghosts. Their conversation moved to Boswell's personal life, his difficulties with his father, and his current idleness and what to do about it.

When Boswell asked Johnson for advice about his studies, Johnson declined, saying that he would have to consider the matter more carefully, indirectly signifying that he would meet with Boswell again. Then Boswell exclaimed, "It is very good of you to allow me to be with you thus. Had it been foretold to me some years ago that I should be passing an evening with the author of *The Rambler,* how should I have exulted." To which Johnson replied, "Sir, I am glad we have met. I hope we shall pass many evenings and mornings too, together!" (Boswell 1980, 291).

Several days later, they met again for supper at the Mitre. In the course of conversation, Boswell contrasted the ease with which he could talk with Johnson to the difficulty he had in communicating with his own father. He expressed regret "that I could not be so easy with my father, though he was not much older than Johnson, and certainly however respectable had not more learning and greater abilities to depress me." He asked Johnson the reason for this, to which Johnson replied, "I am a man of the world, I live in this world, and I take, in some degree, the color of the world as it moves along. Your father is a judge in a remote part of the island, and all his notions are taken from the old world. Besides, there must always be a struggle between a father and son, while one aims at power and the other at independence" (Boswell 1980, 302).

In reply, Boswell expressed fear that his father would force him to become a lawyer, but Johnson reassured him: "You need not be afraid of his forcing you to be a laborious practicing lawyer; this is not in his power. . . . He may be displeased that you are not what he wishes you to be; but that displeasure will not go far. If he insists only on your having as much law as is necessary for a man of property, and then endeavors to get you into Parliament, he is quite in the right" (Boswell 1980, 302–3).

The conversation then turned to Boswell and his studies, and Johnson was now prepared to offer the younger man some advice. He suggested that he keep a journal of his life, to which Boswell responded with considerable pride that he had been keeping a journal for some time. He was worried, however, that it contained "too many little incidents," to which Johnson replied, "There is nothing too little for so little a creature as man. It is by studying little things that we attain the great art of having as little misery and as much happiness as possible" (Boswell 1980, 307).

Several evenings later, they had dinner together again, this time at a local coffee house. Johnson seemed intent on revealing his more personal, vulnerable side to Boswell. He began by telling Boswell that he loved the acquaintance of younger people, for several reasons, including the fact that he did not like to think of himself as growing old; young men had more virtue and more generous sentiments than older men. Then he acknowledged for the first time in their conversations that he had been distressed by melancholy "and for that reason had been obliged to fly from study and meditation, to the dissipating variety of life" (Boswell 1980, 316). Against melancholy, he recommended constant occupation of mind, a great deal of physical exercise, moderation in eating and drinking, and especially no drinking at night. He noted that melancholy individuals are apt to escape to intemperance for relief, which only sank them deeper into misery: "Laboring men who work hard and live sparingly are seldom troubled with low spirits" (Boswell 1980, 316).

They went on to speak on other topics, but this evening was a most memorable one for Boswell, for Johnson had let down his guard and had taken his young friend into his confidence. It happened that Boswell also suffered from melancholy, and on one occasion, many years later, he wrote to Johnson from Scotland to tell him that he needed to see him because he felt that the best way for him to gain relief from it was to be in the company of an old and dear friend. In response, Johnson invited him to come to London if he wished, but he expressed his regret that Boswell had no other, more local means to gain relief. He warned Boswell to avoid negative thoughts, but also cautioned that he should not "hope wholly to reason away your troubles; do not feed them with attention, and they will die imperceptibly away. Fix your thoughts upon your business, fill your intervals with company, and sunshine will again break in upon your mind" (Boswell 1980, 676).

In the end, Boswell did succumb to drinking to combat his melancholy, and, as Johnson had predicted, this remedy only sank him into deeper misery. His last letter from Johnson, twenty-five years after they had first met, written when Johnson was on his deathbed, challenged Boswell's failure to write: "Are you sick, or are you sullen? Whatever be the reason, if it be less than necessity, drive it away; and of the short life that we have, make the best use for yourself and for your friends" (Boswell 1980, 1362). As Johnson had guessed, Boswell had sunk into a deep depression and was drinking heavily: "I unfortunately was so much indisposed during a considerable part of the year, that it was not, or at least I thought it was not, in my power to write my illustrious friend as formerly" (Boswell 1980, 1362).

After Johnson's death, some of their mutual friends remarked on the fact that Boswell had not managed to get back to London to see Johnson before he died. They viewed this as disrespectful, especially in light of all the kindnesses Johnson had shown to him over the years, but Boswell's melancholy had consumed him.

From the first evening that Johnson confessed to his own melancholia, the two men often talked about their common malady. On a visit to Oxford together, they talked one evening about constitutional melancholy. Johnson observed, "A man so afflicted must divert distressing thoughts, and not combat with them." Boswell asked, "May not he think them down?" Johnson: "No, Sir. To attempt to *think them down* is madness. He should have a lamp constantly burning in his bed-chamber during the night, and if wakefully disturbed, take a book, and read, and compose himself to rest. To have the management of the mind is a great art, and it may be attained in a considerable degree by experience and habitual exercise" (Boswell 1980, 690, my emphasis).

Boswell then suggested that amusements might be helpful: "Would it not, for instance, be right for him to take a course of chemistry?" Johnson heartily agreed: "Let him take a course of chemistry, or a course of rope-dancing, or a course of anything to which he is inclined at the time. Let him contrive to have as many retreats for his mind as he can, as many things to which it can fly from itself" (Boswell 1980, 690).

Johnson extolled Robert Burton's *Anatomy of Melancholy*, first published in 1621, noting that while it is too full of quotations, "there is great spirit and great power in what Burton says, *when he writes from his own mind*" (Boswell 1980, 690, my emphasis). Earlier, he had told Boswell that Burton's *Melancholy* was the only book that could get him out of bed two hours sooner than he wanted to get up, suggesting that reading about melancholy can be a useful stimulus to combating it (Boswell 1980, 428).

On another occasion, when they were alone and again discussing melancholy, Johnson noted that "some men, and very thinking men, too, have not these vexing thoughts." Two men in his inner circle of friends came immediately to mind: "Sir Joshua Reynolds is the same all year round, Beauclerk, except when ill and in pain, is the same." Yet "I believe most men have them in the degree *in which they are capable of having them*. If I were in the country, and were distressed by that malady, I would force myself to take a book; and every time I did it I should find it easier. Melancholy, indeed, should be diverted by every means but drinking" (Boswell 1980, 720–21, my emphasis).

In relating this conversation Boswell commends Johnson for his phrase "vexing thoughts," as he had been familiar with the phrase from childhood, for it occurs in the Scottish psalmbook:

> Why art thou cast down, my soul?
> What should discourage thee?
> And why with *vexing thoughts* art thou
> Disquieted in me? [Psalm 43:5].

Thus, their relationship was based on several factors that created a bond of friendship between them. For Boswell, Johnson was a surrogate father, a spiritual mentor, an older man with whom he could talk easily, even impertinently at times, and ask advice. For Johnson, Boswell was a younger man who was not afraid to express generous sentiments (to idealize Johnson to his face!) and was open to receiving advice from an older man. For both, there was a common bond in their common affliction. Especially for Boswell, this common bond was terribly important, for he could see how effective Johnson could be in life despite his disposition to melancholy.

Father surrogates are shadowy figures in a man's lifelong struggle with melancholy. But perhaps this is as it should be, because melancholy itself lives in the shadows of life, wistfully gazing through the lonely windows into the brightly lit room where mother and son frolic and sing in careless abandon, their hearts bursting with everlasting love.

Notes

Chapter 1: *Religious Melancholy and the Lost Object*

1. Rozsika Parker (1995, 59–65) argues that Winnicott's "good enough mother" term has been taken out of its original context in Winnicott's thinking. In her view, Winnicott emphasized mothers' "good enoughness" because he had already stressed mothers' hostility and even hatred for their children. Thus, he was concerned to say that her moments of hatred toward her child do not mean that she is not good enough.

2. Fisher and Fisher (1993) cite several research studies showing that people prone to depression are more realistic in their assessments of situations than are nondepressives. They also cite studies demonstrating the adaptive uses of illusion, especially in cases of severe trauma (p. 10).

Chapter 2: *"That Shape Am I"*

1. See Stephen H. Webb (1995) for a discussion of James's rhetorical strategy of abeyance or deferral.

2. Some would say that this "individualistic" and "noncommunal" definition of religion is not jarring at all, for this is precisely how most Americans today understand themselves to be religious. However, I am taking note here of the many critiques that have been written in recent years by theologians and sociologists of religion concerning "privatistic" religion (e.g., Robert N. Bellah et al., *Habits of the Heart* [1985]).

3. Cotkin (1994) notes that Henry James, Sr., kept his two older sons out of the war, using arguments that he was later to contradict in a Fourth of July oration in Newport

(1994, 33–34). The fact that he "contradicted" himself in this regard raises the question of whether it was not he but Mrs. James who played the decisive role in keeping their older sons out of conflict.

4. Styron also offers a passionate argument against our tendency to call this sickness "depression," preferring the more traditional term — melancholy — that James himself uses: "Depression, most people know, used to be termed 'melancholia,' a word which appears in English as early as the year 1303 and crops up more than once in Chaucer, who in his usage seemed to be aware of its pathological nuances. 'Melancholia' would still appear to be a far more apt and evocative word for the blacker forms of the disorder, but it was usurped by a noun with a bland tonality and lacking any magisterial presence, used indifferently to describe an economic decline or a rut in the ground, a true wimp of a word for such a major illness" (1990, 36–37).

5. William Styron confirms the state of indifference that James here describes, and he also provides a dramatic illustration of the melancholiac's desperate need to be "knifed," as it were, so as to be brought out of this state of indifference. He was watching the tape of a movie set in late nineteenth-century Boston. The characters were moving down the hallway of a music conservatory, beyond the walls of which, from unseen musicians, came a contralto voice singing "a sudden soaring passage from the Brahms Alto Rhapsody." Styron, who had previously decided he would commit suicide later that evening, was literally "struck" by the sound: "This sound, which like all music — indeed, like all pleasure — I had been numbly unresponsive to for months, *pierced my heart like a dagger*" (1990, 66, my emphasis). Later, Styron informs the reader that his mother, who had died when he was thirteen, had sung the Alto Rhapsody in his own hearing (1990, 81). The sound "drew blood," and Styron realized that he could not "commit this desecration on myself" and on "those, so close to me, with whom the memories were bound" (1990, 67).

6. In his chapter in *The Varieties* on "other characteristics" of religion, James discusses the role that "automatisms" have played in the lives of religious individuals, citing "the whole array of Christian saints and heresiarchs" who experienced automatisms of one kind or another: visions, voices, rapt conditions, guiding impressions, "openings," dreams, and trances. Whatever forms these may take, such automatisms corroborate belief: "Incursions from beyond the transmarginal region have a peculiar power to increase conviction" (*VRE*, 478). The scripture texts that entered his mind and kept him from going really insane in the French Sufferer episode were undoubtedly verbal automatisms.

7. These frightening dreams occurred on February 12–13, 1906. Coincidentally, the San Francisco earthquake occurred two months later (April 18) while James was still in the San Francisco area. He took the train into San Francisco so that he could walk through the ruined city, "taking the measure of the fantastic natural spectacle and the behavior of the people" (1991, 553). As he had just delivered his lecture "The Moral Equivalent of War" at Stanford in late February, it would not be inappropriate to suggest that the earthquake was the nearest equivalent he would experience to having actually been in combat. See chap. 2, n. 3.

8. William Styron also emphasizes the fundamental role that loss plays in the progress of depression, as well as its origins: "Loss in all of its manifestations is the touchstone of depression — in the progress of the disease and, most likely, in its origin" (1990, 56). In his case, his mother's death when he was thirteen years old was critical.

9. Henry James's short story "The Jolly Corner" (H. James 1990) has significant similarities to William James's intimate friend account. The protagonist in the story has an encounter with his "alter ego" and finds himself revulsed by its appearance. In *Meaning in Henry James* (1991), Millicent Bell suggests that the protagonist had made a "discovery of the repressed self, which had been 'there all the time,' as the novelist's brother [William] had insisted" (p. 281). James describes the protagonist's alter ego as appearing with hands covering his face, with two fingers of one hand missing, and as "evil, odious, blatant, vulgar," a description not unlike William's perception of the "finite, small, and distressful being" and their father's perception of the "damned shape squatting invisible to me within the precincts of the room, and raying out from his fetid personality influences fatal for life."

10. While some might argue that James's mother would not have reacted to the goings-on at the studio with moral trepidation, I strongly doubt this. It was generally considered a mother's and wife's obligation to protect sons and husbands from immoral influences. Thus, Myers reports that James's wife, Alice, took a "dim view" of his choice of books to read, considering them "dirty" and a "bad influence." He defended his reading of novels and autobiographies, noting: "It is not for the dirt, but for the whole sense of reality of which the dirt is part that I find these books so renovating" (Myers 1986, 38). Of course, in the instance before us, the worry would have been James's susceptibility to homoeroticism. That it was Henry who reacted so emotionally is significant in light of the judgment of many scholars that he was a closeted homosexual (Kaplan 1992, 401–9; Sedgwick 1990, 182–212).

11. If James uses the beasts in support of the melancholiac's vision of the world that *is* seen, he uses them as well to support the religious vision of the world that is *unseen*. In "Is Life Worth Living?" (1956, 32–62), he notes that our domestic animals "are in our human life but not of it. They witness hourly the outward body of events whose inner meaning cannot, by any possible operation, be revealed to their intelligence, — events in which they themselves often play the cardinal part. My terrier bites a teasing boy, for example, and the father demands damages. The dog may be present at every step of the negotiations, and see the money paid, without an inkling of what it all means, without a suspicion that it has anything to do with *him;* and he never can know in his natural dog's life" (1956, 58).

12. Since Henry James, Sr., was working on an exegetical study of the Book of Genesis, it is not inconceivable that he saw his own difficult situation mirrored in its family narratives. The obvious parallel to his own situation was the story of Jacob, who loved the younger sister, Rachel, but was first required to marry the older sister, Leah (Genesis 29–30). If he did in fact have a continuing attraction to Katherine after his marriage to Mary, he would not have been able to avoid seeing his own fate prefigured in the story of Jacob. Especially tormenting for him would be Genesis 30:1ff.: "When Rachel [read Kate] saw that she bore Jacob [read Henry] no children, she envied her sister; and she said to Jacob, 'Give me children, or I shall die!' "

13. Lewis also mentions that while in Dresden, James had the habit of "peering through a telescope from his room on Christianstrasse at the young girls in a boarding school across the street, among them a ravishing Jewish female" (1991, 187). Was this simply another example of his artistic interests? (A pencil sketch with the notation "The lovely young Jewess looking at the large end of the telescope" is reproduced in Myers

1986, 306ff.) Or is it another instance of his being attracted to women of whom his mother would disapprove? (For a similar example of his father's voyeuristic interest in women, see Davis 1995.)

14. For an interesting example of how a powerful psychical experience was *not* interpreted by its experiencer as religious until the religious community insisted on so viewing it, see Michael P. Carroll's "Virgin Mary at LaSalette and Lourdes: Whom Did the Children See?," *Journal for the Scientific Study of Religion* 24 (1985): 56–74.

15. William's brother Henry once commented that he had been troubled "all along just by this particular crookedness of our being so extremely religious without having, as it were, anything in the least classified or striking to show for it" (Kaplan 1992, 20–21).

16. James was not a praying person in the conventional sense. In response to Pratt's question "Do you pray, and if so, why?" James responded, "I can't pray — I feel foolish and artificial" (Brown 1973, 125).

Chapter 3: "A Thrill of Fear"

1. My appreciation to Daniel Beveridge for bringing this article by Almond to my attention and also to Philip C. Almond himself for graciously responding to my request for additional information about the manner in which Otto was reared as a child.

2. Harvey's reference to the Otto household may give the false impression that Otto was married with children. He never married. He did, however, live for some time with his niece, and Harvey's references to the Otto household are in this context. (Personal correspondence, Philip C. Almond, July 11, 1996.)

3. In his appendix to *The Idea of the Holy*, the translator, John W. Harvey, notes that the English word *uncanny* is "a more or less exact rendering of the German 'unheimlich,'" though he has also made use of such English words as *weird* and *eerie* where he felt this was appropriate (Otto 1958, 217).

4. In his discussion of experiences that are analogous to the mysterium tremendum, Otto cites erotic or sexual love and notes how there is something "more," not only in quantity but also in quality, in the phrase "he loves me" when spoken by a girl of her lover than when spoken by a child of its father. This "more," present in experiences of the holy, distinguishes them from mundane experiences (*IH,* 46–47). If it is self-evident that a child's expression of love for its father lacks erotic overtones, what of the boy's expression of love for his mother? In this respect, the silence of Otto's text is not insignificant, especially in light of the importance he ascribes to silence as a means of representing the numinous.

5. Jung's suspicion that there was some "connivance in high places" is further developed in René Girard's *Job: The Victim of His People* (Stanford: Stanford University Press, 1987), which argues that Job was the victim of the community's decision to sacrifice him as a scapegoat, a role that he in turn refused to accept.

Chapter 4: "A Little Sun in His Own Heart"

1. In the essay, Jung associates the child motif with the future and an openness to it: "One of the essential features of the child motif is its futurity. Hence the occurrence of the

child motif in the psychology of the individual signifies as a rule an anticipation of future developments, even though at first sight it may seem like a retrospection configuration. . . . In the individuation process, it anticipates the figure that comes from the synthesis of conscious and unconscious elements in the personality. It is therefore a symbol which unites the opposites; a mediator, bringer of healing, that is, one who makes whole" (Jung and Kerenyi 1963, 83).

Chapter 5: Melancholy and Motherhate

1. The view that *Young Man Luther* is a kind of clinical case study in the psychology of religion is advanced by Paul W. Pruyser, "Erikson's *Young Man Luther:* A New Chapter in the Psychology of Religion," *Journal for the Scientific Study of Religion* 2 (1963): 238–42. Reprinted in Roger A. Johnson (ed.), *Psychohistory and Religion: The Case of Young Man Luther* (1977, 88–96).

2. An especially interesting illustration of the threat of such disintegration is Erikson's brief analysis of William James's "terminal dreams" (Erikson 1968, 204–7). As I note in chap. 2, n. 7, the dreams occurred when James was lecturing at Stanford University in 1906. Erikson says that James apparently "never came as close to a truly psychotic experience as in this dream — a fact which I ascribe to the depth of 'ultimate concerns' at this stage of his life" (1968, 204). He concludes that James, "in his eagerness for and closeness to transcendence, ended by feeling that his dream had been dreamed 'in reality' — by another 'I,' by a mysterious stranger" (1968, 207). I believe that this "mysterious stranger" was James's "abandoned self," and that the dream therefore recapitulated the intimate friend episode.

3. Erikson here makes it sound as though he readily assimilated "the artist in me" into his professional identity as a psychoanalyst. In his autobiographical essay (1975, 17–47), however, he makes clear that he struggled against relinquishing an artist's life and that psychology as such did not attract him. The "self-murder" he attributes to James applies equally to himself. In this regard, his psychoanalyst, Anna Freud, played a crucial role, as she countered his arguments in favor of an artist's career with reassurances that, as artist turned psychoanalyst, he would help his patients to "see."

4. The only aspects of his personal life to which Erikson freely alluded in his writings were his own "crisis of identity" in his twenties and his status in America as an immigrant. When the Black Panther leader Huey P. Newton remarked in a conversation with Erikson that he seldom discussed his personal life except as it related to his political movement, Erikson replied, "I seldom do either. In fact, I only talk about myself in relation to the identity concept. . . . I think one has the right — maybe even the duty — to restrict oneself to that: otherwise everything becomes a kind of self-indulgence" (Erikson 1974, 132).

5. In the final section of *The Life Cycle Completed,* entitled "Historical Relativity and the Psychoanalytic Method," Erikson notes that when Einstein's theory of relativity became a popular idea, it seemed at best to have "unbearably relativistic implications, seemingly undermining the foundations of any firm human 'standpoint'; and yet, it opens a new vista in which relative standpoints are 'reconciled' to each other in fundamental invariance" (1982, 96–97). He suggests that soma, ethos, and psyche (his new words for the somatic, historical, and individual) are relative to each other, and that the individual

with a true "sense of 'I' " will not allow one or another of these "standpoints" a dominating influence.

6. In *A Study of Vermeer,* Edward Snow notes that the soldier "appears to be projected backwards, flattened against the inside of the surface of the canvas, as if to position him just inside the threshold between the viewer's realm and the space the woman occupies" (1994, 82). Conversely, "the woman and the space she occupies appear to recede from the soldier, while he in turn becomes a dark, looming presence, alien and ominous in his place opposite her. . . . There is, from where we look, a cramped, defensive uneasiness about his posture, and an indrawn, evasive quality about his gaze" (1994, 83–84). On the other hand, Snow notes that the defensiveness we attribute to the soldier is not supported by the servant girl's demeanor, which is attentive and receptive: "She manifests a unity, a concentration of being, a capacity to exist at the center of the present moment. . . . The soldier, by contrast, seems peripheral and transitory in this context, *gazing somewhat timidly across a threshold that some inner conflict makes him hesitant to cross*" (1994, 89, my emphasis).

Conclusion

1. I have focused throughout this study on the son's *introjection* of negative emotions (of hate and rage) originally evoked by "the perfect mother." In effect, "she" becomes a hated self-object. What I have not explored is the *projection* of such negative emotions onto others, especially other women, and the abusive forms that such projection may take. To address this issue adequately would be a book-length study in itself. My preliminary judgment, however, is that precisely because these negative emotions are self-directed, melancholiacs are less likely than other men to be overtly abusive of women. On the other hand, as we have seen in the cases of the men studied here, melancholiacs are likely to relate to women in a rather distant, wary, suspicious, and perhaps wounded fashion. Therefore they tend to be experienced by the women in their lives as unemotional and dispassionate, especially in the expression of emotions of tenderness, but as also capable of seemingly inexplicable emotions of anger and hurt, especially when their pride is threatened or challenged.

References

Almond, P. C. 1983. Rudolf Otto: Life and work. *Journal of religious history* 12:305–21.

American Psychiatric Association. 1994. *Diagnostic and statistical manual of mental disorders.* 4th ed. Washington, D.C.: American Psychiatric Association.

Augustine, St. 1992. *The confessions.* H. Chadwick, trans. New York: Oxford University Press.

Bell, M. 1991. *Meaning in Henry James.* Cambridge, Mass.: Harvard University Press.

Bellah, R. N., et al. 1985. *Habits of the heart: Individualism and commitment in American life.* Berkeley: University of California Press.

Boswell, J. 1980. *Life of Johnson.* New York: Oxford University Press.

Brilliant, R. 1991. *Portraiture.* Cambridge, Mass.: Harvard University Press.

Brown, L. B., ed. 1973. *Psychology and religion: Selected readings.* Baltimore, Md.: Penguin Books.

Bryson, N. 1990. *Looking at the overlooked: Four essays on still life painting.* Cambridge, Mass.: Harvard University Press.

Capps, D. 1993. *The depleted self: Sin in a narcissistic age.* Minneapolis: Fortress Press.

———. 1995. *The child's song: The religious abuse of children.* Louisville, Ky.: Westminster/John Knox Press.

——— and J. E. Dittes, eds. 1990. *The hunger of the heart: Reflections on the Confessions of Augustine.* West Lafayette, Ind.: Society for the Scientific Study of Religion (monograph series no. 8).

Carroll, M. P. 1985. The Virgin Mary at LaSalette and Lourdes: Whom did the children see? *Journal for the scientific study of religion* 24:56–74.

Coles, R. 1970. *Erik H. Erikson: The growth of his work.* Boston: Little, Brown and Company.

Cotkin, G. 1994. *William James: Public philosopher.* Urbana: University of Illinois Press.

Crossan, J. D. 1975. *The dark interval: Towards a theology of story.* Niles, Illinois: Argus Communications.

Davis, P. H. 1995. The sky-blue soul: Women's religion in *The varieties.* In D. Capps and J. L. Jacobs, eds., *The struggle for life: A companion to William James's "The varieties of religious experience"* (pp. 163–77). West Lafayette, Ind.: Society for the Scientific Study of Religion (monograph series no. 9).

Decker, H. S. 1991. *Freud, Dora, and Vienna 1900.* New York: Free Press.

Dittes, J. 1977. The investigator as an instrument of investigation: Some exploratory observations on the compleat researcher. In D. Capps, W. H. Capps, and M. G. Bradford, eds., *Encounter with Erikson: Historical interpretation and religious biography* (pp. 347–74). Missoula, Mont.: Scholars Press.

Eakin, P. J. 1985. *Fictions in autobiography: Studies in the art of self-invention.* Princeton: Princeton University Press.

Edel, L., ed. 1974. *Henry James: Selected letters.* Cambridge, Mass.: Belknap Press of Harvard University Press.

Erikson, E. H. 1958. *Young man Luther: A study in psychoanalysis and history.* New York: W. W. Norton.

———. 1959. *Identity and the life cycle.* New York: International Universities Press.

———. 1963. *Childhood and society.* 2d. rev. ed. New York: W. W. Norton.

———. 1964. *Insight and responsibility: Lectures on the ethical implications of psychoanalytic insight.* New York: W. W. Norton.

———. 1968. *Identity: Youth and crisis.* New York: W. W. Norton.

———. 1974. *In search of common ground: Conversations with Erik H. Erikson and Huey P. Newton.* K. Erikson, ed. New York: Dell Publications.

———. 1975. *Life history and the historical moment.* New York: W. W. Norton.

———. 1977. *Toys and reasons: Stages in the ritualization of experience.* New York: W. W. Norton.

———. 1981. The Galilean sayings and the sense of "I." *Yale review* 70:321–62.

———. 1982. *The life cycle completed: A review.* New York: W. W. Norton.

———. 1987. *A way of looking at things: Selected papers from 1930 to 1980.* S. Schlein, ed. New York: W. W. Norton.

Fairchild, R. W. 1987. Issues in contemporary spirituality: The upsurge of spiritual movements. *Princeton Seminary Bulletin* 8:4–16.

Ferrari, L. 1974. The boyhood beatings of Augustine. *Augustinian studies* 5:1–14.

Fisher, G. M. 1990. A ministry of encouragement to those who feel forsaken by God at Ross Christian Church, Ross, Ohio. Nashville, Tenn.: Historical Commission of the Southern Baptist Convention.

Fisher, S., and R. L. Fisher. 1993. *The psychology of adaptation to absurdity: Tactics of make-believe.* Hillsdale, N.J.: Lawrence Erlbaum.

Freud, S. 1958. The "uncanny." In B. Nelson, ed., *On creativity and the unconscious* (pp. 122–61). A. Strachey, trans. New York: Harper and Row.

———. 1961. *Civilization and its discontents.* J. Strachey, trans. New York: W. W. Norton.

———. 1963. Mourning and melancholia. J. Riviere, trans. In P. Rieff, ed., *General psychological theory: Papers on metapsychology* (pp. 164–79). New York: Collier Books.

———. 1964. *The future of an illusion.* W. D. Robson-Scott, trans. Garden City, N.Y.: Doubleday Anchor Books.

Gilligan, C. 1982. *In a different voice: Psychological theory and women's development.* Cambridge, Mass.: Harvard University Press.

Girard, R. 1987. *Job: The victim of his people.* Y. Freccero, trans. Stanford: Stanford University Press.

Goodenough, E. R. 1965. *The psychology of religious experiences.* New York: Basic Books.

Goodwin, A. 1993. The right to remain silent. *Pastoral psychology* 6:359–76.

Greven, P. 1991. *Spare the child: The religious roots of punishment and the psychological impact of physical abuse.* New York: Alfred A. Knopf.

Hawkins, A. H. 1990. St. Augustine: Archetypes of family. In D. Capps and J. Dittes, eds., *The hunger of the heart: Reflections on the Confessions of Augustine* (pp. 237–54). West Lafayette, Ind.: Society for the Scientific Study of Religion (monograph series no. 8).

Holly, C. 1995. *Intensely family: The inheritance of family shame and the autobiographies of Henry James.* Madison: University of Wisconsin Press.

Hutch, R. A. 1995. Over my dead body: A "common sense" test of saintliness. In D. Capps and J. L. Jacobs, eds., *The struggle for life: A companion to William James's "The varieties of religious experience"* (pp. 147–62). West Lafayette, Ind.: Society for the Scientific Study of Religion (monograph series no. 9).

Jackson, S. W. 1986. *Melancholia and depression: From Hippocratic times to modern times.* New Haven: Yale University Press.

James, H. 1990. *The jolly corner and other tales.* R. Gard, ed. New York: Penguin Books.

James, W. 1950. *The principles of psychology.* 2 vols. New York: Dover Publications.

———. 1956. *The will to believe and other essays in popular philosophy.* New York: Dover Publications.

———. 1982. *The varieties of religious experience.* M. E. Marty, ed. New York: Penguin Books.

Jay, M. 1993. *Downcast Eyes: The Denigration of Vision in Twentieth-Century French Thought.* Berkeley: University of California Press.

Johnson, R. A. 1977. Psychohistory as religious narrative: The demonic role of Hans Luther in Erikson's saga of human evolution. In R. A. Johnson, ed., *Psychohistory and religion: The case of "Young man Luther"* (pp. 127–61). Philadelphia: Fortress Press.

Jung, C. G. 1961. *Memories, dreams, reflections.* A. Jaffe, ed., R. and C. Winston, trans. New York: Vintage Books.

———. 1969. *Answer to Job.* R. F. C. Hull, trans. Princeton: Princeton University Press.

——— and C. Kerenyi. 1963. *Essays on a science of mythology: The myth of the divine child and the mysteries of Eleusis.* R. F. C. Hull, trans. Princeton: Princeton University Press.

Kant, I. 1960. *Observations on the feeling of the beautiful and sublime.* J. T. Goldthwait, trans. Berkeley: University of California Press.

Kaplan, B. 1977. Acedia: The decline of desire as the ultimate life crisis. In D. Capps,

W. H. Capps, and M. G. Bradford, eds., *Encounter with Erikson: Historical interpretation and religious biography* (pp. 389–400). Missoula, Mont.: Scholars Press.

Kaplan, F. 1992. *Henry James: The imagination of a genius.* New York: William Morrow.

Kasten, C. O. 1987. Imagination and desire in *The spoils of Poynton* and *What Maisie knew.* In H. Bloom, ed., *Henry James: Modern critical views* (pp. 251–75). New York: Chelsea House.

Kenyon, J. 1993. *Constance.* St. Paul, Minn.: Graywolf Press.

Kierkegaard, S. K. 1983. *Fear and trembling.* H. V. and E. H. Hong, eds. and trans. Princeton: Princeton University Press.

Kohut, H. 1971. *The analysis of the self.* New York: International Universities Press.

——. 1977. *The restoration of the self.* New York: International Universities Press.

——. 1984. *How does analysis cure?* A. Goldberg, ed. Chicago: University of Chicago Press.

—— and E. S. Wolf. 1986. The disorders of the self and their treatment: An outline. In A. P. Morrison, ed., *Essential papers on narcissism* (pp. 175–96). New York: New York University Press.

Kristeva, J. 1989. *Black sun: depression and melancholia.* L. S. Roudiez, trans. New York: Columbia University Press.

Lewis, R. W. B. 1991. *The Jameses: A family narrative.* New York: Farrar, Straus and Giroux.

Meissner, W. W. 1984. *Psychoanalysis and religious experience.* New Haven: Yale University Press.

Miller, A. 1984. *For your own good: Hidden cruelty in child-rearing and the roots of violence.* 2nd. ed. H. and H. Hannum, trans. New York: Farrar, Straus and Giroux.

——. 1990a. *Banished knowledge.* L. Vennewitz, trans. New York: Doubleday.

——. 1990b. *The untouched key: Tracing childhood trauma in creativity and destructiveness.* H. and H. Hannum, trans. New York: Anchor Books.

——. 1991. *Breaking down the wall of silence.* S. Worrall, trans. New York: Dutton Books.

Miller, J. H. 1992. *Illustration.* Cambridge, Mass.: Harvard University Press.

Millett, K. 1969. *Sexual politics.* New York: Simon and Schuster.

Myers, G. E. 1986. *William James: His life and thought.* New Haven: Yale University Press.

Nørager, T. 1995. Blowing alternately hot and cold: William James and the complex strategies of *The varieties.* In D. Capps and J. L. Jacobs, eds., *The struggle for life: A companion to William James's "The varieties of religious experience"* (pp. 61–71). West Lafayette, Ind.: Society for the Scientific Study of Religion (monograph series no. 9).

Otto, R. 1958. *The idea of the holy.* J. W. Harvey, trans. New York: Oxford University Press.

Parker, R. 1995. *Mother love/mother hate: The power of maternal ambivalence.* New York: Basic Books.

Proudfoot, W., and P. Shaver. 1975. Attribution theory and the psychology of religion. *Journal for the scientific study of religion* 14:317–30.

Pruyser, P. W. 1963. Erikson's *Young man Luther*: A new chapter in the psychology of religion. *Journal for the scientific study of religion* 2:238–42.

———. 1968. *A dynamic psychology of religion*. New York: Harper and Row.

———. 1974. *Between belief and unbelief*. New York: Harper and Row.

———. 1976. Lessons from art theory for the psychology of religion. *Journal for the scientific study of religion* 15:1–14.

———. 1983. *The play of the imagination: Toward a psychoanalysis of culture*. New York: International Universities Press.

———. 1987. Where do we go from here? Scenarios for the psychology of religion. *Journal for the scientific study of religion* 26:173–81.

Rigby, P. 1990. Augustine's *Confessions*: The recognition of fatherhood. In D. Capps and J. Dittes, eds., *The hunger of the heart: Reflections on the "Confessions" of Augustine* (pp. 143–65). West Lafayette, Ind.: Society for the Scientific Study of Religion (monograph series no. 8).

Rizzuto, A.-M. 1979. *The birth of the living god: A psychoanalytic study*. Chicago: University of Chicago Press.

Rubin, J. H. 1994. *Religious melancholy and Protestant experience in America*. New York: Oxford University Press.

Sedgwick, E. K. 1990. *Epistemology of the closet*. Berkeley: University of California Press.

Shengold, L. 1989. *Soul murder: The effects of childhood abuse and deprivation*. New Haven: Yale University Press.

Snow, E. 1994. *A study of Vermeer*. Rev. ed. Berkeley: University of California Press.

Strout, C. 1968. William James and the twice-born sick soul. In S. R. Graubard, ed., *Philosophers and kings: Studies in leadership. Proceedings of the American Academy of Arts and Sciences* 97:1062–81.

Styron, W. 1990. *Darkness visible: A memoir of madness*. New York: Random House.

Watzlawick, P. 1983. *The situation is hopeless, but not serious: The pursuit of unhappiness*. New York: W. W. Norton.

Webb, S. H. 1995. The rhetoric of and about excess in William James's *The varieties of religious experience*. *Religion and literature* 27:27–45.

Winnicott, D. W. 1971a. Mirror-role of mother and family in child development. *Playing and reality* (pp. 111–18). London: Tavistock Publications.

———. 1971b. Transitional objects and transitional phenomena. *Playing and reality* (pp. 1–25). London: Tavistock Publications.

Wittkower, R., and M. Wittkower. 1969. *Born under Saturn*. New York: W. W. Norton.

Wood, M. E. 1994. *The writing on the wall: Women's autobiography and the asylum*. Urbana, Ill.: University of Illinois Press.

Index

Adler, Gerhard, 127–28
Aion (Jung), 127, 130, 133
Alline, Henry, 45, 47, 58
Almond, Philip C., 82–83, 89–91, 93, 96, 218n1(1)
Animistic religion, 19, 69, 73–75
Answer to Job (Jung), 2, 6; as controversial, 127–28; on divine evil, 135–37; freedom from God as Jung's motive for, 128; on God's "dark side," 118–20, 130, 138; and *Idea of the Holy*, 133–35; John the Evangelist interpreted in, 128, 137–42; psychic vs. physical facts in, 121–22, 133–34, 141–42; title of interpreted, 132–33; Uriah dream as foreshadowing, 131–32
Anxiety: adult, 155–56; metaphysical, 58–59
Archetypes, numinous, 134, 135, 142
Art, 11; the holy expressed in, 87, 99, 112–13, 115–16, 184; of portraiture,

54, 181–85; of still lifes, 195–98, 220n6
Attribution theory of religious experience, 24–25
Augustine, 1–2, 5, 104, 109–10
Autoeroticism, 48, 49

Bacon, Francis, 185
Bakan, David, 80–81
Belief: James on, 26–27, 32
Bell, Millicent, 217n9
Benz, Ernst, 90
Bible: as matrix, 174–76; mysterium tremendum in, 106, 108–10. *See also* Revelation, Book of
Bismarck, Otto von, 125–26
Bitterness, 9, 17
Bloom, Harold, 68
Boswell, James, 211–14
Bradley, Stephen H., 24–25
Brilliant, Richard, 184–85
Brown, L. B., 26